The Discourses of Epictetus

Special Edition

by

Arrian

As related by

Epictetus

AD 55–AD 135

Translated by

George Long

Special Edition Books

The Discourses of Epictetus – Special Edition
By Arrian
Translated by George Long

Copyright © 2010 by Special Edition Books
All rights reserved. No part of this book may be reproduced or utilized in any form or by any means, electronic or mechanical, including photocopying, recording, or by any information storage and retrieval system, without permission in writing from the publisher, except that brief passages may be quoted by reviewers provided full credit is given.

First Printing – March 2010

Published by
Special Edition Books
El Paso, Texas

ISBN: 1-934255-31-9
ISBN13: 978-1-934255-31-5

Printed in the United States of America

PREFACE

Arrian to Lucius Gellius, with wishes for his happiness:

I neither wrote these "Discourses of Epictetus" in the way in which a man might write such things; nor did I make them public myself, inasmuch as I declare that I did not even write them. But whatever I heard him say, the same I attempted to write down in his own words as nearly as possible, for the purpose of preserving them as memorials to myself afterward of the thoughts and the freedom of speech of Epictetus.

Accordingly, the "Discourses" are naturally such as a man would address without preparation to another, not such as a man would write with the view of others reading them. Now, being such, I do not know how they fell into the hands of the public, without either my consent or my knowledge.

But it concerns me little if I shall be considered incompetent to write; and it concerns Epictetus not at all if any man shall despise his words; for at the time when he uttered them it was plain that he had no other purpose than to move the minds of his hearers to the best things. If, indeed, these "Discourses" should produce this effect, they will have, I think, the result which the words of philosophers ought to have. But if they shall not, let those who read them know that, when Epictetus delivered them, the hearer could not avoid being affected in the way that Epictetus wished him to be. But if the "Discourses" themselves, as they are written, do not effect this result, it may be that the fault is mine, or, it may be, that the thing is unavoidable.

Farewell!

Discourses of Epictetus

The Discourses of Epictetus

TABLE OF CONTENTS

PREFACE	i
CONTENTS	iii
INTRODUCTION	vii

BOOK ONE

Chapter		Page
1	Of the things which are in our Power, and not in our Power.	1
2	How a Man on every occasion can maintain his Proper Character.	3
3	How a man should proceed from the principle of God being the father of all men to the rest.	6
4	Of progress or improvement.	7
5	Against the academics.	9
6	Of providence.	10
7	Of the use of sophistical arguments, and hypothetical, and the like.	13
8	That the faculties are not safe to the uninstructed.	15
9	How from the fact that we are akin to God a man may proceed to the consequences.	16
10	Against those who eagerly seek preferment at Rome.	19
11	Of natural affection.	20
12	Of contentment.	23
13	How everything may he done acceptably to the gods.	25
14	That the deity oversees all things.	26
15	What philosophy promises.	27
16	Of providence.	28
17	That the logical art is necessary.	30
18	That we ought not to he angry with the errors of others.	32
19	How we should behave to tyrants.	34
20	About reason, how it contemplates itself.	36
21	Against those who wish to be admired.	37
22	On precognitions.	38
23	Against Epicurus.	40
24	How we should struggle with circumstances.	41
25	On the same.	43
26	What is the law of life.	45
27	In how many ways appearances exist, and what aids we should provide against them.	47
28	That we ought not to he angry with men; and what are the small and the great things among men.	49
29	On constancy.	51
30	What we ought to have ready in difficult circumstances.	55

The Discourses of Epictetus

TABLE OF CONTENTS

BOOK TWO

Chapter		Page
1	That confidence is not inconsistent with caution.	56
2	Of Tranquillity.	59
3	To those who recommend persons to philosophers.	61
4	Against a person who had once been detected in adultery.	62
5	How magnanimity is consistent with care.	63
6	Of indifference.	65
7	How we ought to use divination.	67
8	What is the nature of the good.	68
9	That when we cannot fulfill that which the character of a man promises, we assume the character of a philosopher.	70
10	How we may discover the duties of life from names.	72
11	What the beginning of philosophy is.	74
12	Of disputation or discussion.	76
13	On anxiety.	78
14	To Naso.	80
15	To or against those who obstinately persist in what they have determined.	82
16	That we do not strive to use our opinions about good and evil.	84
17	How we must adapt preconceptions to particular cases.	87
18	How we should struggle against appearances.	90
19	Against those who embrace, philosophical opinions only in words.	92
20	Against the Epicureans and Academics.	95
21	Of inconsistency.	98
22	On friendship.	100
23	On the power of speaking.	103
24	To a person who was one of those who was not valued by him.	107
25	That logic is necessary.	109
26	What is the property of error.	110

The Discourses of Epictetus

TABLE OF CONTENTS

BOOK THREE

Chapter		Page
1	Of finery in dress.	111
2	In what a man ought to be exercised who has made proficiency; and that we neglect the chief things.	115
3	What is the matter on which a good man should he employed, and in what we ought chiefly to practice ourselves.	117
4	Against a person who showed his partisanship in an unseemly way in a theatre.	119
5	Against those who on account of sickness go away home.	120
6	Miscellaneous.	122
7	To the administrator of the free cities who was an Epicurean.	123
8	How we must exercise ourselves against appearances.	126
9	To a certain rhetorician who was going up to Rome on a suit.	127
10	In what manner we ought to bear sickness.	129
11	Certain miscellaneous matters.	131
12	About exercise.	132
13	What solitude is, and what kind of person a solitary man is.	134
14	Certain miscellaneous matters.	136
15	That we ought to proceed with circumspection to everything.	137
16	That we ought with caution to enter, into familiar intercourse with men.	138
17	On providence.	139
18	That we ought not to be disturbed by any news.	140
19	What is the condition of a common kind of man and of a philosopher.	141
20	That we can derive advantage from all external things.	142
21	Against those who readily come to the profession of sophists.	144
22	About cynicism.	146
23	To those who read and discuss for the sake of ostentation.	154
24	That we ought not to be moved by a desire of those things which are not in our power.	157
25	To those who fall off from their purpose.	165
26	To those who fear want.	166

The Discourses of Epictetus

TABLE OF CONTENTS

BOOK FOUR

Chapter		Page
1	About freedom.	169
2	On familiar intimacy.	182
3	What things we should exchange for other things.	183
4	To those who are desirous of passing life in tranquility.	184
5	Against the quarrelsome and ferocious.	188
6	Against those who lament over being pitied.	191
7	On freedom from fear.	194
8	Against those who hastily rush into the use of the philosophic dress.	198
9	To a person who had been changed to a character of shamelessness.	204
10	What things we ought to despise, and what things we ought to value.	204
11	About Purity.	207
12	On attention.	210
13	Against or to those who readily tell their own affairs.	212

THE ENCHIRIDIDON, OR MANUAL	214
FRAGMENTS OF THE LOST BOOKS OF EPICTETUS	227

INTRODUCTION

OF the life of Epictetus little need be said. His biography is his character, and this lies open in his books, where the fine spirit of an earnest and noble soul still breathes. He was born in Phrygia, about the middle of the first century. His mother was a slave; his father is unknown. Epictetus is not his name, but is a Greek word which denotes his servile condition. In his youth he became the property of Epaphroditus, a freedman of Nero's, who permitted him to attend the lectures of Musonius Rufus, one of the most celebrated teachers in Rome. Having acquired freedom, he began himself to give lessons; but he was soon sent into exile, together with the other philosophers, by the Emperor Domitian.

Settling at Nicopolis, in Epirus (the modern Albania), he opened a school, and continued to teach the doctrines of stoicism to the time of his death, at the age, it is supposed, of nearly a hundred years. He was feeble in body, lame, poor, and unmarried, living alone until he took an old woman into his house to care for an orphan whom he had adopted. He wrote nothing, but talked with his pupils in a familiar way of whatever concerns the conduct of life. Arrian, his favorite disciple, took notes of his conversations, not with a view to publication, but for his own use. When, however, without his knowledge, they had fallen into the hands of several, he edited them himself. Thus we owe to an accident the existence of these "Discourses," which form one of the world's vital books. The "Manual" is a collection of aphorisms taken substantially from the larger work.

Epictetus was not the founder of a new philosophy. Zeno, the originator of the Stoic system, was his master, and Zeno himself derived his fundamental principles from Antisthenes, the author of the cynic school and the friend of Socrates.

The Greeks are the creators of philosophy, and their earliest attempt at systematic thought was an effort to understand Nature. But they soon learned that it was necessary to begin from within, since to know anything man must first know himself. Thus the problem of the conduct of life forced itself upon them. This is the constant preoccupation of Socrates, who was born five hundred years before Epictetus. He taught that the good is to be sought not in outward things, nor in the indulgence of appetite, but in virtue, which for him, however, is an intellectual rather than a moral habit. His calm and rational temper led him to the belief that man always acts in accordance with his knowledge, does what insight shows him to be useful to himself. He who does evil, does it from a mistake of judgment. Sin is error. Virtue, then, being chiefly knowledge, may be taught, and to teach it is the philosopher's life work. But Socrates moved in a circle from which there was no escape. To know the useful is virtue. But what is the useful? That which makes for virtue.

Antisthenes does not attempt to determine the meaning of the good. He simply declares that virtue is the only good, and, in his view, virtue is the intelligent conduct of life. Right life is the essential good; virtue is its sown reward, and one need not look to its results. It is, in the midst of whatever vicissitudes, a sure possession. The virtuous man is independent of events, and stands secure against fate and fortune. The world is full of things he does not need; he seeks not wealth, nor fame, nor honor, nor pleasure. however, holding that man is by nature social, require that he lead a social life. The social ideal of the sage is that of a universal ethical community, and he is indifferent to forms of government and to actually existing states. He is a citizen of the world, demands justice and sympathy for all, and refuses to recognize the division of mankind into Greeks and barbarians.

Zeno, the Stoic, born in Cyprus about 340 B. C, is the heir of the Cynics. The sage, as he conceives the truly wise and virtuous man, is first of all independent of the world, since only on this condition can he be free and find happiness in himself alone; and as what is external is but little subject to human will, he must overcome the world within himself by gaining the mastery over the feelings and desires which it excites. To be self-contained and self-sufficient, to remain unmoved in the presence of good or of evil fortune, imperturbable though the universe be shattered, is the goal he must strive to reach. If he can not defend himself against the excitations of feeling, he will at least refuse his assent, and thereby prevent them from becoming passions. His ideal is apathy, absence of emotion. The course of things may bring him pleasure and pain, but since he holds that the one is not a good, the other not an evil, he retains his equanimity. Virtue is his sole good, and the only evil is to permit passion to conquer reason. This withdrawal of the individual within himself, however it may be modified and supplemented, is an essential element in the Stoic's conception of life. Reason, from his point of view, is not only man's nature, but that of the universe, while the impulses of the senses are irrational. The soul, as part of the World-Reason, must therefore exclude from itself all excitation of feeling. To live in harmony with Nature is to rise into a sphere where the senses cease to trouble; it is to live in communion with the cosmic power, from which all things proceed, in cheerful obedience to the eternal destiny which, being the will of God, is the divine law. Likewise man accepts this life as his first and highest duty. It is the task which Reason imposes upon him.

The chief stress is laid upon the worth of moral personality, upon the paramount value of the good that lies within, though the duty of co-operating with one's fellowmen for the general welfare is inculcated. The metaphysical principle is pantheistic, and involves fatalism; but the Stoics, preoccupied exclusively with moral ideas and interests, cared little for logical consistency, and stoutly asserted the freedom of' the will, holding fast to liberty of choice and to the universality of causation.

Though of Greek origin, stoicism attained its highest practical significance in Rome, where its doctrines seemed to be suited to the character of the people. Those stern, self-controlled, and brave men were attracted by a system which emphasized the value of independence, courage, and imperturbability. They found in it a source of the moral enthusiasm which the pagan religions had no power to inspire. They were drawn to the society of the philosophers, received them into their houses, and became their disciples. By daily intercourse with these earnest and austere teachers, such men as Scipio and Laelius, as Brutus, Cato, and Cicero, were formed. The prestige and authority of the preachers of stoicism were heightened by the general corruption which was undermining the state, and the public calamities which were becoming more and more frequent.

The noblest souls, despairing of the cause of liberty, withdrew from politics, and sought consolation in a philosophy which taught them how to bear the ills of life and how to die. In Rome, where only what is practical was rightly appreciated, little attention was given to the metaphysical presuppositions of stoicism, and the great teachers, losing sight of the logical requirements of the system, took what seemed to them true and to the purpose wherever it was found. Indeed, contradiction and inconsistency did not repel, as we have seen, the early Stoics, and in its Roman development the philosophy became more and more eclectic.

Epictetus, Seneca, and Marcus Aurelius are the three famous names of this later school of stoicism, and they are all teachers of the conduct of life, in love with inner perfection, and comparatively heedless of mere speculation. In the midst of the general decadence and threatening collapse of the civilized world, they sought to rouse conscience; and as the pagan religion could do nothing for them, they strove to give a kind of sacredness to human wisdom. To derive profit from their works it is not necessary to understand their theories. All that is required is an open mind and a tractable heart. What is speculative disappears in the presence of the practical worth of the truths they utter. To read them aright we need an attentive and devout spirit rather than an acute and curious intellect.

Of these three teachers of the later stoicism, Epictetus is the noblest character and the greatest authority. His life is more completely in harmony with his doctrine. He rises in moral elevation to the level of his maxims and precepts. His purity equals his insight. He is the venerable sage. He is the saint of a philosophical religion, a man who from an abject condition raised himself to the worthiest dispositions of mind and heart, who in the midst of a corrupt society remained unstained and faithful, his thought fixed on the highest moral ideals, and following to the end his vocation as a preacher of righteousness—a slave, a cripple, a pauper, as his epitaph declares, but dear to the gods. He has drawn for us an ideal of the Stoic sage, in which his own character is portrayed. He accuses neither God nor man; he controls desire; he knows not anger, nor resentment, nor envy, nor pity; he fences himself with virtuous shame. He has nothing to conceal; he does not fear exile or death, for wherever and however he is there also is God. But it is not enough that he be good in and for himself. He is a messenger sent by Zeus to instruct men concerning good and evil, to point out to them that they walk in wrong ways. He must cry out: "Oh, mortals, whither are ye hasting? Why do ye tumble about, like the blind? The good is not in the body; it is not in wealth, or power, or empire; it lies in yourselves. God has sent you one to teach you by his example. Take notice of me that I am without a country, without a house, without an estate, without a servant: I lie on the ground; have no wife, no children, no coat, but have only earth and heaven and one poor cloak. And what need I? Am I not without sorrow, without fear? Am I not free? Did I ever blame God or man? Did I ever accuse any one? Have any of you seen me look discontented?" Epictetus is direct, plain, and earnest in his speech. His style is bare of ornament, vigorous, and incisive. He is always serious, often stern, and at times pathetic. He does not deliver finished discourses, is heedless of rhetorical ornament, and wholly intent on improving his hearers by inciting them to the love and practice of virtue. He is not so much an orator as a brave, genuine man, whose whole being vibrates in his words, which are vital and electric. They are the honest and fearless expression of what he thinks in his heart, of what he feels and lives. They are the utterance of what is deepest and permanent in man. and therefore they never lose the power to stimulate and nourish faith in the worth of a life led in obedience to the divine commands. The simple and straightforward manner in which he speaks the highest truth has made him a favorite not with scholars merely, but with all classes of readers. Whoever is persuaded that life is chiefly conduct may derive help from him. Only the learned can read Plato with profit and the fewest of these study him, "But an ordinary mind may find in Epictetus a friend and teacher, for his philosophy is of the most practical character and easily understood. Wisdom consists in knowing how to distinguish between what is our own and what is not ours. Our will, our opinions, desires, inclinations, and aversions are ours; the rest—body, possessions, honor, and reputation—is not ours. The divine law bids us hold fast to what is our own, and make no claim to what is not ours. God in endowing us with free will gives us control over what is ours, but other things he has not placed in our power. A man's business is with himself, with learning to think rightly and will wisely. Here he is master, here he has full control. Let him give heed to this, and in other things resign himself with a cheerful heart to the guidance of the all-wise Father, who rules the whole. Since we can not determine the course of Nature, it is our duty to accept with courage and resignation whatever befalls. If money, or friend, or wife, or child taken is from us, let us remember that they never were ours; they were but lent to us, and have been returned to the owner. Shall we complain when he asks us to restore what belongs to him? But it lies with us to have an independent soul and a victorious will, to remain imperturbable, serene, reverent, and thankful, despite disgrace and misfortune, which can not touch our inmost being or deprive us of freedom and virtue. These are the sole good, and so long as they are ours all else is unimportant. Will that things happen as they do, and nothing shall happen contrary to thy will. But how shall I bear the wrongs which the wicked inflict? May not God choose his agents to demand of thee what he has lent. Thou art but a player to whom a role has been assigned. Take cheerfully whatever character is given thee, whether it be that of a beggar or that of a king. Thy sole business is to act well the part to which God has appointed thee. Think of him as often as thou breathest, and let thy whole study and desire be to know and do his will.

For Epictetus a virtuous life is not a means, but an end. The sage does right not from the hope of prosperity and good name, not that he may have health of body and mind, not because wise behavior produces a contented and happy temper, but he does what is just, avoids what is base, without thought of reward or punishment, impelled solely by a sense of duty. He clings to virtue though virtue be his death sentence, and though he have no expectation of a future life. He makes no sacrifice in abandoning all things for virtue, for virtue is his only good. He who wishes to please men, who desires to be known and praised even for his virtue, is not a lover of virtue, as he who loves money or pleasure or glory is not a lover of mankind. The wise man's will rolls like a wheel with steady and even motion toward the one eternal goal, to which the universe also is drawn. "If there be any worth in thee, O man, learn to walk alone and to converse with thyself!"

In the "Manual" Epictetus appears as a stern, uncompromising Stoic. In the "Discourses" we find him in the midst of his friends and disciples, where he takes a more human and sympathetic tone. Here he infuses into his morality the glow of religion, which makes it vital and effective. We are not always made to feel that virtue lacks vigor, unless it be hard and repellent, that pride heightens truth, or that insolence is a mark of goodness, or that harshness is zeal, or modest assertion of opinion a compromise with error. We almost seem to hear Thrasea declare that he fears to hate even vice too much, lest perchance he come to hate his fellow-men. It is in the "Discourses" that he tells us that the true Stoic is " the father of mankind; that all men are his sons and all women his daughters. He attends to all, takes care of all. Is it from impertinence that he rebukes those he meets? He does it as a father, as a brother, as a minister of the common parent, Zeus." He does not marry, he has no children, he accepts no office, that nothing may interfere with the work which God has given him to do. He is careful of his health and appearance, lest he repel those whom he wishes to attract. Above all, he is clean of heart,

Introduction to the Discourses of Epictetus

for how, if he is himself guilty, shall he reprove others? He watches and labors for men, becomes purer day by day; he rules all his thoughts as the friend, as the minister of the gods, as a partner in the empire of Zeus. He has, besides, so much patience as to appear to the vulgar insensible and like a stone; "for there is this fine circumstance connected with the character of a Cynic: that he must be beaten like an ass, and yet when beaten must love those who beat him as the father, as the brother of all."

Epictetus does not reject the pantheism of the Stoics nor the polytheism of his age, but whatever his theological opinions, which seem to have been vague, he does not think of God as an indeterminate somewhat, but as a person to whom he is bound by ties of obedience, reverence, and love; and though he often speaks of the gods, the Supreme Being is never absent from his mind. He is the creator of the world and the ruler of all things. He can not conceive that the universe should have come into existence or should continue without God. The glory and harmony of the creation fill him with devout enthusiasm. "What can I, a lame old man, do other than praise God? Were I a nightingale, I should perform the office of a nightingale; were I a swan, that of a swan; but as I am a rational being, I must praise God. This is my work, this I do, nor shall I cease from the task while life is left me. And upon you also I call to intone this hymn." With his last breath he hopes still to continue his sacred song: "Nothing but thanks to thee do I utter, because thou hast deemed me worthy to partake with thee of life's feast, to behold thy works, and to follow thy government of the world." Day and night he is mindful of the divine commands; his thoughts are raised to Heaven, and in earthly things he sees God, not as the Creator alone, but also as the Father who watches over his children and has care of even the least among them.

Epictetus takes what seems to him true and good wherever it be found. He has no respect for mere theory, and prizes only the knowledge which is brought to bear on the conduct of life. The beginning of philosophy, he says, is the turning from intellectual conceit and the recognition of one's own helplessness in the most indispensable things. To talk like a Stoic is easy; to live like one is difficult. He challenges his hearers to show him one whose life is in harmony with his principles. And yet all that is needed is the will. Will, and thou art free. From within come salvation and ruin. If the heart is set upon external things, a god can not rescue thee. But let us forget the past, he cries, and begin anew. God has placed us in the midst of the battle of life; we have sworn to be true to him, our king and leader, to defend at whatever cost the post he has assigned us. "I am thine. Where will'st thou that I live—in Rome, or Athens, or Thebes, or on the desert island of Gyara? Only, be mindful of me there."

Introduction to the Discourses of Epictetus

Epictetus is not a Christian: he knows nothing of God's anger and mercy, of guilt and punishment, of redemption and forgiveness. In contradiction with his doctrine of providence, he holds to the old Stoic tradition which permits suicide, and in certain cases makes it a duty. He who can live content wherever God places him is ready to quit the tabernacle of the soul if the house is too full of smoke. Though not a Christian, he certainly knew something of the Christian religion. He lived in Rome as student and teacher of philosophy from the year 73 to 95, and at this time Christianity had penetrated even the higher circles of Roman society; and the charge of atheism which caused Domitian to send the philosophers into exile led him also to banish the Christians, many of whom suffered martyrdom while Epictetus was delivering his discourses at Nicopolis. He takes occasion to mention the heroism with which these Galileans, as he calls them, met death. They die without fear, he says, not from ignorance of the danger, nor from weariness of life, nor from madness, nor yet from philosophic conviction, but from habit. Galileans is not the name by which the Roman writers of this period designate the Christians. They did not call themselves Galileans, and to the Jews they were known as Nazarenes. It is probable, therefore, that Epictetus found the word in the New Testament writings, where the epithet is not infrequently applied to the followers of Jesus. Galen, who was educated in the Stoic philosophy and who lived but a short time after Epictetus, speaks of the contempt for death shown by "those men who are called Christians." He goes on to say that their doctrines are delivered in parables, which are more easily understood than abstruse arguments, and that their lives are in many respects like to that of the true philosophers. In fact, while the world view of the Stoic differs radically from the Christian, the moral teaching of the pagan philosopher and of the follower of Christ is often much the same. Both attach the highest importance to religious faith and sentiment; both hold that virtue is the chief good; both emphasize the principle of liberty, and draw from it that of free personality; both declare that man holds his earthly possessions as a steward of the divine owner, to whom he is responsible for the use he makes of them.

John Lancaster Spalding

BOOK ONE

CHAPTER 1

Of the things which are in our Power, and not in our Power

Of all the faculties, you will find not one which is capable of contemplating itself; and, consequently, not capable either of approving or disapproving. How far does the grammatic art possess the contemplating power? As far as forming a judgment about what is written and spoken. And how far music? As far as judging about melody. Does either of them then contemplate itself? By no means. But when you must write something to your friend, grammar will tell you what words you must write; but whether you should write or not, grammar will not tell you. And so it is with music as to musical sounds; but whether you should sing at the present time and play on the lute, or do neither, music will not tell you. What faculty then will tell you? That which contemplates both itself and all other things. And what is this faculty? The rational faculty; for this is the only faculty that we have received which examines itself, what it is, and what power it has, and what is the value of this gift, and examines all other faculties: for what else is there which tells us that golden things are beautiful, for they do not say so themselves? Evidently it is the faculty which is capable of judging of appearances. What else judges of music, grammar, and other faculties, proves their uses and points out the occasions for using them? Nothing else.

As then it was fit to be so, that which is best of all and supreme over all is the only thing which the gods have placed in our power, the right use of appearances; but all other things they have not placed in our power. Was it because they did not choose? I indeed think that, if they had been able, they would have put these other things also in our power, but they certainly could not. For as we exist on the earth, and are bound to such a body and to such companions, how was it possible for us not to be hindered as to these things by externals?

But what says Zeus? "Epictetus, if it were possible, I would have made both your little body and your little property free and not exposed to hindrance. But now be not ignorant of this: this body is not yours, but it is clay finely tempered. And since I was not able to do for you what I have mentioned, I have given you a small portion of us, this faculty of pursuing an object and avoiding it, and the faculty of desire and aversion, and, in a word, the faculty of using the appearances of things; and if you will take care of this faculty and consider it your only possession, you will never be hindered, never meet with impediments; you will not lament, you will not blame, you will not flatter any person."

"Well, do these seem to you small matters?" I hope not. "Be content with them then and pray to the gods." But now when it is in our power to look after one thing, and to attach ourselves to it, we prefer to look after many things, and to be bound to many things, to the body and to property, and to brother and to friend, and to child and to slave. Since, then, we are bound to many things, we are depressed by them and dragged down. For this reason, when the weather is not fit for sailing, we sit down and torment ourselves, and continually look out to see what wind is blowing. "It is north." What is that to us? "When will the west wind blow?" When it shall choose, my good man, or when it shall please Aeolus; for God has not made you the manager of the winds, but Aeolus. What then? We must make the best use that we can of the things which are in our power, and use the rest according to their nature. What is their nature then? As God may please.

"Must I, then, alone have my head cut off?" What, would you have all men lose their heads that you may be consoled? Will you not stretch out your neck as Lateranus did at Rome when Nero ordered him to be beheaded? For when he had stretched out his neck, and received a feeble blow, which made him draw it in for a moment, he stretched it out again. And a little before, when he was visited by Epaphroditus, Nero's freedman, who asked him about the cause of offense which he had given, he said, "If I choose to tell anything, I will tell your master."

What then should a man have in readiness in such circumstances? What else than "What is mine, and what is not mine; and permitted to me, and what is not permitted to me." I must die. Must I then die lamenting? I must be put in chains. Must I then also lament? I must go into exile. Does any man then hinder me from going with smiles and cheerfulness and contentment? "Tell me the secret which you possess." I will not, for this is in my power. "But I will put you in chains." Man, what are you talking about? Me in chains? You may fetter my leg, but my will not even Zeus himself can overpower. "I will throw you into prison." My poor body, you mean. "I will cut your head off." When, then, have I told you that my head alone cannot be cut off? These are the things which philosophers should meditate on, which they should write daily, in which they should exercise themselves.

Thrasea used to say, "I would rather be killed to-day than banished to-morrow." What, then, did Rufus say to him? "If you choose death as the heavier misfortune, how great is the folly of your choice? But if, as the lighter, who has given you the choice? Will you not study to be content with that which has been given to you?"

What, then, did Agrippinus say? He said, "I am not a hindrance to myself." When it was reported to him that his trial was going on in the Senate, he said, "I hope it may turn out well; but it is the fifth hour of the day"—this was the time when he was used to exercise himself and then take the cold bath—"let us go and take our exercise." After he had taken his exercise, one comes and tells him, "You have been condemned." "To banishment," he replies, "or to death?" "To banishment." "What about my property?" "It is not taken from you." "Let us go to Aricia then," he said, "and dine."

This it is to have studied what a man ought to study; to have made desire, aversion, free from hindrance, and free from all that a man would avoid. I must die. If now, I am ready to die. If, after a short time, I now dine because it is the dinner-hour; after this I will then die. How? Like a man who gives up what belongs to another.

CHAPTER 2

How a Man on every occasion can maintain his Proper Character

To the rational animal only is the irrational intolerable; but that which is rational is tolerable. Blows are not naturally intolerable. "How is that?" See how the Lacedaemonians endure whipping when they have learned that whipping is consistent with reason. "To hang yourself is not intolerable." When, then, you have the opinion that it is rational, you go and hang yourself. In short, if we observe, we shall find that the animal man is pained by nothing so much as by that which is irrational; and, on the contrary, attracted to nothing so much as to that which is rational.

But the rational and the irrational appear such in a different way to different persons, just as the good and the bad, the profitable and the unprofitable. For this reason, particularly, we need discipline, in order to learn how to adapt the preconception of the rational and the irrational to the several things conformably to nature. But in order to determine the rational and the irrational, we use not only the of external things, but we consider also what is appropriate to each person. For to one man it is consistent with reason to hold a chamber pot for another, and to look to this only, that if he does not hold it, he will receive stripes, and he will not receive his food: but if he shall hold the pot, he will not suffer anything hard or disagreeable. But to another man not only does the holding of a chamber pot appear intolerable for himself, but intolerable also for him to allow another to do this office for him. If, then, you ask me whether you should hold the chamber pot or not, I shall say to you that the receiving of food is worth more than the not receiving of it, and the being scourged is a greater indignity than not being scourged; so that if you measure your interests by these things, go and hold the chamber pot. "But this," you say, "would not be worthy of me." Well, then, it is you who must introduce this consideration into the inquiry, not I; for it is you who know yourself, how much you are worth to yourself, and at what price you sell yourself; for men sell themselves at various prices.

For this reason, when Florus was deliberating whether he should go down to Nero's spectacles and also perform in them himself, Agrippinus said to him, "Go down": and when Florus asked Agrippinus, "Why do not you go down?" Agrippinus replied, "Because I do not even deliberate about the matter." For he who has once brought himself to deliberate about such matters, and to calculate the value of external things, comes very near to those who have forgotten their own character. For why do you ask me the question, whether death is preferable or life? I say "life." "Pain or pleasure?" I say "pleasure." But if I do not take a part in the tragic acting, I shall have my head struck off. Go then and take a part, but I will not. "Why?" Because you consider yourself to be only one thread of those which are in the tunic. Well then it was fitting for you to take care how you should be like the rest of men, just as the thread has no design to be anything superior to the other threads. But I wish to be purple, that small part which is bright, and makes all the rest appear graceful and beautiful. Why then do you tell me to make myself like the many? and if I do, how shall I still be purple?

Priscus Helvidius also saw this, and acted conformably. For when Vespasian sent and commanded him not to go into the senate, he replied, "It is in your power not to allow me to be a member of the senate, but so long as I am, I must go in." "Well, go in then," says the emperor, "but say nothing." "Do not ask my opinion, and I will be silent." "But I must ask your opinion." "And I must say what I think right." "But if you do, I shall put you to death." "When then did I tell you that I am immortal? You will do your part, and I will do mine: it is your part to kill; it is mine to die, but not in fear: yours to banish me; mine to depart without sorrow."

What good then did Priscus do, who was only a single person? And what good does the purple do for the toga? Why, what else than this, that it is conspicuous in the toga as purple, and is displayed also as a fine example to all other things? But in such circumstances another would have replied to Caesar who forbade him to enter the senate, "I thank you for sparing me." But such a man Vespasian would not even have forbidden to enter the senate, for he knew that he would either sit there like an earthen vessel, or, if he spoke, he would say what Caesar wished, and add even more.

In this way an athlete also acted who was in danger of dying unless his private parts were amputated. His brother came to the athlete, who was a philosopher, and said, "Come, brother, what are you going to do? Shall we amputate this member and return to the gymnasium?" But the athlete persisted in his resolution and died. When someone asked Epictetus how he did this, as an athlete or a philosopher, "As a man," Epictetus replied, "and a man who had been proclaimed among the athletes at the Olympic games and had contended in them, a man who had been familiar with such a place, and not merely anointed in Baton's school. Another would have allowed even his head to be cut off, if he could have lived without it. Such is that regard to character which is so strong in those who have been accustomed to introduce it of themselves and conjoined with other things into their deliberations."

"Come, then, Epictetus, shave yourself." "If I am a philosopher," I answer, "I will not shave myself." "But I will take off your head?" If that will do you any good, take it off.

Some person asked, "How then shall every man among us perceive what is suitable to his character?" How, he replied, does the bull alone, when the lion has attacked, discover his own powers and put himself forward in defense of the whole herd? It is plain that with the powers the perception of having them is immediately conjoined; and, therefore, whoever of us has such powers will not be ignorant of them. Now a bull is not made suddenly, nor a brave man; but we must discipline ourselves in the winter for the summer campaign, and not rashly run upon that which does not concern us.

Only consider at what price you sell your own will; if for no other reason, at least for this, that you sell it not for a small sum. But that which is great and superior perhaps belongs to Socrates and such as are like him. "Why then, if we are naturally such, are not a very great number of us like him?" Is it true then that all horses become swift, that all dogs are skilled in tracking footprints? "What, then, since I am naturally dull, shall I, for this reason, take no pains?" I hope not. Epictetus is not superior to Socrates; but if he is not inferior, this is enough for me; for I shall never be a Milo, and yet I do not neglect my body; nor shall I be a Croesus, and yet I do not neglect my property; nor, in a word, do we neglect looking after anything because we despair of reaching the highest degree.

CHAPTER 3

How a man should proceed from the principle of God being the father of all men to the rest

If a man should be able to assent to this doctrine as he ought, that we are all sprung from God in an especial manner, and that God is the father both of men and of gods, I suppose that he would never have any ignoble or mean thoughts about himself. But if Caesar should adopt you, no one could endure your arrogance; and if you know that you are the son of Zeus, will you not be elated? Yet we do not so; but since these two things are mingled in the generation of man, body in common with the animals, and reason and intelligence in common with the gods, many incline to this kinship, which is miserable and mortal; and some few to that which is divine and happy. Since then it is of necessity that every man uses everything according to the opinion which he has about it, those, the few, who think that they are formed for fidelity and modesty and a sure use of appearances have no mean or ignoble thoughts about themselves; but with the many it is quite the contrary. For they say, "What am I? A poor, miserable man, with my wretched bit of flesh." Wretched. Indeed; but you possess something better than your "bit of flesh." Why then do you neglect that which is better, and why do you attach yourself to this?

Through this kinship with the flesh, some of us inclining to it become like wolves, faithless and treacherous and mischievous: some become like lions, savage and untamed; but the greater part of us become foxes and other worse animals. For what else is a slanderer and a malignant man than a fox, or some other more wretched and meaner animal? See, then, and take care that you do not become some one of these miserable things.

CHAPTER 4

Of progress or improvement

He who is making progress, having learned from philosophers that desire means the desire of good things, and aversion means aversion from bad things; having learned too that happiness and tranquility are not attainable by man otherwise than by not failing to obtain what he desires, and not falling into that which he would avoid; such a man takes from himself desire altogether and defers it, but he employs his aversion only on things which are dependent on his will. For if he attempts to avoid anything independent of his will, he knows that sometimes he will fall in with something which he wishes to avoid, and he will be unhappy. Now if virtue promises good fortune and tranquility and happiness, certainly also the progress toward virtue is progress toward each of these things. For it is always true that to whatever point the perfecting of anything leads us, progress is an approach toward this point.

How then do we admit that virtue is such as I have said, and yet seek progress in other things and make a display of it? What is the product of virtue? Tranquility. Who then makes improvement? It is he who has read many books of Chrysippus? But does virtue consist in having understood Chrysippus? If this is so, progress is clearly nothing else than knowing a great deal of Chrysippus. But now we admit that virtue produces one thing. and we declare that approaching near to it is another thing, namely, progress or improvement. "Such a person," says one, "is already able to read Chrysippus by himself." Indeed, sir, you are making great progress. What kind of progress? But why do you mock the man? Why do you draw him away from the perception of his own misfortunes? Will you not show him the effect of virtue that he may learn where to look for improvement? Seek it there, wretch, where your work lies. And where is your work? In desire and in aversion, that you may not be disappointed in your desire, and that you may not fall into that which you would avoid; in your pursuit and avoiding, that you commit no error; in assent and suspension of assent, that you be not deceived. The first things, and the most necessary, are those which I have named. But if with trembling and lamentation you seek not to fall into that which you avoid, tell me how you are improving.

Do you then show me your improvement in these things? If I were talking to an athlete, I should say, "Show me your shoulders"; and then he might say, "Here are my halters." You and your halters look to that. I should reply, "I wish to see the effect of the halters." So, when you say: "Take the treatise on the active powers, and see how I have studied it." I reply, "Slave, I am not inquiring about this, but how you exercise pursuit and avoidance, desire and aversion, how your design and purpose and prepare yourself, whether conformably to nature or not. If conformably, give me evidence of it, and I will say that you are making progress: but if not conformably, be gone, and not only expound your books, but write such books yourself; and what will you gain by it? Do you not know that the whole book costs only five denarii? Does then the expounder seem to be worth more than five denarii? Never, then, look for the matter itself in one place, and progress toward it in another."

Where then is progress? If any of you, withdrawing himself from externals, turns to his own will to exercise it and to improve it by labor, so as to make it conformable to nature, elevated, free, unrestrained, unimpeded, faithful, modest; and if he has learned that he who desires or avoids the things which are not in his power can neither be faithful nor free, but of necessity he must change with them and be tossed about with them as in a tempest, and of necessity must subject himself to others who have the power to procure or prevent what he desires or would avoid; finally, when he rises in the morning, if he observes and keeps these rules, bathes as a man of fidelity, eats as a modest man; in like manner, if in every matter that occurs he works out his chief principles as the runner does with reference to running, and the trainer of the voice with reference to the voice — this is the man who truly makes progress, and this is the man who has not traveled in vain. But if he has strained his efforts to the practice of reading books, and labors only at this, and has traveled for this, I tell him to return home immediately, and not to neglect his affairs there; for this for which he has traveled is nothing. But the other thing is something, to study how a man can rid his life of lamentation and groaning, and saying, "Woe to me," and "wretched that I am," and to rid it also of misfortune and disappointment and to learn what death is, and exile, and prison, and poison, that he may be able to say when he is in fetters, "Dear Crito, if it is the will of the gods that it be so, let it be so"; and not to say, "Wretched am I, an old man; have I kept my gray hairs for this?" Who is it that speaks thus? Do you think that I shall name some man of no repute and of low condition? Does not Priam say this? Does not Oedipus say this? Nay, all kings say it! For what else is tragedy than the perturbations of men who value externals exhibited in this kind of poetry? But if a man must learn by fiction that no external things which are independent of the will concern us, for this? part I should like this fiction, by the aid of which I should live happily and undisturbed. But you must consider for yourselves what you wish.

What then does Chrysippus teach us? The reply is, "to know that these things are not false, from which happiness comes and tranquility arises. Take my books, and you will learn how true and conformable to nature are the things which make me free from perturbations." O great good fortune! O the great benefactor who points out the way! To

Triptolemus all men have erected temples and altars, because he gave us food by cultivation; but to him who discovered truth and brought it to light and communicated it to all, not the truth which shows us how to live, but how to live well, who of you for this reason has built an altar, or a temple, or has dedicated a statue, or who worships God for this? Because the gods have given the vine, or wheat, we sacrifice to them: but because they have produced in the human mind that fruit by which they designed to show us the truth which relates to happiness, shall we not thank God for this?

CHAPTER 5

Against the academics

If a man, said Epictetus, opposes evident truths, it is not easy to find arguments by which we shall make him change his opinion. But this does not arise either from the man's strength or the teacher's weakness; for when the man, though he has been confuted, is hardened like a stone, how shall we then be able to deal with him by argument?

Now there are two kinds of hardening, one of the understanding, the other of the sense of shame, when a man is resolved not to assent to what is manifest nor to desist from contradictions. Most of us are afraid of mortification of the body, and would contrive all means to avoid such a thing, but we care not about the soul's mortification. And indeed with regard to the soul, if a man be in such a state as not to apprehend anything, or understand at all, we think that he is in a bad condition: but if the sense of shame and modesty are deadened, this we call even power.

Do you comprehend that you are awake? "I do not," the man replies, "for I do not even comprehend when in my sleep I imagine that I am awake." Does this appearance then not differ from the other? "Not at all," he replies. Shall I still argue with this man? And what fire or what iron shall I apply to him to make him feel that he is deadened? He does perceive, but he pretends that he does not. He's even worse than a dead man. He does not see the contradiction: he is in a bad condition. Another does see it, but he is not moved, and makes no improvement: he is even in a worse condition. His modesty is extirpated, and his sense of shame; and the rational faculty has not been cut off from him, but it is brutalized. Shall I name this strength of mind? Certainly not, unless we also name it such in catamites, through which they do and say in public whatever comes into their head.

CHAPTER 6

Of providence

From everything which is or happens in the world, it is easy to praise Providence, if a man possesses these two qualities, the faculty of seeing what belongs and happens to all persons and things, and a grateful disposition. If he does not possess these two qualities, one man will not see the use of things which are and which happen; another will not be thankful for them, even if he does know them. If God had made colors, but had not made the faculty of seeing them, what would have been their use? None at all. On the other hand, if He had made the faculty of vision, but had not made objects such as to fall under the faculty, what in that case also would have been the use of it? None at all. Well, suppose that He had made both, but had not made light? In that case, also, they would have been of no use. Who is it, then, who has fitted this to that and that to this? And who is it that has fitted the knife to the case and the case to the knife? Is it no one? And, indeed, from the very structure of things which have attained their completion, we are accustomed to show that the work is certainly the act of some artificer, and that it has not been constructed without a purpose. Does then each of these things demonstrate the workman, and do not visible things and the faculty of seeing and light demonstrate Him? And the existence of male and female, and the desire of each for conjunction, and the power of using the parts which are constructed, do not even these declare the workman? If they do not, let us consider the constitution of our understanding according to which, when we meet with sensible objects, we simply receive impressions from them, but we also select something from them, and subtract something, and add, and compound by means of them these things or those, and, in fact, pass from some to other things which, in a manner, resemble them: is not even this sufficient to move some men, and to induce them not to forget the workman? If not so, let them explain to us what it is that makes each several thing, or how it is possible that things so wonderful and like the contrivances of art should exist by chance and from their own proper motion?

What, then, are these things done in us only. Many, indeed, in us only, of which the rational animal had peculiar need; but you will find many common to us with irrational animals. Do they them understand what is done? By no means. For use is one thing, and understanding is another: God had need of irrational animals to make use of appearances, but of us to understand the use of appearances. It is therefore enough for them to eat and to drink, and to sleep and to copulate, and to do all the other things which they severally do. But for us, to whom He has given also the faculty, these things are not sufficient; for unless we act in a proper and orderly manner, and conformably to the nature and constitution of each thing, we shall never attain our true end. For where the constitutions of living beings are different, there also the acts and the ends are different. In those animals, then, whose constitution is adapted only to use, use alone is enough: but in an animal which has also the power of understanding the use, unless there be the due exercise of the understanding, he will never attain his proper end. Well then God constitutes every animal, one to be eaten, another to serve for agriculture, another to supply cheese, and another for some like use; for which purposes what need is there to understand appearances and to be able to distinguish them? But God has introduced man to be a spectator of God and of His works; and not only a spectator of them, but an interpreter. For this reason it is shameful for man to begin and to end where irrational animals do, but rather he ought to begin where they begin, and to end where nature ends in us; and nature ends in contemplation and understanding, in a way of life conformable to nature. Take care then not to die without having been spectators of these things.

But you take a journey to Olympia to see the work of Phidias, and all of you think it a misfortune to die without having seen such things. But when there is no need to take a journey, and where a man is, there he has the works (of God) before him, will you not desire to see and understand them? Will you not perceive either what you are, or what you were born for, or what this is for which you have received the faculty of sight? But you may say, "There are some things disagreeable and troublesome in life." And are there none in Olympia? Are you not scorched? Are you not pressed by a crowd? Are you not without comfortable means of bathing? Are you not wet when it rains? Have you not abundance of noise, clamor, and other disagreeable things? But I suppose that setting all these things off against the magnificence of the spectacle, you bear and endure. Well, then, and have you not received faculties by which you will be able to bear all that happens? Have you not received greatness of soul? Have you not received manliness? Have you not received endurance? And why do I trouble myself about anything that can happen if I possess greatness of soul? What shall distract my mind or disturb me, or appear painful? Shall I not use the power for the purposes for which I received it, and shall I grieve and lament over what happens?

"Yes, but my nose runs." For what purpose then, slave, have you hands? Is it not that you may wipe your nose? "Is it, then, consistent with reason that there should be running of noses in the world?" Nay, how much better it is to wipe your nose than to find fault. What do you think that Hercules would have been if there had not been such a lion, and hydra, and stag, and boar, and certain unjust and bestial men, whom Hercules used to drive away and clear out? And what would he have been doing if there had been nothing of the kind? Is it not plain that he would have wrapped himself up and have slept? In the first place, then he would not have been a Hercules, when he was dreaming away all his life in such luxury and case; and even if he had been one what would have been the use of him? and what the use of his arms, and of the strength of the other parts of his body, and his endurance and noble spirit, if such circumstances and occasions had not roused and exercised him? "Well, then, must a man provide for himself such means of exercise, and to introduce a lion from some place into his country, and a boar and a hydra?" This would be folly and madness: but as they did exist, and were found, they were useful for showing what Hercules was and for exercising him. Come then do you also having observed these things look to the faculties which you have, and when you have looked at them, say: "Bring now, O Zeus, any difficulty that Thou pleasest, for I have means given to me by Thee and powers for honoring myself through the things which happen." You do not so; but you sit still, trembling for fear that some things will happen, and weeping, and lamenting and groaning for what does happen: and then you blame the gods. For what is the consequence of such meanness of spirit but impiety? And yet God has not only given us these faculties; by which we shall be able to bear everything that happens without being depressed or broken by it; but, like a good king and a true father, He has given us these faculties free from hindrance, subject to no compulsion unimpeded, and has put them entirely in our own power, without even having reserved to Himself any power of hindering or impeding. You, who have received these powers free and as your own, use them not: you do not even see what you have received, and from whom; some of you being blinded to the giver, and not even acknowledging your benefactor, and others, through meanness of spirit, betaking yourselves to fault finding and making charges against God. Yet I will show to you that you have powers and means for greatness of soul and manliness but what powers you have for finding fault and making accusations, do you show me.

CHAPTER 7

Of the use of sophistical arguments, and hypothetical, and the like

The handling of sophistical and hypothetical arguments, and of those which derive their conclusions from questioning, and in a word the handling of all such arguments, relates to the duties of life, though the many do not know this truth. For in every matter we inquire how the wise and good man shall discover the proper path and the proper method of dealing with the matter. Let, then, people either say that the grave man will not descend into the contest of question and answer, or that, if he does descend into the contest, he will take no care about not conducting himself rashly or carelessly in questioning and answering. But if they do not allow either the one or the other of these things, they must admit that some inquiry ought to be made into those topics on which particularly questioning and answering are employed. For what is the end proposed in reasoning? To establish true propositions, to remove the false, to withhold assent from those which are not plain. Is it enough then to have learned only this? "It is enough," a man may reply. Is it, then, also enough for a man, who would not make a mistake in the use of coined money, to have heard this precept, that he should receive the genuine drachmae and reject the spurious? "It is not enough." What, then, ought to be added to this precept? What else than the faculty which proves and distinguishes the genuine and the spurious drachmae? Consequently also in reasoning what has been said is not enough; but is it necessary that a man should acquire the faculty of examining and distinguishing the true and the false, and that which is not plain? "It is necessary." Besides this, what is proposed in reasoning? "That you should accept what follows from that which you have properly granted." Well, is it then enough in this case also to know this? It is not enough; but a man must learn how one thing is a consequence of other things, and when one thing follows from one thing, and when it follows from several collectively. Consider, then if it be not necessary that this power should also be acquired by him who purposes to conduct himself skillfully in reasoning, the power of demonstrating himself the several things which he has proposed, and the power of understanding the demonstrations of others, including of not being deceived by sophists, as if they were demonstrating. Therefore there has arisen among us the practice and exercise of conclusive arguments and figures, and it has been shown to be necessary.

But in fact in some cases we have properly granted the premises or assumptions, and there results from them something; and though it is not true, yet none the less it does result. What then ought I to do? Ought I to admit the falsehood? And how is that possible? Well, should I say that I did not properly grant that which we agreed upon? "But you are not allowed to do even this." Shall I then say that the consequence does not arise through what has been conceded? "But neither is it allowed." What then must be done in this case? Consider if it is not this: as to have borrowed is not enough to make a man still a debtor, but to this must be added the fact that he continues to owe the money and that the debt is not paid, so it is not enough to compel you to admit the inference that you have granted the premises, but you must abide by what you have granted. Indeed, if the premises continue to the end such as they were when they were granted, it is absolutely necessary for us to abide by what we have granted, and we must accept their consequences: but if the premises do not remain such as they were when they were granted, it is absolutely necessary for us also to withdraw from what we granted, and from accepting what does not follow from the words in which our concessions were made. For the inference is now not our inference, nor does it result with our assent, since we have withdrawn from the premises which we granted. We ought then both to examine such kind of premises, and such change and variation of them, by which in the course of questioning or answering, or in making the syllogistic conclusion, or in any other such way, the premises undergo variations, and give occasion to the foolish to be confounded, if they do not see what conclusions are. For what reason ought we to examine? In order that we may not in this matter be employed in an improper manner nor in a confused way.

And the same in hypotheses and hypothetical arguments; for it is necessary sometimes to demand the granting of some hypothesis as a kind of passage to the argument which follows. Must we then allow every hypothesis that is proposed, or not allow every one? And if not everyone, which should we allow? And if a man has allowed an hypothesis, must he in every case abide by allowing it? or must he sometimes withdraw from it, but admit the consequences and not admit contradictions? Yes; but suppose that a man says, "If you admit the hypothesis of a possibility, I will draw you to an impossibility." With such a person shall a man of sense refuse to enter into a contest, and avoid discussion and conversation with him? But what other man than the man of sense can use argumentation and is skillful in questioning and answering, and incapable of being cheated and deceived by false reasoning? And shall he enter into the contest, and yet not take care whether he shall engage in argument not rashly and not carelessly? And if he does not take care, how can he be such a man as we conceive him to be? But without some such exercise and preparation, can he maintain a continuous and consistent argument? Let them show this; and all these speculations become superfluous, and are absurd and inconsistent with our notion of a good and serious man.

Why are we still indolent and negligent and sluggish, and why do we seek pretences for not laboring and not being watchful in cultivating our reason? "If then I shall make a mistake in these matters may I not have killed my father?" Slave, where was there a father in this matter that you could kill him? What, then, have you done? The only fault that was possible here is the fault which you have committed. This is the very remark which I made to Rufus when he blamed me for not having discovered the one thing omitted in a certain syllogism: "I suppose," I said, "that I have burnt the Capitol." "Slave," he replied, "was the thing omitted here the Capitol?" Or are these the only crimes, to burn the Capitol and to kill your father? But for a man to use the appearances resented to him rashly and foolishly and carelessly, not to understand argument, nor demonstration, nor sophism, nor, in a word, to see in questioning and answering what is consistent with that which we have granted or is not consistent; is there no error in this?

CHAPTER 8

That the faculties are not safe to the uninstructed

In as many ways as we can change things which are equivalent to one another, in just so many ways we can change the forms of arguments and enthymemes in argumentation. This is an instance: "If you have borrowed and not repaid, you owe me the money: you have not borrowed and you have not repaid; then you do not owe me the money." To do this skillfully is suitable to no man more than to the philosopher; for if the enthymeme is all imperfect syllogism. it is plain that he who has been exercised in the perfect syllogism must be equally expert in the imperfect also.

"Why then do we not exercise ourselves and one another in this manner?" Because, I reply, at present, though we are not exercised in these things and not distracted from the study of morality, by me at least, still we make no progress in virtue. What then must we expect if we should add this occupation? and particularly as this would not only be an occupation which would withdraw us from more necessary things, but would also be a cause of self conceit and arrogance, and no small cause. For great is the power of arguing and the faculty of persuasion, and particularly if it should be much exercised, and also receive additional ornament from language: and so universally, every faculty acquired by the uninstructed and weak brings with it the danger of these persons being elated and inflated by it. For by what means could one persuade a young man who excels in these matters that he ought not to become an appendage to them, but to make them an appendage to himself? Does he not trample on all such reasons, and strut before us elated and inflated, not enduring that any man should reprove him and remind him of what he has neglected and to what he has turned aside?

"What, then, was not Plato a philosopher?" I reply, "And was not Hippocrates a physician? but you see how Hippocrates speaks." Does Hippocrates, then, speak thus in respect of being a physician? Why do you mingle things which have been accidentally united in the same men? And if Plato was handsome and strong, ought I also to set to work and endeavor to become handsome or strong, as if this was necessary for philosophy, because a certain philosopher was at the same time handsome and a philosopher? Will you not choose to see and to distinguish in respect to what men become philosophers, and what things belong to belong to them in other respects? And if I were a philosopher, ought you also to be made lame? What then? Do I take away these faculties which you possess? By no means; for neither do I take away the faculty of seeing. But if you ask me what is the good of man, I cannot mention to you anything else than that it is a certain disposition of the will with respect to appearances.

The Discourses of Epictetus

CHAPTER 9

How from the fact that we are akin to God a man may proceed to the consequences

If the things are true which are said by the philosophers about the kinship between God and man, what else remains for men to do then what Socrates did? Never in reply to the question, to what country you belong, say that you are an Athenian or a Corinthian, but that you are a citizen of the world. For why do you say that you are an Athenian, and why do you not say that you belong to the small nook only into which your poor body was cast at birth? Is it not plain that you call yourself an Athenian or Corinthian from the place which has a greater authority and comprises not only that small nook itself and all your family, but even the whole country from which the stock of your progenitors is derived down to you? He then who has observed with intelligence the administration of the world, and has learned that the greatest and supreme and the most comprehensive community is that which is composed of men and God, and that from God have descended the seeds not only to my father and grandfather, but to all beings which are generated on the earth and are produced, and particularly to rational beings—for these only are by their nature formed to have communion with God, being by means of reason conjoined with Him—why should not such a man call himself a citizen of the world, why not a son of God, and why should he be afraid of anything which happens among men? Is kinship with Caesar or with any other of the powerful in Rome sufficient to enable us to live in safety, and above contempt and without any fear at all? and to have God for your maker and father and guardian, shall not this release us from sorrows and fears?

But a man may say, "Whence shall I get bread to eat when I have nothing?"

And how do slaves, and runaways, on what do they rely when they leave their masters? Do they rely on their lands or slaves, or their vessels of silver? They rely on nothing but themselves, and food does not fail them. And shall it be necessary for one among us who is a philosopher to travel into foreign parts, and trust to and rely on others, and not to take care of himself, and shall he be inferior to irrational animals and more cowardly, each of which, being self-sufficient, neither fails to get its proper food, nor to find a suitable way of living, and one conformable to nature?

I indeed think that the old man ought to be sitting here, not to contrive how you may have no mean thoughts nor mean and ignoble talk about yourselves, but to take care that there be not among us any young men of such a mind that, when they have recognized their kinship to God, and that we are fettered by these bonds, the body, I mean, and its possessions, and whatever else on account of them is necessary to us for the economy and commerce of life, they should intend to throw off these things as if they were burdens painful and intolerable, and to depart to their kinsmen. But this is the labor that your teacher and instructor ought to be employed upon, if he really were what he should be. You should come to him and say, "Epictetus, we can no longer endure being bound to this poor body, and feeding it and giving it drink, and rest, and cleaning it, and for the sake of the body complying with the wishes of these and of those. Are not these things indifferent and nothing to us, and is not death no evil? And are we not in a manner kinsmen of God, and did we not come from Him? Allow us to depart to the place from which we came; allow us to be released at last from these bonds by which we are bound and weighed down. Here there are robbers and thieves and courts of justice, and those who are named tyrants, and think that they have some power over us by means of the body and its possessions. Permit us to show them that they have no power over any man." And I on my part would say, "Friends, wait for God; when He shall give the signal and release you from this service, then go to Him; but for the present endure to dwell in this place where He has put you: short indeed is this time of your dwelling here, and easy to bear for those who are so disposed: for what tyrant or what thief, or what courts of justice, are formidable to those who have thus considered as things of no value the body and the possessions of the body? Wait then, do not depart without a reason."

Something like this ought to be said by the teacher to ingenuous youths. But now what happens? The teacher is a lifeless body, and you are lifeless bodies. When you have been well filled to-day, you sit down and lament about the morrow, how you shall get something to eat. Wretch, if you have it, you will have it; if you have it not, you will depart from life. The door is open. Why do you grieve? where does there remain any room for tears? and where is there occasion for flattery? why shall one man envy another? why should a man admire the rich or the powerful, even if they be both very strong and of violent temper? for what will they do to us? We shall not care for that which they can do; and what we do care for, that they cannot do. How did Socrates behave with respect to these matters? Why, in what other way than a man ought to do who was convinced that he was a kinsman of the gods? "If you say to me now," said Socrates to his judges, "'We will acquit you on the condition that you no longer discourse in the way in which you have hitherto discoursed, nor trouble either our young or our old men,' I shall answer, 'you make yourselves ridiculous by thinking that, if one of our commanders has appointed me to a certain post, it is my duty to keep and maintain it, and to resolve to die a thousand times rather than desert it; but if God has put us in any place and way of life, we ought to desert it.'" Socrates speaks like a man who is really a kinsman of the gods. But we think about ourselves as if we were only stomachs, and intestines, and shameful parts; we fear, we desire; we flatter those who are able to help us in these matters, and we fear them also.

A man asked me to write to Rome about him, a man who, as most people thought, had been unfortunate, for formerly he was a man of rank and rich, but had been stripped of all, and was living here. I wrote on his behalf in a submissive manner; but when he had read the letter, he gave it back to me and said, "I wished for your help, not your pity: no evil has happened to me."

Thus also Musonius Rufus, in order to try me, used to say: "This and this will befall you from your master"; and I replied that these were things which happen in the ordinary course of human affairs. "Why, then," said he, "should I ask him for anything when I can obtain it from you?" For, in fact, what a man has from himself, it is superfluous and foolish to receive from another? Shall I, then, who am able to receive from myself greatness of soul and a generous spirit, receive from you land and money or a magisterial office? I hope not: I will not be so ignorant about my own possessions. But when a man is cowardly and mean, what else must be done for him than to write letters as you would about a corpse. "Please to grant us the body of a certain person and a sextarius of poor blood." For such a person is, in fact, a carcass and a sextarius of blood, and nothing more. But if he were anything more, he would know that one man is not miserable through the means of another.

CHAPTER 10

Against those who eagerly seek preferment at Rome

If we applied ourselves as busily to our own work as the old men at Rome do to those matters about which they are employed, perhaps we also might accomplish something. I am acquainted with a man older than myself who is now superintendent of corn at Rome, and remember the time when he came here on his way back from exile, and what he said as he related the events of his former life, and how he declared that with respect to the future after his return he would look after nothing else than passing the rest of his life in quiet and tranquility. "For how little of life," he said, remains for me." I replied, "You will not do it, but as soon as you smell Rome, you will forget all that you have said; and if admission is allowed even into the imperial palace, you will gladly thrust yourself in and thank God." "If you find me, Epictetus," he answered, "setting even one foot within the palace, think what you please." Well, what then did he do? Before he entered the city he was met by letters from Caesar, and as soon as he received them he forgot all, and ever after has added one piece of business to another. I wish that I were now by his side to remind him of what he said when he was passing this way and to tell him how much better a seer I am than he is.

Well, then, do I say that man is an animal made for doing nothing? Certainly not. But why are we not active? For example, as to myself, as soon as day comes, in a few words I remind myself of what I must read over to my pupils; then forthwith I say to myself, "But what is it to me how a certain person shall read? the first thing for me is to sleep." And indeed what resemblance is there between what other persons do and what we do? If you observe what they do, you will understand. And what else do they do all day long than make up accounts, inquire among themselves, give and take advice about some small quantity of grain, a bit of land, and such kind of profits? Is it then the same thing to receive a petition and to read in it: "I entreat you to permit me to export a small quantity of corn"; and one to this effect: "I entreat you to learn from Chrysippus what is the administration of the world, and what place in it the rational animal holds; consider also who you are, and what is the nature of your good and bad." Are these things like the other, do they require equal care, and is it equally base to neglect these and those? Well, then, are we the only persons who are lazy and love sleep? No; but much rather you young men are. For we old men, when we see young men amusing themselves, are eager to play with them; and if I saw you active and zealous, much more should I be eager myself to join you in your serious pursuits.

CHAPTER 11

Of natural affection

When he was visited by one of the magistrates, Epictetus inquired of him about several particulars, and asked if he had children and a wife. The man replied that he had; and Epictetus inquired further, how he felt under the circumstances. "Miserable," the man said. Then Epictetus asked, "In what respect," for men do not marry and beget children in order to be wretched, but rather to be happy. "But I," the man replied, "am so wretched about my children that lately, when my little daughter was sick and was supposed to be in danger, I could not endure to stay with her, but I left home till a person sent me news that she had recovered." Well then, said Epictetus, do you think that you acted right? "I acted naturally," the man replied. But convince me of this that you acted naturally, and I will convince you that everything which takes place according to nature takes place rightly. "This is the case," said the man, "with all or at least most fathers." I do not deny that: but the matter about which we are inquiring is whether such behavior is right; for in respect to this matter we must say that tumors also come for the good of the body, because they do come; and generally we must say that to do wrong is natural, because nearly all or at least most of us do wrong. Do you show me then how your behavior is natural. "I cannot," he said; "but do you rather show me how it is not according to nature and is not rightly done.

Well, said Epictetus, if we were inquiring about white and black, what criterion should we employ for distinguishing between them? "The sight," he said. And if about hot and cold, and hard and soft, what criterion? "The touch." Well then, since we are inquiring about things which are according to nature, and those which are done rightly or not rightly, what kind of criterion do you think that we should employ? "I do not know," he said. And yet not to know the criterion of colors and smells, and also of tastes, is perhaps no great harm; but if a man do not know the criterion of good and bad, and of things according to nature and contrary to nature, does this seem to you a small harm? "The greatest harm." Come tell me, do all things which seem to some persons to be good and becoming rightly appear such; and at present as to Jews and Syrians and Egyptians and Romans, is it possible that the opinions of all of them in respect to food are right? "How is it possible?" he said. Well, I suppose it is absolutely necessary that, if the opinions of the Egyptians are right, the opinions of the rest must be wrong: if the opinions of the Jews are right, those of the rest cannot be right. "Certainly." But where there is ignorance, there also there is want of learning and training in things which are necessary. He assented to this. You then, said Epictetus, since you know this, for the future will employ yourself seriously about nothing else, and will apply your mind to nothing else than to learn the criterion of things which are according to nature, and by using it also to determine each several thing. But in the present matter I have so much as this to aid you toward what you wish. Does affection to those of your family appear to you to be according to nature and to be good? "Certainly." Well, is such affection natural and good, and is a thing consistent with reason not good? "By no means." Is then that which is consistent with reason in contradiction with affection? "I think not." You are right, for if it is otherwise, it is necessary that one of the contradictions being according to nature, the other must be contrary to nature. Is it not so? "It is," he said. Whatever, then, we shall discover to be at the same time affectionate and also consistent with reason, this we confidently declare to be right and good. "Agreed." Well then to leave your sick child and to go away is not reasonable, and I suppose that you will not say that it is; but it remains for us to inquire if it is consistent with affection. "Yes, let us consider." Did you, then, since you had an affectionate disposition to your child, do right when you ran off and left her; and has the mother no affection for the child? "Certainly, she has." Ought, then, the mother also to have left her, or ought she not? "She ought not." And the nurse, does she love her? "She does." Ought, then, she also to have left her? "By no means." And the pedagogue, does he not love her? "He does love her." Ought, then, he also to have deserted her? and so should the child have been left alone and without help on account of the great affection of you, the parents, and of those about her, or should she have died in the hands of those who neither loved her nor cared for her? "Certainly not." Now this is unfair and unreasonable, not to allow those who have equal affection with yourself to do what you think to be proper for yourself to do because you have affection. It is absurd. Come then, if you were sick, would you wish your relations to be so affectionate, and all the rest, children and wife, as to leave you alone and deserted? "By no means." And would you wish to be so loved by your own that through their excessive affection you would always be left alone in sickness? or for this reason would you rather pray, if it were possible, to be loved by your enemies and deserted by them? But if this is so, it results that your behavior was not at all an affectionate act.

Well then, was it nothing which moved you and induced you to desert your child? and how is that possible? But it might be something of the kind which moved a man at Rome to wrap up his head while a horse was running which he favored; and when contrary to expectation the horse won, he required sponges to recover from his fainting fit. What then is the thing which moved? The exact discussion of this does not belong to the present occasion perhaps; but it is enough to be convinced of this, if what the philosophers say is true, that we must not look for it anywhere without, but in all cases it is one and the same thing which is the cause of our doing or not doing something, of saying or not saying something, of being elated or depressed, of avoiding anything or pursuing: the very thing which is now the cause to me and to you, to you of coming to me and sitting and hearing, and to me of saying what I do say. And what is this? Is it any other than our will to do so? "No other." But if we had willed otherwise, what else should we have been doing than that which we willed to do? This, then, was the cause of Achilles' lamentation, not the death of Patroclus; for another man does not behave thus on the death of his companion; but it was because he chose to do so. And to you this was the very cause of your then running away, that you chose to do so; and on the other side, if you should stay with her, the reason will be the same. And now you are going to Rome because you choose; and if you should change your mind, you will not go thither. And in a word, neither death nor exile nor pain nor anything of the kind is the cause of our doing anything or not doing; but our own opinions and our wills.

Do I convince you of this or not? "You do convince me." Such, then, as the causes are in each case, such also are the effects. When, then, we are doing anything not rightly, from this day we shall impute it to nothing else than to the will from which we have done it: and it is that which we shall endeavor to take away and to extirpate more than the tumors and abscesses out of the body. And in like manner we shall give the same account of the cause of the things which we do right; and we shall no longer allege as causes of any evil to us, either slave or neighbor, or wife or children, being persuaded that, if we do not think things to he what we do think them to be, we do not the acts which follow from such opinions; and as to thinking or not thinking, that is in our power and not in externals. "It is so," he said. From this day then we shall inquire into and examine nothing else, what its quality is, or its state, neither land nor slaves nor horses nor dogs, nothing else than opinions. "I hope so." You see, then, that you must become a Scholasticus, an animal whom all ridicule, if you really intend to make an examination of your own opinions: and that this is not the work of one hour or day, you know yourself.

CHAPTER 12

Of contentment

With respect to gods, there are some who say that a divine being does not exist: others say that it exists, but is inactive and careless, and takes no forethought about anything; a third class say that such a being exists and exercises forethought, but only about great things and heavenly things, and about nothing on the earth; a fourth class say that a divine being exercises forethought both about things on the earth and heavenly things, but in a general way only, and not about things severally. There is a fifth class to whom Ulysses and Socrates belong, who say: "I move not without thy knowledge."

Before all other things, then, it is necessary to inquire about each of these opinions, whether it is affirmed truly or not truly. For if there are no gods, how is it our proper end to follow them? And if they exist, but take no care of anything, in this case also how will it be right to follow them? But if indeed they do exist and look after things, still if there is nothing communicated from them to men, nor in fact to myself, how even so is it right? The wise and good man, then, after considering all these things, submits his own mind to him who administers the whole, as good citizens do to the law of the state. He who is receiving instruction ought to come to the instructed with this intention: How shall I follow the gods in all things, how shall I be contented with the divine administration, and how can I become free?" For he is free to whom everything happens according, to his will, and whom no man can hinder. "What then, is freedom madness?" Certainly not: for madness and freedom do not consist. "But," you say, "I would have everything result just as I like, and in whatever way I like." You are mad, you are beside yourself. Do you not know that freedom is a noble and valuable thing? But for me inconsiderately to wish for things to happen as I inconsiderately like, this appears to be not only not noble, but even most base. For how do we proceed in the matter of writing? Do I wish to write the name of Dion as I choose? No, but I am taught to choose to write it as it ought to be written. And how with respect to music? In the same manner. And what universally in every art or science? Just the same. If it were not so, it would be of no value to know anything, if knowledge were adapted to every man's whim. Is it, then, in this alone, in this which is the greatest and the chief thing, I mean freedom, that I am permitted to will inconsiderately? By no means; but to be instructed is this, to learn to wish that everything may happen as it does. And how do things happen? As the disposer has disposed them? And he has appointed summer and winter, and abundance and scarcity, and virtue and vice, and all such opposites for the harmony of the whole; and to each of us he has given a body, and parts of the body, and possessions, and companions.

Remembering, then, this disposition of things we ought to go to be instructed, not that we may change the constitution of things—for we have not the power to do it, nor is it better that we should have the power-but in order that, as the things around us are what they are and by nature exist, we may maintain our minds in harmony with them things which happen. For can we escape from men? and how is it possible? And if we associate with them, can we chance them? Who gives us the power? What then remains, or what method is discovered of holding commerce with them? Is there such a method by which they shall do what seems fit to them, and we not the less shall be in a mood which is conformable to nature? But you are unwilling to endure and are discontented: and if you are alone, you call it solitude; and of you are with men, you call them knaves and robbers; and you find fault with your own parents and children, and brothers and neighbors. But you ought when you are alone to call this condition by the name of tranquility and freedom, and to think yourself like to the gods; and when you are with many, you ought not to call it crowd, nor trouble, nor uneasiness, but festival and assembly, and so accept all contentedly.

What, then, is the punishment of those who do not accept? It is to be what they are. Is any person dissatisfied with being alone, let him be alone. Is a man dissatisfied with his parents? let him be a bad son, and lament. Is he dissatisfied with his children? let him be a bad father. "Cast him into prison." What prison? Where he is already, for he is there against his will; and where a man is against his will, there he is in prison. So Socrates was not in prison, for he was there willingly. "Must my leg then be lamed?" Wretch, do you then on account of one poor leg find fault with the world? Will you not willingly surrender it for the whole? Will you not withdraw from it? Will you not gladly part with it to him who gave it? And will you be vexed and discontented with the things established by Zeus, which he with the Moirae who were present and spinning the thread of your generation, defined and put in order? Know you not how small a part you are compared with the whole. I mean with respect to the body, for as to intelligence you are not inferior to the gods nor less; for the magnitude of intelligence is not measured by length nor yet by height, but by thoughts.

Will you not, then, choose to place your good in that in which you are equal to the gods? "Wretch that I am to have such a father and mother." What, then, was it permitted to you to come forth, and to select, and to say: "Let such a man at this moment unite with such a woman that I may be produced?" It was not permitted, but it was a necessity for your parents to exist first, and then for you to be begotten. Of what kind of parents? Of such as they were. Well then, since they are such as they are, is there no remedy given to you? Now if you did not know for what purpose you possess the faculty of vision, you would be unfortunate and wretched if you closed your eyes when colors were brought before them; but in that you possess greatness of soul and nobility of spirit for every event that may happen, and you know not that you possess them, are you not more unfortunate and wretched? Things are brought close to you which are proportionate to the power which you possess, but you turn away this power most particularly at the very time when you ought to maintain it open and discerning. Do you not rather thank the gods that they have allowed you to be above these things which they have not placed in your power; and have made you accountable only for those which are in your power? As to your parents, the gods have left you free from responsibility; and so with respect to your brothers, and your body, and possessions, and death and life. For what, then, have they made you responsible? For that which alone is in your power, the proper use of appearances. Why then do you draw on yourself the things for which you are not responsible? It is, indeed, a giving of trouble to yourself.

CHAPTER 13

How everything may he done acceptably to the gods

When someone asked, how may a man eat acceptably to the gods, he answered: If he can eat justly and contentedly, and with equanimity, and temperately and orderly, will it not be also acceptably to the gods? But when you have asked for warm water and the slave has not heard, or if he did hear has brought only tepid water, or he is not even found to be in the house, then not to be vexed or to burst with passion, is not this acceptable to the gods? "How then shall a man endure such persons as this slave?" Slave yourself, will you not bear with your own brother, who has Zeus for his progenitor, and is like a son from the same seeds and of the same descent from above? But if you have been put in any such higher place, will you immediately make yourself a tyrant? Will you not remember who you are, and whom you rule? that they are kinsmen, that they are brethren by nature, that they are the offspring of Zeus? "But I have purchased them, and they have not purchased me." Do you see in what direction you are looking, that it is toward the earth, toward the pit, that it is toward these wretched laws of dead men? but toward the laws of the gods you are not looking.

CHAPTER 14

That the deity oversees all things

When a person asked him how a man could be convinced that all his actions are under the inspection of God, he answered, Do you not think that all things are united in one? "I do," the person replied. Well, do you not think that earthly things have a natural agreement and union with heavenly things "I do." And how else so regularly as if by God's command, when He bids the plants to flower, do they flower? when He bids them to send forth shoots, do they shoot? when He bids them to produce fruit, how else do they produce fruit? when He bids the fruit to ripen, does it ripen? when again He bids them to cast down the fruits, how else do they cast them down? and when to shed the leaves, do they shed the leaves? and when He bids them to fold themselves up and to remain quiet and rest, how else do they remain quiet and rest? And how else at the growth and the wane of the moon, and at the approach and recession of the sun, are so great an alteration and change to the contrary seen in earthly things? But are plants and our bodies so bound up and united with the whole, and are not our souls much more? and our souls so bound up and in contact with God as parts of Him and portions of Him; and does not God perceive every motion of these parts as being His own motion connate with Himself? Now are you able to think of the divine administration, and about all things divine, and at the same time also about human affairs, and to be moved by ten thousand things at the same time in your senses and in your understanding, and to assent to some, and to dissent from others, and again as to some things to suspend your judgment; and do you retain in your soul so many impressions from so many and various things, and being moved by them, do you fall upon notions similar to those first impressed, and do you retain numerous arts and the memories of ten thousand things; and is not God able to oversee all things, and to be present with all, and to receive from all a certain communication? And is the sun able to illuminate so large a part of the All, and to leave so little not illuminated, that part only which is occupied by the earth's shadow; and He who made the sun itself and makes it go round, being a small part of Himself compared with the whole, cannot He perceive all things?

"But I cannot," the man may reply, "comprehend all these things at once." But who tells you that you have equal power with Zeus? Nevertheless he has placed by every man a guardian, every man's Demon, to whom he has committed the care of the man, a guardian who never sleeps, is never deceived. For to what better and more careful guardian could He have entrusted each of us? When, then, you have shut the doors and made darkness within, remember never to say that you are alone, for you are not; but God is within, and your Demon is within, and what need have they of light to see what you are doing? To this God you ought to swear an oath just as the soldiers do to Caesar. But they who are hired for pay swear to regard the safety of Caesar before all things; and you who have received so many and such great favors, will you not swear, or when you have sworn, will you not abide by your oath? And what shall you swear? Never to be disobedient, never to make any charges, never to find fault with anything that he has given, and never unwillingly to do or to suffer anything, that is necessary. Is this oath like the soldier's oath? The soldiers swear not to prefer any man to Caesar: in this oath men swear to honor themselves before all.

CHAPTER 15

What philosophy promises

When a man was consulting him how he should persuade his brother to cease being angry with him, Epictetus replied: Philosophy does not propose to secure for a man any external thing. If it did philosophy would be allowing something which is not within its province. For as the carpenter's material is wood, and that of the statuary is copper, so the matter of the art of living is each man's life. "What then is my brother's?" That again belongs to his own art; but with respect to yours, it is one of the external things, like a piece of land, like health, like reputation. But Philosophy promises none of these. "In every circumstance I will maintain," she says, "the governing part conformable to nature." Whose governing part? "His in whom I am," she says.

"How then shall my brother cease to be angry with me?" Bring him to me and I will tell him. But I have nothing to say to you about his anger.

When the man, who was consulting him, said, "I seek to know this— how, even if my brother is not reconciled to me, shall I maintain myself in a state conformable to nature?" Nothing great, said Epictetus, is produced suddenly, since not even the grape or the fig is. If you say to me now that you want a fig, I will answer to you that it requires time: let it flower first, then put forth fruit, and then ripen. Is, then, the fruit of a fig-tree not perfected suddenly and in one hour, and would you possess the fruit of a man's mind in so short a time and so easily? Do not expect it, even if I tell you.

CHAPTER 16

Of providence

Do not wonder if for other animals than man all things are provided for the body, not only food and drink, but beds also, and they have no need of shoes nor bed materials, nor clothing; but we require all these additional things. For, animals not being made for themselves, but for service, it was not fit for them to be made so as to need other things. For consider what it would be for us to take care not only of ourselves, but also about cattle and asses, how they should be clothed, and how shod, and how they should eat and drink. Now as soldiers are ready for their commander, shod, clothed and armed: but it would be a hard thing, for the chiliarch to go round and shoe or clothe his thousand men; so also nature has formed the animals which are made for service, all ready, prepared, and requiring no further care. So one little boy with only a stick drives the cattle.

But now we, instead of being thankful that we need not take the same care of animals as of ourselves, complain of God on our own account; and yet, in the name of Zeus and the gods, any one thing of those which exist would be enough to make a man perceive the providence of God, at least a man who is modest and grateful. And speak not to me now of the great things, but only of this, that milk is produced from grass, and cheese from milk, and wool from skins. Who made these things or devised them? "No one," you say. Oh, amazing shamelessness and stupidity!

Well, let us omit the works of nature and contemplate her smaller acts. Is there anything less useful than the hair on the chin? What then, has not nature used this hair also in the most suitable manner possible? Has she not by it distinguished the male and the female? does not the nature of every man forthwith proclaim from a distance, "I am a man; as such approach me, as such speak to me; look for nothing else; see the signs"? Again, in the case of women, as she has mingled something softer in the voice, so she has also deprived them of hair (on the chin). You say: "Not so; the human animal ought to have been left without marks of distinction, and each of us should have been obliged to proclaim, 'I am a man.' But how is not the sign beautiful and becoming, and venerable? how much more beautiful than the cock's comb, how much more becoming than the lion's mane? For this reason we ought to preserve the signs which God has given, we ought not to throw them away, nor to confound, as much as we can, the distinctions of the sexes.

Are these the only works of providence in us? And what words are sufficient to praise them and set them forth according to their worth? For if we had understanding, ought we to do anything else both jointly and severally than to sing hymns and bless the deity, and to tell of his benefits? Ought we not when we are digging and ploughing and eating to sing this hymn to God? "Great is God, who has given us such implements with which we shall cultivate the earth: great is God who has given us hands, the power of swallowing, a stomach, imperceptible growth, and the power of breathing while we sleep." This is what we ought to sing on every occasion, and to sing the greatest and most divine hymn for giving us the faculty of comprehending these things and using a proper way. Well then, since most of you have become blind, ought there not to be some man to fill this office, and on behalf of all to sing the hymn to God? For what else can I do, a lame old man, than sing hymns to God? If then I was a nightingale, I would do the part of a nightingale: if I were a swan, I would do like a swan. But now I am a rational creature, and I ought to praise God: this is my work; I do it, nor will I desert this post, so long as I am allowed to keep it; and I exhort you to join in this same song.

CHAPTER 17

That the logical art is necessary

Since reason is the faculty which analyzes and perfects the rest, and it ought itself not to be unanalyzed, by what should it be analyzed? for it is plain that this should be done either by itself or by another thing. Either, then, this other thing also is reason, or something else superior to reason; which is impossible. But if it is reason, again who shall analyze that reason? For if that reason does this for itself, our reason also can do it. But we shall require something else, the thing, will go on to infinity and have no end. Reason therefore is analyzed by itself. "Yes: but it is more urgent to cure (our opinions) and the like." Will you then hear about those things? Hear. But if you should say, "I know not whether you are arguing truly or falsely," and if I should express myself in any way ambiguously, and you should say to me, " Distinguish," I will bear with you no longer, and I shall say to "It is more urgent." This is the reason, I suppose, why they place the logical art first, as in the measuring of corn we place first the examination of the measure. But if we do not determine first what is a modius, and what is a balance, how shall we be able to measure or weigh anything?

In this case, then, if we have not fully learned and accurately examined the criterion of all other things, by which the other things are learned, shall we be able to examine accurately and to learn fully anything else? "Yes; but the modius is only wood, and a thing which produces no fruit." But it is a thing which can measure corn. "Logic also produces no fruit." As to this indeed we shall see: but then even if a man should rant this, it is enough that logic has the power of distinguishing and examining other things, and, as we may say, of measuring and weighing them. Who says this? Is it only Chrysippus, and Zeno, and Cleanthes? And does not Antisthenes say so? And who is it that has written that the examination of names is the beginning of education? And does not Socrates say so? And of whom does Xenophon write, that he began with the examination of names, what each name signified? Is this then the great and wondrous thing to understand or interpret Chrysippus? Who says this? What then is the wondrous thing? To understand the will of nature. Well then do you apprehend it yourself by your own power? and what more have you need of? For if it is true that all men err involuntarily, and you have learned the truth, of necessity you must act right. "But in truth I do not apprehend the will of nature." Who then tells us what it is? They say that it is Chrysippus. I proceed, and I inquire what this interpreter of nature says. I begin not to understand what he says; I seek an interpreter of Chrysippus. "Well, consider how this is said, just as if it were said in the Roman tongue." What then is this superciliousness of the interpreter? There is no superciliousness which can justly he charged even to

Chrysippus, if he only interprets the will of nature, but does not follow it himself; and much more is this so with his interpreter. For we have no need of Chrysippus for his own sake, but in order that we may understand nature. Nor do we need a diviner on his own account, but because we think that through him we shall know the future and understand the signs given by the gods; nor do we need the viscera of animals for their own sake, but because through them signs are given; nor do we look with wonder on the crow or raven, but on God, who through them gives signs?

I go then to the interpreter of these things and the sacrificer, and I say, "Inspect the viscera for me, and tell me what signs they give." The man takes the viscera, opens them, and interprets them: "Man," he says, "you have a will free by nature from hindrance and compulsion; this is written here in the viscera. I will show you this first in the matter of assent. Can any man hinder you from assenting to the truth? No man can. Can any man compel you to receive what is false? No man can. You see that in this matter you have the faculty of the will free from hindrance, free from compulsion, unimpeded." Well, then, in the matter of desire and pursuit of an object, is it otherwise? And what can overcome pursuit except another pursuit? And what can overcome desire and aversion except another desire and aversion? But, you object: "If you place before me the fear of death, you do compel me." No, it is not what is placed before you that compels, but your opinion that it is better to do so-and-so than to die. In this matter, then, it is your opinion that compelled you: that is, will compelled will. For if God had made that part of Himself, which He took from Himself and gave to us, of such a nature as to be hindered or compelled either by Himself or by another, He would not then be God nor would He be taking care of us as He ought. "This," says the diviner, "I find in the victims: these are the things which are signified to you. If you choose, you are free; if you choose, you will blame no one: you will charge no one. All will be at the same time according to your mind and the mind of God." For the sake of this divination I go to this diviner and to the philosopher, not admiring him for this interpretation, but admiring the things which he interprets.

CHAPTER 18

That we ought not to be angry with the errors of others

If what philosophers say is true, that all men have one principle, as in the case of assent the persuasion that a thing is so, and in the case of dissent the persuasion that a thing is not so, and in the case of a suspense of judgment the persuasion that a thing is uncertain, so also in the case of a movement toward anything the persuasion that a thing is for a man's advantage, and it is impossible to think that one thing is advantageous and to desire another, and to judge one thing to be proper and to move toward another, why then are we angry with the many? "They are thieves and robbers," you may say. What do you mean by thieves and robbers? "They are mistaken about good and evil." Ought we then to be angry with them, or to pity them? But show them their error, and you will see how they desist from their errors. If they do not see their errors, they have nothing superior to their present opinion.

"Ought not then this robber and this adulterer to be destroyed?" By no means say so, but speak rather in this way: "This man who has been mistaken and deceived about the most important things, and blinded, not in the faculty of vision which distinguishes white and black, but in the faculty which distinguishes good and bad, should we not destroy him?" If you speak thus, you will see how inhuman this is which you say, and that it is just as if you would say, "Ought we not to destroy this blind and deaf man?" But if the greatest harm is the privation of the greatest things, and the greatest thing in every man is the will or choice such as it ought to be, and a man is deprived of this will, why are you also angry with him? Man, you ought not to be affected contrary to nature by the bad things of another. Pity him rather: drop this readiness to be offended and to hate, and these words which the many utter: "These accursed and odious fellows." How have you been made so wise at once? and how are you so peevish? Why then are we angry? Is it because we value so much the things of which these men rob us? Do not admire your clothes, and then you will not be angry with the thief. Do not admire the beauty of your wife, and you will not be angry with the adulterer. Learn that a thief and an adulterer have no place in the things which are yours, but in those which belong to others and which are not in your power. If you dismiss these things and consider them as nothing, with whom are you still angry? But so long as you value these things, be angry with yourself rather than with the thief and the adulterer. Consider the matter thus: you have fine clothes; your neighbor has not: you have a window; you wish to air the clothes. The thief does not know wherein man's good consists, but he thinks that it consists in having fine clothes, the very thing which you also think. Must he not then come and take them away? When you show a cake to greedy persons, and swallow it all yourself, do you expect them not to snatch it from you? Do not provoke them: do not have a window: do not air your clothes. I also lately had an iron lamp placed by the side of my household gods: hearing a noise at the door, I ran down, and found that the lamp had been carried off. I reflected that he who had taken the lamp had done nothing strange. What then? To-morrow, I said, you will find an earthen lamp: for a man only loses that which he has. "I have lost my garment." The reason is that you had a garment. "I have pain in my head." Have you any pain in your horns? Why then are you troubled? for we only lose those things, we have only pains about those things which we possess.

"But the tyrant will chain." What? the leg. "He will take away." What? the neck. What then will he not chain and not take away? the will. This is why the ancients taught the maxim, "Know thyself." Therefore we ought to exercise ourselves in small things and, beginning with them, to proceed to the greater. "I have pain in the head." Do not say, "Alas!" "I have pain in the ear." Do not say, "Alas!" And I do not say that you are not allowed to groan, but do not groan inwardly; and if your slave is slow in bringing a bandage, do not cry out and torment yourself, and say, "Everybody hates me": for who would not hate such a man? For the future, relying on these opinions, walk about upright, free; not trusting to the size of your body, as an athlete, for a man ought not to be invincible in the way that an ass is.

Who then is the invincible? It is he whom none of the things disturb which are independent of the will. Then examining one circumstance after another I observe, as in the case of an athlete; he has come off victorious in the first contest: well then, as to the second? and what if there should be great heat? and what, if it should be at Olympia? And the same I say in this case: if you should throw money in his way, he will despise it. Well, suppose you put a young girl in his way, what then? and what, if it is in the dark? what if it should be a little reputation, or abuse; and what, if it should be praise; and what if it should be death? He is able to overcome all. What then if it be in heat, and what if it is in the rain, and what if he be in a melancholy mood, and what if he be asleep? He will still conquer. This is my invincible athlete.

CHAPTER 19

How we should behave to tyrants

If a man possesses any superiority, or thinks that he does, when he does not, such a man, if he is uninstructed, will of necessity be puffed up through it. For instance, the tyrant says, "I am master of all." And what can you do for me? Can you give me desire which shall have no hindrance? How can you? Have you the infallible power of avoiding what you would avoid? Have you the power of moving toward an object without error? And how do you possess this power? Come, when you are in a ship, do you trust to yourself or to the helmsman? And when you are in a chariot, to whom do you trust but to the driver? And how is it in all other arts? Just the same. In what then lies your power? "All men pay respect to me." Well, I also pay respect to my platter, and I wash it and wipe it; and for the sake of my oil flask, I drive a peg into the wall. Well then, are these things superior to me? No, but they supply some of my wants, and for this reason I take care of them. Well, do I not attend to my ass? Do I not wash his feet? Do I not clean him? Do you not know that every man has regard to himself, and to you just the same as he has regard to his ass? For who has regard to you as a man? Show me. Who wishes to become like you? Who imitates you, as he imitates Socrates? "But I can cut off your head." You say right. I had forgotten that I must have regard to you, as I would to a fever and the bile, and raise an altar to you, as there is at Rome an altar to fever.

What is it then that disturbs and terrifies the multitude? is it the tyrant and his guards? I hope that it is not so. It is not possible that what is by nature free can be disturbed by anything else, or hindered by any other thing than by itself. But it is a man's own opinions which disturb him: for when the tyrant says to a man, "I will chain your leg," he who values his leg says, "Do not; have pity": but he who values his own will says, "If it appears more advantageous to you, chain it." "Do you not care?" I do not care. "I will show you that I am master." You cannot do that. Zeus has set me free: do you think that he intended to allow his own son to be enslaved? But you are master of my carcass: take it. "So when you approach me, you have no regard to me?" No, but I have regard to myself; and if you wish me to say that I have regard to you also, I tell you that I have the same regard to you that I have to my pipkin.

This is not a perverse self-regard, for the animal is constituted so as to do all things for itself. For even the sun does all things for itself; nay, even Zeus himself. But when he chooses to be the Giver of rain and the Giver of fruits, and the Father of gods and men, you see that he cannot obtain these functions and these names, if he is not useful to man; and, universally, he has made the nature of the rational animal such that it cannot obtain any one of its own proper interests, if it does not contribute something to the common interest. In this manner and sense it is not unsociable for a man to do everything, for the sake of himself. For what do you expect? that a man should neglect himself and his own interest? And how in that case can there be one and the same principle in all animals, the principle of attachment to themselves?

What then? when absurd notions about things independent of our will, as if they were good and bad, lie at the bottom of our opinions, we must of necessity pay regard to tyrants; for I wish that men would pay regard to tyrants only, and not also to the bedchamber men. How is it that the man becomes all at once wise, when Caesar has made him superintendent of the close stool? How is it that we say immediately, "Felicion spoke sensibly to me." I wish he were ejected from the bedchamber, that he might again appear to you to be a fool.

Epaphroditus had a shoemaker whom he sold because he was good for nothing. This fellow by some good luck was bought by one of Caesar's men, and became Caesar's shoemaker. You should have seen what respect Epaphroditus paid to him: "How does the good Felicion do, I pray?" Then if any of us asked, "What is master doing?" the answer "He is consulting about something with Felicion." Had he not sold the man as good for nothing? Who then made him wise all at once? This is an instance of valuing something else than the things which depend on the will.

Has a man been exalted to the tribuneship? All who meet him offer their congratulations; one kisses his eyes, another the neck, and the slaves kiss his hands. He goes to his house, he finds torches lighted. He ascends the Capitol: he offers a sacrifice of the occasion. Now who ever sacrificed for having had good desires? for having acted conformably to nature? For in fact we thank the gods for those things in which we place our good.

A person was talking to me to-day about the priesthood of Augustus. I say to him: "Man, let the thing alone: you will spend much for no purpose." But he replies, "Those who draw up agreements will write any name." Do you then stand by those who read them, and say to such persons, "It is I whose name is written there;" And if you can now be present on all such occasions, what will you do when you are dead? "My name will remain." Write it on a stone, and it will remain. But come, what remembrance of you will there be beyond Nicopolis? "But I shall wear a crown of gold." If you desire a crown at all, take a crown of roses and put it on, for it will be more elegant in appearance.

CHAPTER 20

About reason, how it contemplates itself

Every art and faculty contemplates certain things especially. When then it is itself of the same kind with the objects which it contemplates, it must of necessity contemplate itself also: but when it is of an unlike kind, it cannot contemplate itself. For instance, the shoemaker's art is employed on skins, but itself is entirely distinct from the material of skins: for this reason it does not contemplate itself. Again, the grammarian's art is employed about articulate speech; is then the art also articulate speech? By no means. For this reason it is not able to contemplate itself. Now reason, for what purpose has it been given by nature? For the right use of appearances. What is it then itself? A system of certain appearances. So by its nature it has the faculty of contemplating itself so. Again, sound sense, for the contemplation of what things does it belong to us? Good and evil, and things which are neither. What is it then itself? Good. And want of sense, what is it? Evil. Do you see then that good sense necessarily contemplates both itself and the opposite? For this reason it is the chief and the first work of a philosopher to examine appearances, and to distinguish them, and to admit none without examination. You see even in the matter of coin, in which our interest appears to be somewhat concerned, how we have invented an art, and how many means the assayer uses to try the value of coin, the sight, the touch, the smell, and lastly the hearing. He throws the coin down, and observes the sound, and he is not content with its sounding once, but through his great attention he becomes a musician. In like manner, where we think that to be mistaken and not to be mistaken make a great difference, there we apply great attention to discovering the things which can deceive. But in the matter of our miserable ruling faculty, yawning and sleeping, we carelessly admit every appearance, for the harm is not noticed.

When then you would know how careless you are with respect to good and evil, and how active with respect to things which are indifferent, observe how you feel with respect to being deprived of the sight of eyes, and how with respect of being deceived, and you will discover you are far from feeling as you ought to in relation to good and evil. "But this is a matter which requires much preparation, and much labor and study." Well then do you expect to acquire the greatest of arts with small labor? And yet the chief doctrine of philosophers is brief. If you would know, read Zeno's writings and you will see. For how few words it requires to say man's end is to follow the god's, and that the nature of good is a proper use of appearances. But if you say "What is 'God,' what is 'appearance,' and what is 'particular' and what is 'universal nature'? then indeed many words are necessary. If then Epicures should come and say that the good must be in the body; in this case also many words become necessary, and we must be taught what is the leading principle in us, and the fundamental and the substantial; and as it is not probable that the good of a snail is in the shell, is it probable that the good of a man is in the body? But you yourself, Epicurus, possess something better than this. What is that in you which deliberates, what is that which examines everything, what is that which forms a judgment about the body itself, that it is the principle part? and why do you light your lamp and labor for us, and write so many books? is it that we may not be ignorant of the truth, who we are, and what we are with respect to you? Thus the discussion requires many words.

CHAPTER 21

Against those who wish to be admired

When a man holds his proper station in life, he does not gape after things beyond it. Man, what do you wish to happen to you? "I am satisfied if I desire and avoid conformably to nature, if I employ movements toward and from an object as I am by nature formed to do, and purpose and design and assent." Why then do you strut before us as if you had swallowed a spit? "My wish has always been that those who meet me should admire me, and those who follow me should exclaim, 'Oh, the great philosopher.'" Who are they by whom you wish to be admired? Are they not those of whom you are used to say that they are mad? Well then do you wish to be admired by madmen?

CHAPTER 22

On precognitions

Precognitions are common to all men, and precognition is not contradictory to precognition. For who of us does not assume that Good is useful and eligible, and in all circumstances that we ought to follow and pursue it? And who of us does not assume that justice is beautiful and becoming? When, then, does the contradiction arise? It arises in the adaptation of the precognitions to the particular cases. When one man says, "He has done well: he is a brave man," and another says, "Not so; but he has acted foolishly"; then the disputes arise among men. This is the dispute among the Jews and the Syrians and the Egyptians and the Romans; not whether holiness should be preferred to all things and in all cases should be pursued, but whether it is holy to eat pig's flesh or not holy. You will find this dispute also between Agamemnon and Achilles; for call them forth. What do you say, Agamemnon ought not that to be done which is proper and right? "Certainly." Well, what do you say, Achilles? do you not admit that what is good ought to be done? "I do most certainly." Adapt your precognitions then to the present matter. Here the dispute begins. Agamemnon says, "I ought not to give up Chryseis to her father." Achilles says, "You ought." It is certain that one of the two makes a wrong adaptation of the precognition of ought" or "duty." Further, Agamemnon says, "Then if I ought to restore Chryseis, it is fit that I take his prize from some of you." Achilles replies, "Would you then take her whom I love?" "Yes, her whom you love." "Must I then be the only man who goes without a prize? and must I be the only man who has no prize?" Thus the dispute begins.

What then is education? Education is the learning how to adapt the natural precognitions to the particular things conformably to nature; and then to distinguish that of things some are in our power, but others are not; in our power are will and all acts which depend on the will; things not in our power are the body, the parts of the body, possessions, parents, brothers, children, country, and, generally, all with whom we live in society. In what, then, should we place the good? To what kind of things shall we adapt it? "To the things which are in our power?" Is not health then a good thing, and soundness of limb, and life? and are not children and parents and country? Who will tolerate you if you deny this?

Let us then transfer the notion of good to these things. is it possible, then, when a man sustains damage and does not obtain good things, that he can be happy? "It is not possible." And can he maintain toward society a proper behavior? He cannot. For I am naturally formed to look after my own interest. If it is my interest to have an estate in land, it is my interest also to take it from my neighbor. If it is my interest to have a garment, it is my interest also to steal it from the bath. This is the origin of wars, civil commotions, tyrannies, conspiracies. And how shall I be still able to maintain my duty toward Zeus? for if I sustain damage and am unlucky, he takes no care of me; and what is he to me if he allows me to be in the condition in which I am? I now begin to hate him. Why, then, do we build temples, why set up statues to Zeus, as well as to evil demons, such as to Fever; and how is Zeus the Saviour, and how the Giver of rain, and the Giver of fruits? And in truth if we place the nature of Good in any such things, all this follows.

What should we do then? This is the inquiry of the true philosopher who is in labor. "Now I do not see what the Good is nor the Bad. Am I not mad? Yes." But suppose that I place the good somewhere among the things which depend on the will: all will laugh at me. There will come some grey-head wearing many gold rings on his fingers and he will shake his head and say, "Hear, my child. It is right that you should philosophize; but you ought to have some brains also: all this that you are doing is silly. You learn the syllogism from philosophers; but you know how to act better than philosophers do." Man, why then do you blame me, if I know? What shall I say to this slave? If I am silent, he will burst. I must speak in this way: "Excuse me, as you would excuse lovers: I am not my own master: I am mad."

CHAPTER 23

Against Epicurus

Even Epicurus perceives that we are by nature social, but having once placed our good in the husk he is no longer able to say anything else. For on the other hand he strongly maintains this, that we ought not to admire nor to accept anything which is detached from the nature of good; and he is right in maintaining this. How then are we [suspicious], if we have no natural affection to our children? Why do you advise the wise man not to bring up children? Why are you afraid that he may thus fall into trouble? For does he fall into trouble on account of the mouse which is nurtured in the house? What does he care if a little mouse in the house makes lamentation to him? But Epicurus knows that if once a child is born, it is no longer in our power not to love it nor care about it. For this reason, Epicurus says that a man who has any sense also does not engage in political matters; for he knows what a man must do who is engaged in such things; for, indeed, if you intend to behave among men as you do among a swarm of flies, what hinders you? But Epicurus, who knows this, ventures to say that we should not bring up children. But a sheep does not desert its own offspring, nor yet a wolf; and shall a man desert his child? What do you mean? that we should be as silly as sheep? but not even do they desert their offspring: or as savage as wolves, but not even do wolves desert their young. Well, who would follow your advice, if he saw his child weeping after falling on the ground? For my part I think that, even if your mother and your father had been told by an oracle that you would say what you have said, they would not have cast you away.

CHAPTER 24

How we should struggle with circumstances

It is circumstances which show what men are. Therefore when a difficulty falls upon you, remember that God, like a trainer of wrestlers, has matched you with a rough young man. "For what purpose?" you may say, Why, that you may become an Olympic conqueror; but it is not accomplished without sweat. In my opinion no man has had a more profitable difficulty than you have had, if you choose to make use of it as an athlete would deal with a young antagonist. We are now sending a scout to Rome; but no man sends a cowardly scout, who, if he only hears a noise and sees a shadow anywhere, comes running back in terror and reports that the enemy is close at hand. So now if you should come and tell us, "Fearful is the state of affairs at Rome, terrible is death, terrible is exile; terrible is calumny; terrible is poverty; fly, my friends; the enemy is near"; we shall answer, "Begone, prophesy for yourself; we have committed only one fault, that we sent such a scout."

Diogenes, who was sent as a scout before you, made a different report to us. He says that death is no evil, for neither is it base: he says that fame is the noise of madmen. And what has this spy said about pain, about pleasure, and about poverty? He says that to be naked is better than any purple robe, and to sleep on the bare ground is the softest bed; and he gives as a proof of each thing that he affirms his own courage, his tranquility his freedom, and the healthy appearance and compactness of his body. "There is no enemy he says; "all is peace." How so, Diogenes? "See," he replies, "if I am struck, if I have been wounded, if I have fled from any man." This is what a scout ought to be. But you come to us and tell us one thing after another. Will you not go back, and you will see clearer when you have laid aside fear?

What then shall I do? What do you do when you leave a ship? Do you take away the helm or the oars? What then do you take away? You take what is your own, your bottle and your wallet; and now if you think of what is your own, you will never claim what belongs to others. The emperor says, "Lay aside your laticlave." See, I put on the angusticlave. "Lay aside this also." See, I have only my toga. "Lay aside your toga." See, I am naked. "But you still raise my envy." Take then all my poor body; when, at a man's command, I can throw away my poor body, do I still fear him?

"But a certain person will not leave to me the succession to his estate." What then? had I forgotten that not one of these things was mine. How then do we call them mine? just as we call the bed in the inn. If, then, the innkeeper at his death leaves you the beds, all well;

but if he leaves them to another, he will have them, and you will seek another bed. If then you shall not find one, you will sleep on the ground: only sleep with a good will and snore, and remember that tragedies have their place among the rich and kings and tyrants, but no poor man fills a part in the tragedy, except as one of the chorus. Kings indeed commence with prosperity: "ornament the palaces with garlands," then about the third or fourth act they call out, "O Cithaeron, why didst thou receive me?" Slave, where are the crowns, where the diadem? The guards help thee not at all. When then you approach any of these persons, remember this that you are approaching a tragedian, not the actor but Oedipus himself. But you say, "Such a man is happy; for he walks about with many," and I also place myself with the many and walk about with many. In sum remember this: the door is open; be not more timid than little children, but as they say, when the thing does not please them, "I will play no loner," so do you, when things seem to you of such a kind, say I will no longer play, and begone: but if you stay, do not complain.

CHAPTER 25

On the same

If these things are true, and if we are not silly, and are not acting hypocritically when we say that the good of man is in the will, and the evil too, and that everything else does not concern us, why are we still disturbed, why are we still afraid? The things about which we have been busied are in no man's power: and the things which are in the power of others, we care not for. What kind of trouble have we still?

"But give me directions." Why should I give you directions? has not Zeus given you directions? Has he not given to you what is your own free from hindrance and free from impediment, and what is not your own subject to hindrance and impediment? What directions then, what kind of orders did you bring when you came from him? Keep by every means what is your own; do not desire what belongs to others. Fidelity is your own, virtuous shame is your own; who then can take these things from you? who else than yourself will hinder you from using them? But how do you act? when you seek what is not your own, you lose that which is your own. Having such promptings and commands from Zeus, what kind do you still ask from me? Am I more powerful than he, am I more worthy of confidence? But if you observe these, do you want any others besides? "Well, but he has not given these orders" you will say. Produce your precognitions, produce the proofs of philosophers, produce what you have often heard, and produce what you have said yourself, produce what you have read, produce what you have meditated on (and you will then see that all these things are from God). How long, then, is it fit to observe these precepts from God, and not to break up the play? As long as the play is continued with propriety. In the Saturnalia a king is chosen by lot, for it has been the custom to play at this game. The king commands: "Do you drink," "Do you mix the wine," "Do you sing," "Do you go," "Do you come." I obey that the game may be broken up through me. But if he says, "Think that you are in evil plight": I answer, "I do not think so"; and who compel me to think so? Further, we agreed to play Agamemnon and Achilles. He who is appointed to play Agamemnon says to me, "Go to Achilles and tear from him Briseis." I go. He says, "Come," and I come.

For as we behave in the matter of hypothetical arguments, so ought we to do in life. "Suppose it to be night." I suppose that it is night. "Well then; is it day?" No, for I admitted the hypothesis that it was night. "Suppose that you think that it is night?" Suppose that I do. "But also think that it is night." That is not consistent with the hypothesis. So in this case also: "Suppose that you are unfortunate." Well, suppose so. "Are you then unhappy?" Yes. "Well, then, are you troubled with an unfavorable demon?" Yes. "But think also that you are in misery." This is not consistent with the hypothesis; and Another forbids me to think so.

How long then must we obey such orders? As long as it is profitable; and this means as long as I maintain that which is becoming and consistent. Further, some men are sour and of bad temper, and they say, "I cannot sup with this man to be obliged to hear him telling daily how he fought in Mysia: 'I told you, brother, how I ascended the hill: then I began to be besieged again.'" But another says, "I prefer to get my supper and to hear him talk as much as he likes." And do you compare these estimates: only do nothing in a depressed mood, nor as one afflicted, nor as thinking that you are in misery, for no man compels you to that. Has it smoked in the chamber? If the smoke is moderate, I will stay; if it is excessive, I go out: for you must always remember this and hold it fast, that the door is open. Well, but you say to me, "Do not live in Nicopolis." I will not live there. "Nor in Athens." I will not live in Athens. "Nor in Rome." I will not live in Rome. "Live in Gyarus." I will live in Gyarus, but it seems like a great smoke to live in Gyarus; and I depart to the place where no man will hinder me from living, for that dwelling-place is open to all; and as to the last garment, that is the poor body, no one has any power over me beyond this. This was the reason why Demetrius said to Nero, "You threaten me with death, but nature threatens you." If I set my admiration on the poor body, I have given myself up to be a slave: if on my little possessions, I also make myself a slave: for I immediately make it plain with what I may be caught; as if the snake draws in his head, I tell you to strike that part of him which he guards; and do you he assured that whatever part you choose to guard, that part your master will attack. Remembering this, whom will you still flatter or fear?

"But I should like to sit where the Senators sit." Do you see that you are putting yourself in straits, you are squeezing yourself. "How then shall I see well in any other way in the amphitheatre?" Man, do not be a spectator at all; and you will not be squeezed. Why do you give yourself trouble? Or wait a little, and when the spectacle is over, seat yourself in the place reserved for the Senators and sun yourself. For remember this general truth, that it is we who squeeze ourselves, who put ourselves in straits; that is, our opinions squeeze us and put us in straits. For what is it to be reviled? Stand by a stone and revile it; and what will you gain? If, then, a man listens like a stone, what profit is there to the reviler? But if the reviler has as a stepping-stone the weakness of him who is reviled, then he accomplishes something. "Strip him." What do you mean by "him"? Lay hold of his garment, strip it off. "I have insulted you." Much good may it do you.

This was the practice of Socrates: this was the reason why he always had one face. But we choose to practice and study anything rather than the means by which we shall be unimpeded and free. You say, "Philosophers talk paradoxes." But are there no paradoxes in the other arts? and what is more paradoxical than to puncture a man's eye in order that he may see? If any one said this to a man ignorant of the surgical art, would he not ridicule the speaker? Where is the wonder then if in philosophy also many things which are true appear paradoxical to the inexperienced?

CHAPTER 26

What is the law of life

When a person was reading hypothetical arguments, Epictetus said: This also is an hypothetical law that we must accept what follows from the hypothesis. But much before this law is the law of life, that we must act conformably to nature. For if in every matter and circumstance we wish to observe what is natural, it is plain that in everything we ought to make it our aim that is consequent shall not escape us, and that we do not admit the contradictory. First, then, philosophers exercise us in theory, which is easier; and then next they lead us to the more difficult things; for in theory, there is nothing which draws us away from following what is taught; but in the matters of life, many are the things which distract us. He is ridiculous, then, who says that he wishes to begin with the matters of real life, for it is not easy to begin with the more difficult things; and we ought to employ this fact as an argument to those parents who are vexed at their children learning philosophy: "Am I doing wrong then, my father, and do I not know what is suitable to me and becoming? If indeed this can neither be learned nor taught, why do you blame me? but if it can he taught, teach me; and if you cannot, allow me to learn from those who say that they know how to teach. For what do you think? do you suppose that I voluntarily fall into evil and miss the good? I hope that it may not be so. What is then the cause of my doing wrong? Ignorance. Do you not choose then that I should get rid of my ignorance? Who was ever taught by anger the art of a pilot or music? Do you think then that by means of your anger I shall learn the art of life?" He only is allowed to speak in this way who has shown such an intention. But if a man only intending to make a display at a banquet and to show that he is acquainted with hypothetical arguments reads them and attends the philosophers, what other object has he than that some man of senatorian rank who sits by him may admire? For there are the really great materials, and the riches here appear to be trifles there. This is the reason why it is difficult for a man to be master of the appearances, where the things which disturb the judgment are great. I know a certain person who complained, as he embraced the knees of Epaphroditus, that he had only one hundred and fifty times ten thousand denarii remaining. What then did Epaphroditus do? Did he laugh at him, as we slaves of Epaphroditus did? No, but he cried out with amazement, "Poor man, how did you keep silence, how did you endure it?"

When Epictetus had reproved the person who was reading the hypothetical arguments, and the teacher who had suggested the reading was laughing at the reader, Epictetus said to the teacher: "You are laughing at yourself; you did not prepare the young man nor did you ascertain whether he was able to understand these matters; but perhaps you are only employing him as a reader." Well then, said Epictetus, if a man has not ability enough to understand a complex, do we trust him in, giving praise, do we trust him in giving blame, do we allow that he is able to form a judgment about good or bad? and if such a man blames any one, does the man care for the blame? and if he praises any one, is the man elated, when in such small matters as an hypothetical syllogism he who praises cannot see what is consequent on the hypothesis?

This then is the beginning of philosophy, a man's perception of the state of his ruling faculty; for when a man knows that it is weak, then he will not employ it on things of the greatest difficulty. But at present, if men cannot swallow even a morsel, they buy whole volumes and attempt to devour them; and this is the reason why they vomit them up or suffer indigestion: and then come gripings, defluxes, and fevers. Such men ought to consider what their ability is. In theory it is easy to convince an ignorant person; but in the affairs of real life no one offers himself to be convinced, and we hate the man who has convinced us. But Socrates advised us not to live a life which is not subjected to examination.

CHAPTER 27

In how many ways appearances exist, and what aids we should provide against them

Appearances to us in four ways: for either things appear as they are; or they are not, and do not even appear to be; or they are, and do not appear to be; or they are not, and yet appear to be. Further, in all these cases to form a right judgment is the office of an educated man. But whatever it is that annoys us, to that we ought to apply a remedy. If the sophisms of Pyrrho and of the Academics are what annoys, we must apply the remedy to them. If it is the persuasion of appearances, by which some things appear to be good, when they are not good, let us seek a remedy for this. If it is habit which annoys us, we must try to seek aid against habit. What aid then can we find against habit, The contrary habit. You hear the ignorant say: "That unfortunate person is dead: his father and mother are overpowered with sorrow; he was cut off by an untimely death and in a foreign land." Here the contrary way of speaking: tear yourself from these expressions: oppose to one habit the contrary habit; to sophistry oppose reason, and the exercise and discipline of reason; against persuasive appearances we ought to have manifest precognitions, cleared of all impurities and ready to hand.

When death appears an evil, we ought to have this rule in readiness, that it is fit to avoid evil things, and that death is a necessary thing. For what shall I do, and where shall I escape it? Suppose that I am not Sarpedon, the son of Zeus, nor able to speak in this noble way: "I will go and I am resolved either to behave bravely myself or to give to another the opportunity of doing so; if I cannot succeed in doing anything myself, I will not grudge another the doing of something noble." Suppose that it is above our power to act thus; is it not in our power to reason thus? Tell me where I can escape death: discover for me the country, show me the men to whom I must go, whom death does not visit. Discover to me a charm against death. If I have not one, what do you wish me to do? I cannot escape from death. Shall I not escape from the fear of death, but shall I die lamenting and trembling? For the origin of perturbation is this, to wish for something, and that this should not happen. Therefore if I am able to change externals according to my wish, I change them; but if I cannot, I am ready to tear out the eyes of him who hinders me. For the nature of man is not to endure to be deprived of the good, and not to endure the falling into the evil. Then, at last, when I am neither able to change circumstances nor to tear out the eyes of him who hinders me, I sit down and groan, and abuse whom I can, Zeus and the rest of the gods. For if they do not care for me, what are they to me? "Yes, but you will be an impious man." In what respect then will it be worse for me than it is now? To sum up, remember this that unless piety and your interest be in the same thing, piety cannot be maintained in any man. Do not these things seem necessary?

Let the followers of Pyrrho and the Academics come and make their objections. For I, as to my part, have no leisure for these disputes, nor am I able to undertake the defense of common consent. If I had a suit even about a bit of land, I would call in another to defend my interests. With what evidence then am I satisfied? With that which belongs to the matter in hand. How indeed perception is effected, whether through the whole body or any part, perhaps I cannot explain: for both opinions perplex me. But that you and I are not the same, I know with perfect certainty. "How do you know it?" When I intend to swallow anything, I never carry it to your b month, but to my own. When I intend to take bread, I never lay hold of a broom, but I always go to the bread as to a mark. And you yourselves who take away the evidence of the senses, do you act otherwise? Who among you, when he intended to enter a bath, ever went into a mill?

What then? Ought we not with all our power to hold to this also, the maintaining of general opinion, and fortifying ourselves against the arguments which are directed against it? Who denies that we ought to do this? Well, he should do it who is able, who has leisure for it; but as to him who trembles and is perturbed and is inwardly broken in heart, he must employ his time better on something else.

CHAPTER 28

That we ought not to be angry with men; and what are the small and the great things among men

What is the cause of assenting to anything? The fact that it appears to be true. It is not possible then to assent to that which appears not to be true. Why? Because this is the nature of the understanding, to incline to the true, to be dissatisfied with the false, and in matters uncertain to withhold assent. What is the proof of this? "Imagine, if you can, that it is now night." It is not possible. "Take away your persuasion that it is day." It is not possible. "Persuade yourself or take away your persuasion that the stars are even in number." It is impossible. When, then, any man assents to that which is false, be assured that he did not intend to assent to it as false, for every soul is unwillingly deprived of the truth, as Plato says; but the falsity seemed to him to be true. Well, in acts what have we of the like kind as we have here truth or falsehood? We have the fit and the not fit, the profitable and the unprofitable, that which is suitable to a person and that which is not, and whatever is like these. Can, then, a man think that a thing is useful to him and not choose it? He cannot. How says Medea?

"'Tis true I know what evil I shall do,
But passion overpowers the better council.'"

She thought that to indulge her passion and take vengeance on her husband was more profitable than to spare her children. "It was so; but she was deceived." Show her plainly that she is deceived, and she will not do it; but so long as you do not show it, what can she follow except that which appears to herself? Nothing else. Why, then, are you angry with the unhappy woman that she has been bewildered about the most important things, and is become a viper instead of a human creature? And why not, if it is possible, rather pity, as we pity the blind and the lame, those who are blinded and maimed in the faculties which are supreme?

Whoever, then, clearly remembers this, that to man the measure of every act is the appearance—whether the thing appears good or bad: if good, he is free from blame; if bad, himself suffers the penalty, for it is impossible that he who is deceived can be one person, and he who suffers another person—whoever remembers this will not be angry with any man, will not be vexed at any man, will not revile or blame any man, nor hate nor quarrel with any man.

"So then all these great and dreadful deeds have this origin, in the appearance?" Yes, this origin and no other. The Iliad is nothing else than appearance and the use of appearances. It appeared to Paris to carry off the wife of Menelaus: it appeared to Helen to follow him. If then it had appeared to Menelaus to feel that it was a gain to be deprived of such a wife, what would have happened? Not only would the Iliad have been lost, but the Odyssey also. "On so small a matter then did such great things depend?" But what do you mean by such great things? Wars and civil commotions, and the destruction of many men and cities. And what great matter is this? "Is it nothing?" But what great matter is the death of many oxen, and many sheep, and many nests of swallows or storks being burnt or destroyed? "Are these things, then, like those?" Very like. Bodies of men are destroyed, and the bodies of oxen and sheep; the dwellings of men are burnt, and the nests of storks. What is there in this great or dreadful? Or show me what is the difference between a man's house and a stork's nest, as far as each is a dwelling; except that man builds his little houses of beams and tiles and bricks, and the stork builds them of sticks and mud. "Are a stork and a man, then, like things?" What say you? In body they are very much alike.

"Does a man then differ in no respect from a stork?" Don't suppose that I say so; but there is no difference in these matters. "In what, then, is the difference?" Seek and you will find that there is a difference in another matter. See whether it is not in a man the understanding of what he does, see if it is not in social community, in fidelity, in modesty, in steadfastness, in intelligence. Where then is the great good and evil in men? It is where the difference is. If the difference is preserved and remains fenced round, and neither modesty is destroyed, nor fidelity, nor intelligence, then the man also is preserved; but if any of these things is destroyed and stormed like a city, then the man too perishes; and in this consist the great things. Paris, you say, sustained great damage, then, when the Hellenes invaded and when they ravaged Troy, and when his brothers perished. By no means; for no man is damaged by an action which is not his own; but what happened at that time was only the destruction of storks' nests: now the ruin of Paris was when he lost the character of modesty, fidelity, regard to hospitality, and to decency. When was Achilles ruined? Was it when Patroclus died? Not so. But it happened when he began to be angry, when he wept for a girl, when he forgot that he was at Troy not to get mistresses, but to fight. These things are the ruin of men, this is being besieged, this is the destruction of cities, when right opinions are destroyed, when they are corrupted.

"When, then, women are carried off, when children are made captives, and when the men are killed, are these not evils?" How is it then that you add to the facts these opinions? Explain this to me also. "I shall not do that; but how is it that you say that these are not evils?" Let us come to the rules: produce the precognitions: for it is because this is neglected that we cannot sufficiently wonder at what men do. When we intend to judge of weights, we do not judge by guess: where we intend to judge of straight and crooked, we do not judge by guess. In all cases where it is our interest to know what is true in any matter, never will any man among us do anything by guess. But in things which depend on the first and on the only cause of doing right or wrong, of happiness or unhappiness, of being unfortunate or fortunate, there only we are inconsiderate and rash. There is then nothing like scales, nothing like a rule: but some appearance is presented, and straightway I act according to it. Must I then suppose that I am superior to Achilles or Agamemnon, so that they by following appearances do and suffer so many evils: and shall not the appearance be sufficient for me? And what tragedy has any other beginning? The Atreus of Euripides, what is it? An appearance. The Oedipus of Sophocles, what is it? An appearance. The Phoenix? An appearance. The Hippolytus? An appearance. What kind of a man then do you suppose him to be who pays no regard to this matter? And what is the name of those who follow every appearance? "They are called madmen." Do we then act at all differently?

CHAPTER 29

On constancy

The being of the Good is a certain Will; the being of the Bad is a certain kind of Will. What then are externals? Materials for the Will, about which the will being conversant shall obtain its own good or evil. How shall it obtain the good? If it does not admire the materials; for the opinions about the materials, if the opinions are right, make the will good: but perverse and distorted opinions make the will bad. God has fixed this law, and says, "If you would have anything good, receive it from yourself." You say, "No, but I have it from another." Do not so: but receive it from yourself. Therefore when the tyrant threatens and calls me, I say, "Whom do you threaten If he says, "I will put you in chains," I say, "You threaten my hands and my feet." If he says, "I will cut off your head," I reply, "You threaten my head." If he says, "I will throw you into prison," I say, "You threaten the whole of this poor body." If he threatens me with banishment, I say the same. "Does he, then, not threaten you at all?" If I feel that all these things do not concern me, he does not threaten me at all; but if I fear any of them, it is I whom he threatens. Whom then do I fear? the master of what? The master of things which are in my own power? There is no such master. Do I fear the master of things which are not in my power? And what are these things to me?

"Do you philosophers then teach us to despise kings?" I hope not. Who among us teaches to claim against them the power over things which they possess? Take my poor body, take my property, take my reputation, take those who are about me. If I advise any persons to claim these things, they may truly accuse me. "Yes, but I intend to command your opinions also." And who has given you this power? How can you conquer the opinion of another man? "By applying terror to it," he replies, "I will conquer it." Do you not know that opinion conquers itself, and is not conquered by another? But nothing else can conquer Will except the Will itself. For this reason, too, the law of God is most powerful and most just, which is this: "Let the stronger always be superior to the weaker." "Ten are stronger than one." For what? For putting in chains, for killing, for dragging whither they choose, for taking away what a man has. The ten therefore conquer the one in this in which they are stronger. "In what then are the ten weaker," If the one possess right opinions and the others do not. "Well then, can the ten conquer in this matter?" How is it possible? If we were placed in the scales, must not the heavier draw down the scale in which it is?

"How strange, then, that Socrates should have been so treated by the Athenians." Slave, why do you say Socrates? Speak of the thing as it is: how strange that the poor body of

Socrates should have been carried off and dragged to prison by stronger men, and that any one should have given hemlock to the poor body of Socrates, and that it should breathe out the life. Do these things seem strange. do they seem unjust, do you on account of these things blame God? Had Socrates then no equivalent for these things, Where, then, for him was the nature of good? Whom shall we listen to, you or him? And what does Socrates say? "Anytus and Meletus can kill me, but they cannot hurt me": and further, he says, "If it so pleases God, so let it be."

But show me that he who has the inferior principles overpowers him who is superior in principles. You will never show this, nor come near showing it; for this is the law of nature and of God that the superior shall always overpower the inferior. In what? In that in which it is superior. One body is stronger than another: many are stronger than one: the thief is stronger than he who is not a thief. This is the reason why I also lost my lamp, because in wakefulness the thief was superior to me. But the man bought the lamp at this price: for a lamp he became a thief, a faithless fellow, and like a wild beast. This seemed to him a good bargain. Be it so. But a man has seized me by the cloak, and is drawing me to the public place: then others bawl out, "Philosopher, what has been the use of your opinions? see you are dragged to prison, you are going to be beheaded." And what system of philosophy could f have made so that, if a stronger man should have laid hold of my cloak, I should not be dragged off; that if ten men should have laid hold of me and cast me into prison, I should not be cast in? Have I learned nothing else then? I have learned to see that everything which happens, if it be independent of my will, is nothing to me. I may ask if you have not gained by this. Why then do you seek advantage in anything else than in that in which you have learned that advantage is?

Then sitting in prison I say: "The man who cries out in this way neither hears what words mean, nor understands what is said, nor does he care at all to know what philosophers say or what they do. Let him alone."

But now he says to the prisoner, "Come out from your prison." If you have no further need of me in prison, I come out: if you should have need of me again, I will enter the prison. "How long will you act thus?" So long as reason requires me to be with the body: but when reason does not require this, take away the body, and fare you well. Only we must not do it inconsiderately, nor weakly, nor for any slight reason; for, on the other hand, God does not wish it to be done, and he has need of such a world and such inhabitants in it. But if he sounds the signal for retreat, as he did to Socrates, we must obey him who gives the signal, as if he were a general.

"Well, then, ought we to say such things to the many?" Why should we? Is it not enough for a man to be persuaded himself? When children come clapping their hands and crying out, "To-day is the good Saturnalia," do we say, "The Saturnalia are not good?" By no means, but we clap our hands also. Do you also then, when you are not able to make a man change his mind, be assured that he is a child, and clap your hands with him, and if you do not choose to do this, keep silent.

A man must keep this in mind; and when he is called to any such difficulty, he should know that the time is come for showing if he has been instructed. For he who is come into a difficulty is like a young man from a school who has practiced the resolution of syllogisms; and if any person proposes to him an easy syllogism, he says, "Rather propose to me a syllogism which is skillfully complicated that I may exercise myself on it." Even athletes are dissatisfied with slight young men, and say "He cannot lift me." "This is a youth of noble disposition." But when the time of trial is come, one of you must weep and say, "I wish that I had learned more." A little more of what? If you did not learn these things in order to show them in practice, why did you learn them? I think that there is some one among you who are sitting here, who is suffering like a woman in labor, and saying, "Oh, that such a difficulty does not present itself to me as that which has come to this man; oh, that I should be wasting my life in a corner, when I might be crowned at Olympia. When will any one announce to me such a contest?" Such ought to be the disposition of all of you. Even among the gladiators of Caesar there are some who complain grievously that they are not brought forward and matched, and they offer up prayers to God and address themselves to their superintendents entreating that they might fight. And will no one among you show himself such? I would willingly take a voyage for this purpose and see what my athlete is doing, how he is studying his subject. "I do not choose such a subject," he says. Why, is it in your power to take what subject you choose? There has been given to you such a body as you have, such parents, such brethren, such a country, such a place in your country: then you come to me and say, "Change my subject." Have you not abilities which enable you to manage the subject which has been given to you? "It is your business to propose; it is mine to exercise myself well." However, you do not say so, but you say, "Do not propose to me such a tropic, but such: do not urge against me such an objection, but such." There will be a time, perhaps, when tragic actors will suppose that they are masks and buskins and the long cloak. I say, these things, man, are your material and subject. Utter something that we may know whether you are a tragic actor or a buffoon; for both of you have all the rest in common. If any one then should take away the tragic actor's buskins and his mask, and introduce him on the stage as a phantom, is the tragic actor lost, or does he still remain? If he has voice, he still remains.

An example of another kind. "Assume the governorship of a province." I assume it, and when I have assumed it, I show how an instructed man behaves. "Lay aside the laticlave and, clothing yourself in rags, come forward in this character." What then have I not the power of displaying a good voice? How, then, do you now appear? As a witness summoned by God. "Come forward, you, and bear testimony for me, for you are worthy to be brought forward as a witness by me: is anything external to the will good or bad? do I hurt any man? have I made every man's interest dependent on any man except himself?" What testimony do you give for God? "I am in a wretched condition, Master, and I am unfortunate; no man cares for me, no man gives me anything; all blame me, all speak ill of me." Is this the evidence that you are going to give, and disgrace his summons, who has conferred so much honor on you, and thought you worthy of being called to bear such testimony?

But suppose that he who has the power has declared, "I judge you to be impious and profane." What has happened to you? "I have been judged to be impious and profane?" Nothing else? "Nothing else." But if the same person had passed judgment on an hypothetical syllogism, and had made a declaration, "the conclusion that, if it is day, it is light, I declare to be false," what has happened to the hypothetical syllogism? who is judged in this case? who has been condemned? the hypothetical syllogism, or the man who has been deceived by it? Does he, then, who has the power of making any declaration about you know what is pious or impious? Has he studied it, and has he learned it? Where? From whom? Then is it the fact that a musician pays no regard to him who declares that the lowest chord in the lyre is the highest; nor yet a geometrician, if he declares that the lines from the centre of a circle to the circumference are not equal; and shall he who is really instructed pay any regard to the uninstructed man when he pronounces judgment on what is pious and what is impious, on what is just and unjust? Oh, the signal wrong done by the instructed. Did they learn this here?

Will you not leave the small arguments about these matters to others, to lazy fellows, that they may sit in a corner and receive their sorry pay, or grumble that no one gives them anything; and will you not come forward and make use of what you have learned? For it is not these small arguments that are wanted now: the writings of the Stoics are full of them. What then is the thing which is wanted? A man who shall apply them, one who by his acts shall bear testimony to his words. Assume, I, entreat you, this character, that we may no longer use in the schools the examples of the ancients but may have some example of our own.

To whom then does the contemplation of these matters belong? To him who has leisure, for man is an animal that loves contemplation. But it is shameful to contemplate these things as runaway slaves do; we should sit, as in a theatre, free from distraction, and listen at one time to the tragic actor, at another time to the lute-player; and not do as slaves do. As soon as the slave has taken his station he praises the actor and at the same time looks round: then if any one calls out his master's name, the slave is immediately frightened and disturbed. It is shameful for philosophers thus to contemplate the works of nature. For what is a master? Man is not the master of man; but death is, and life and pleasure and pain; for if he comes without these things, bring Caesar to me and you will see how firm I am. But when he shall come with these things, thundering and lightning, and when I am afraid of them, what do I do then except to recognize my master like the runaway slave? But so long as I have any respite from these terrors, as a runaway slave stands in the theatre, so do I: I bathe, I drink, I sing; but all this I do with terror and uneasiness. But if I shall release myself from my masters, that is from those things by means of which masters are formidable, what further trouble have I, what master have I still?

"What then, ought we to publish these things to all men?" No, but we ought to accommodate ourselves to the ignorant and to say: "This man recommends to me that which he thinks good for himself: I excuse him." For Socrates also excused the jailer, who had the charge of him in prison and was weeping when Socrates was going to drink the poison, and said, "How generously he laments over us." Does he then say to the jailer that for this reason we have sent away the women? No, but he says it to his friends who were able to hear it; and he treats the jailer as a child.

CHAPTER 30

What we ought to have ready in difficult circumstances

When you are going into any great personage, remember that Another also from above sees what is going on, and that you ought to please Him rather than the other. He, then, who sees from above asks you: "In the schools what used you to say about exile and bonds and death and disgrace?" I used to say that they are things indifferent. "What then do you say of them now? Are they changed at all?" No. "Are you changed then?" No. "Tell me then what things are indifferent?" The things which are independent of the will. "Tell me, also, what follows from this." The things which are independent of the will are nothing to me. "Tell me also about the Good, what was your opinion?" A will such as we ought to have and also such a use of appearances. "And the end, what is it?" To follow Thee. "Do you say this now also?" I say the same now also.

Then go into the great personage boldly and remember these things; and you will see what a youth is who has studied these things when he is among men who have not studied them. I indeed imagine that you will have such thoughts as these: "Why do we make so great and so many preparations for nothing? Is this the thing which men name power? Is this the antechamber? this the men of the bedchamber? this the armed guards? Is it for this that I listened to so many discourses? All this is nothing: but I have been preparing myself for something great."

BOOK TWO

CHAPTER 1

That confidence is not inconsistent with caution

The opinion of the philosophers, perhaps, seems to some to be a paradox; but still let us examine as well as we can, if it is true that it is possible to do everything both with caution and with confidence. For caution seems to be in a manner contrary to confidence, and contraries are in no way consistent. That which seems to many to be a paradox in the matter under consideration in my opinion is of this kind: if we asserted that we ought to employ caution and in the same things, men might justly accuse us of bringing together things which cannot be united. But now where is the difficulty in what is said? for if these things are true, which have been often said and often proved, that the nature of good is in the use of appearances, and the nature of evil likewise, and that things independent of our will do not admit either the nature of evil nor of good, what paradox do the philosophers assert if they say that where things are not dependent on the will, there you should employ confidence, but where they are dependent on the will, there you should employ caution? For if the bad consists in a bad exercise of the will, caution ought only to be used where things are dependent on the will. But if things independent of the will and not in our power are nothing to us, with respect to these we must employ confidence; and thus we shall both be cautious and confident, and indeed confident because of our caution. For by employing caution toward things which are really bad, it will result that we shall have confidence with respect to things which are not so.

We are then in the condition of deer; when they flee from the huntsmen's feathers in fright, whither do they turn and in what do they seek refuge as safe? They turn to the nets, and thus they perish by confounding things which are objects of fear with things that they ought not to fear. Thus we also act: in what cases do we fear? In things which are independent of the will. In what cases, on the contrary, do we behave with confidence, as if there were no danger? In things dependent on the will. To be deceived then, or to act rashly, or shamelessly or with base desire to seek something, does not concern us at all, if we only hit the mark in things which are independent of our will. But where there is death, or exile or pain or infamy, there we attempt or examine to run away, there we are struck with terror. Therefore, as we may expect it to happen with those who err in the greatest matters, we convert natural confidence into audacity, desperation, rashness, shamelessness; and we convert natural caution and modesty into cowardice and meanness, which are full of fear and confusion. For if a man should transfer caution to those things in which the will may be exercised and the acts of the will, he will immediately, by willing to be cautious, have also the power of avoiding what he chooses: but if he transfer it to the things which are not in his power and will, and attempt to avoid the things which are in the power of others, he will of necessity fear, he will be unstable, he will be disturbed. For death or pain is not formidable, but the fear of pain or death. For this reason we commend the poet who said

Not death is evil, but a shameful death.

Confidence then ought to be employed against death, and caution against the fear of death. But now we do the contrary, and employ against death the attempt to escape; and to our opinion about it we employ carelessness, rashness and indifference. These things Socrates properly used to call "tragic masks"; for as to children masks appear terrible and fearful from inexperience, we also are affected in like manner by events for no other reason than children are by masks. For what is a child? Ignorance. What is a child? Want of knowledge. For when a child knows these things, he is in no way inferior to us. What is death? A "tragic mask." Turn it and examine it. See, it does not bite. The poor body must be separated from the spirit either now or later, as it was separated from it before. Why, then, are you troubled, if it be separated now? for if it is not separated now, it will be separated afterward. Why? That the period of the universe may be completed, for it has need of the present, and of the future, and of the past. What is pain? A mask. Turn it and examine it. The poor flesh is moved roughly, then, on the contrary, smoothly. If this does not satisfy you, the door is open: if it does, bear. For the door ought to be open for all occasions; and so we have no trouble.

What then is the fruit of these opinions? It is that which ought to he the most noble and the most becoming to those who are really educated, release from perturbation, release from fear, freedom. For in these matters we must not believe the many, who say that free persons only ought to be educated, but we should rather believe the philosophers, who say that the educated only are free. "How is this?" In this manner. Is freedom anything else than the power of living as we choose? "Nothing else." Tell me then, ye men, do you wish to live in error? "We do not." No one then who lives in error is free. Do you wish to live in fear? Do you wish to live in sorrow? Do you wish to live in perturbation? "By no means." No one, then, who is in a state of fear or sorrow or perturbation is free; but whoever is delivered from sorrows and fears and perturbations, he is at the same time also delivered from servitude. How then can we continue to believe you, most dear legislators, when you say, "We only allow free persons to be educated?" For philosophers say we allow none to be free except the educated; that is, God does not allow it. "When then a man has turned round before the praetor his own slave, has he done nothing?" He has done something. "What?" He has turned round his own slave before the praetor. "Has he done nothing, more?" Yes: he is also bound to pay for him the tax called the twentieth. "Well then, is not the man who has gone through this ceremony become free?" No more than he is become free from perturbations. Have you who are able to turn round others no master? is not money your master, or a girl or a boy, or some tyrant, or some friend of the tyrant? why do you tremble then when you are going off to any trial of this kind? It is for this reason that I often say: Study and hold in readiness these principles by which you may determine what those things are with reference to which you ought to have confidence, and those things with reference to which you ought to be cautious: courageous in that which does not depend on your will; cautious in that which does depend on it.

"Well have I not read to you, and do you not know what I was doing?" In what? "In my little dissertations." Show me how you are with respect to desire and aversion; and show if you do not fail in getting what you wish, me and if you do not fall into the things which you would avoid: but as to these long and labored sentences, you will take them and blot them out.

"What then did not Socrates write?" And who wrote so much? But how? As he could not always have at hand one to argue against his principles or to be argued against in turn, he used to argue with and examine himself, and he was always treating at least some one subject in a practical way. These are the things which a philosopher writes. But little dissertations and that method, which I speak of, he leaves to others, to the stupid, or to those happy men who being free from perturbations have leisure, or to such as are too foolish to reckon consequences.

And will you now, when the opportunity invites, go and display those things which you possess, and recite them, and make an idle show, and say, "See how I make dialogues?" Do not so, my man: but rather say: "See how I am not disappointed of that which I desire. See how I do not fall into that which I would avoid. Set death before me, and you will see. Set before me pain, prison, disgrace and condemnation." This is the proper display of a young man who is come out of the schools. But leave the rest to others, and let no one ever hear you say a word about these things; and if any man commends you for them, do not allow it; but think that you are nobody and know nothing. Only show that you know this, how never to be disappointed in your desire and how never to fall into that which you would avoid. Let others labor at forensic causes, problems and syllogisms: do you labor at thinking about death, chains, the rack, exile; and do all this with confidence and reliance on him who has called you to these sufferings, who has judged you worthy of the place in which, being stationed, you will show what things the rational governing power can do when it takes its stand against the forces which are not within the power of our will. And thus this paradox will no longer appear either impossible or a paradox, that a man ought to be at the same time cautious and courageous: courageous toward the things which do not depend on the will, and cautious in things which are within the power of the will.

CHAPTER 2

Of Tranquility

Consider, you who are going into court, what you wish to maintain and what you wish to succeed in. For if you wish to maintain a will conformable to nature, you have every security, every facility, you have no troubles. For if you wish to maintain what is in your own power and is naturally free, and if you are content with these, what else do you care for? For who is the master of such things? Who can take them away? If you choose to be modest and faithful, who shall not allow you to be so? If you choose not to be restrained or compelled, who shall compel you to desire what you think that you ought not to desire? who shall compel you to avoid what you do not think fit to avoid? But what do you say? The judge will determine against you something that appears formidable; but that you should also suffer in trying to avoid it, how can he do that? When then the pursuit of objects and the avoiding of them are in your power, what else do you care for? Let this be your preface, this your narrative, this your confirmation, this your victory, this your peroration, this your applause.

Therefore Socrates said to one who was reminding him to prepare for his trial, "Do you not think then that I have been preparing for it all my life?" By what kind of preparation? "I have maintained that which was in my own power." How then? "I have never done anything unjust either in my private or in my public life."

But if you wish to maintain externals also, your poor body, your little property and your little estimation, I advise you to make from this moment all possible preparation, and then consider both the nature of your judge and your adversary. If it is necessary to embrace his knees, embrace his knees; if to weep, weep; if to groan, groan. For when you have subjected to externals what is your own, then be a slave and do not resist, and do not sometimes choose to be a slave, and sometimes not choose, but with all your mind be one or the other, either free or a slave, either instructed or uninstructed, either a well-bred cock or a mean one, either endure to be beaten until you die or yield at once; and let it not happen to you to receive many stripes and then to yield. But if these things are base, determine immediately: "Where is the nature of evil and good? It is where truth is: where truth is and where nature is, there is caution: where truth is, there is courage where nature is."

For what do you think? do you think that, if Socrates had wished to preserve externals, he would have come forward and said: "Anytus and Meletus can certainly kill me, but to harm me they are not able?" Was he so foolish as not to see that this way leads not to the preservation of life and fortune, but to another end? What is the reason then that he takes no account of his adversaries, and even irritates them? Just in the same way my friend Heraclitus, who had a little suit in Rhodes about a bit of land, and had proved to the judges that his case was just, said, when he had come to the peroration of his speech, "I will neither entreat you nor do I care what judgment you will give, and it is you rather than I who are on your trial." And thus he ended the business. What need was there of this? Only do not entreat; but do not also say, "I. do not entreat"; unless there is a fit occasion to irritate purposely the judges, as was the case with Socrates. And you, if you are preparing such a peroration, why do you wait, why do you obey the order to submit to trial? For if you wish to be crucified, wait and the cross will come: but if you choose to submit and to plead your cause as well as you can, you must do what is consistent with this object, provided you maintain what is your own.

For this reason also it is ridiculous to say, "Suggest something to me." What should I suggest to you? "Well, form my mind so as to accommodate itself to any event." Why that is just the same as if a man who is ignorant of letters should say, "Tell me what to write when any name is proposed to me." For if I should tell him to write Dion, and then another should come and propose to him not the name of Dion but that of Theon, what will be done? what will he write? But if you behave practiced writing, you are also prepared to write anything that is required. If you are not, what. can I now suggest? For if circumstances require something else, what will you say or what will you do? Remember, then, this general precept and you will need no suggestion. But if you gape after externals, you must of necessity ramble up and down in obedience to the will of your master. And who is the master? He who has the power over the things which you seek to gain or try to avoid.

CHAPTER 3

To those who recommend persons to philosophers

Diogenes said well to one who asked from him letters of recommendation, "That you are a man he said, "he will know as soon as he sees you; and he will know whether you are good or bad, if he is by experience skillful to distinguish the good and the bad; but if he is without experience, he will never know, if I write to him ten thousand times." For it is just the same as if a drachma asked to be recommended to a person to be tested. If he is skillful in testing silver, he will know what you are, for you will recommend yourself. We ought then in life also to have some skill as in the case of silver coin that a man may be able to say, like the judge of silver, "Bring me any drachma and I will test it." But in the case of syllogisms I would say, "Bring any man that you please, and I will distinguish for you the man who knows how to resolve syllogisms and the man who does not." Why? Because I know how to resolve syllogisms. I have the power, which a man must have who is able to discover those who have the power of resolving syllogisms. But in life how do I act? At one time I call a thing good, and at another time bad. What is the reason? The contrary to that which is in the case of syllogisms, ignorance and inexperience.

CHAPTER 4

Against a person who had once been detected in adultery

As Epictetus was saying that man is formed for fidelity, and that he who subverts fidelity subverts the peculiar characteristic of men, there entered one of those who are considered to be men of letters, who had once been detected in adultery in the city. Then Epictetus continued: But if we lay aside this fidelity for which we are formed and make designs against our neighbor's wife, what are we are we doing? What else but destroying and overthrowing? Whom? The man of fidelity, the man of modesty, the man of sanctity. Is this all? And are we not overthrowing neighborhood, and friendship, and the community; and in what place are we putting ourselves? How shall I consider you, man? As a neighbor, as a friend? What kind of one? As a citizen? Wherein shall I trust you? So if you were an utensil so worthless that a man could not use you, you would be pitched out on the dung heaps, and no man would pick you up. But if, being a man, you are unable to fill any place which befits a man, what shall we do with you? For suppose that you cannot hold the place of a friend, can you hold the place of a slave? And who will trust you? Are you not then content that you also should be pitched somewhere on a dung heap, as a useless utensil, and a bit of dung? Then will you say, "No man, cares for me, a man of letters"? They do not, because you are bad and useless. It is just as if the wasps complained because no man cares for them, but all fly from them, and if a man can, he strikes them and knocks them down. You have such a sting that you throw into trouble and pain any man that you wound with it. What would you have us do with you? You have no place where you can be put.

"What then, are not women common by nature?" So I say also; for a little pig is common to all the invited guests, but when the portions have been distributed, go, if you think it right, and snatch up the portion of him who reclines next to you, or slyly steal it, or place your hand down by it and lay hold of it, and if you cannot tear away a bit of the meat, grease your fingers and lick them. A fine companion over cups, and Socratic guest indeed! "Well, is not the theatre common to the citizens?" When then they have taken their seats, come, if you think proper, and eject one of them. In this way women also are common by nature. When, then, the legislator, like the master of a feast, has distributed them, will you not also look for your own portion and not filch and handle what belongs to another. "But I am a man of letters and understand Archedemus." Understand Archedemus then, and be an adulterer, and faithless, and instead of a man, be a wolf or an ape: for what is the difference?

CHAPTER 5

How magnanimity is consistent with care

Things themselves are indifferent; but the use of them is not indifferent. How then shall a man preserve firmness and tranquility, and at the same time be careful and neither rash nor negligent? If he imitates those who play at dice. The counters are indifferent; the dice are indifferent. How do I know what the cast will be? But to use carefully and dexterously the cast of the dice, this is my business. Thus in life also the chief business is this: distinguish and separate things, and say, "Externals are not in my power: will is in my power. Where shall I seek the good and the bad? Within, in the things which are my own." But in what does not belong to you call nothing either good or bad, or profit or damage or anything of the kind.

"What then? Should we use such things carelessly?" In no way: for this on the other hand is bad for the faculty of the will, and consequently against nature; but we should act carefully because the use is not indifferent and we should also act with firmness and freedom from perturbations because the material is indifferent. For where the material is not indifferent, there no man can hinder me nor compel me. Where I can be hindered and compelled the obtaining of those things is not in my power, nor is it good or bad; but the use is either bad or good, and the use is in my power. But it is difficult to mingle and to bring together these two things, the carefulness of him who is affected by the matter and the firmness of him who has no regard for it; but it is not impossible; and if it is, happiness is impossible. But we should act as we do in the case of a voyage. What can I do? I can choose the master of the ship, the sailors, the day, the opportunity. Then comes a storm. What more have I to care for? for my part is done. The business belongs to another—the master. But the ship is sinking—what then have I to do? I do the only things that I can, not to be drowned full of fear, nor screaming, nor blaming God, but knowing that what has been produced must also perish: for I am not an immortal being, but a man, a part of the whole, as an hour is a part of the day: I must be present like the hour, and past like the hour. What difference, then, does it make to me how I pass away, whether by being suffocated or by a fever, for I must pass through some such means?

This is just what you will see those doing who play at ball skillfully. No one cares about the ball being good or bad, but about throwing and catching it. In this therefore is the skill, this the art, the quickness, the judgment, so that if I spread out my lap I may not be able to catch it, and another, if I throw, may catch the ball. But if with perturbation and fear we receive or throw the ball, what kind of play is it then, and wherein shall a man be steady, and how shall a man see the order in the game? But one will say, "Throw"; or,

"Do not throw"; and another will say, "You have thrown once." This is quarreling, not play.

Socrates, then, knew how to play at ball. How?" By using pleasantry in the court where he was tried. "Tell me," he says, "Anytus, how do you say that I do not believe in God. The Demons, who are they, think you? Are they not sons of Gods, or compounded of gods and men?" When Anytus admitted this, Socrates said, "Who then, think you, can believe that there are mules, but not asses"; and this he said as if he were playing at ball. And what was the ball in that case? Life, chains, banishment, a draught of poison, separation from wife and leaving children orphans. These were the things with which he was playing; but still he did play and threw the ball skillfully. So we should do: we must employ all the care of the players, but show the same indifference about the ball. For we ought by all means to apply our art to some external material, not as valuing the material, but, whatever it may be, showing our art in it. Thus too the weaver does not make wool, but exercises his art upon such as he receives. Another gives you food and property and is able to take them away and your poor body also. When then you have received the material, work on it. If then you come out without having suffered anything, all who meet you will congratulate you on your escape; but he who knows how to look at such things, if he shall see that you have behaved properly in the matter, will commend you and be pleased with you; and if he shall find that you owe your escape to any want of proper behavior, he will do the contrary. For where rejoicing is reasonable, there also is congratulation reasonable.

How then is it said that some external things are according to nature and others contrary to nature? It is said as it might be said if we were separated from union: for to the foot I shall say that it is according to nature for it to be clean; but if you take it as a foot and as a thing not detached, it will befit it both to step into the mud and tread on thorns, and sometimes to be cut off for the benefit of the whole body; otherwise it is no longer a foot. We should think in some way about ourselves also. What are you? A man. If you consider yourself as detached from other men, it is according to nature to live to old age, to be rich, to be healthy. But if you consider yourself as a man and a part of a certain whole, it is for the sake of that whole that at one time you should be sick, at another time take a voyage and run into danger, and at another time be in want, and, in some cases, die prematurely. Why then are you troubled? Do you not know, that as a foot is no longer a foot if it is detached from the body, so you are no longer a man if you are separated from other men. For what is a man? A part of a state, of that first which consists of Gods and of men; then of that which is called next to it, which is a small image of the universal state. "What then must I be brought to trial; must another have a fever, another sail on the sea, another die, and another be condemned?" Yes, for it is impossible in such a body, in such a universe of things, among so many living together, that such things should not happen, some to one and others to others. It is your duty then, since you are come here, to say what you ought, to arrange these things as it is fit. Then some one says, "I shall charge you with doing me wrong." Much good may it do you: I have done my part; but whether you also have done yours, you must look to that; for there is some danger of this too, that it may escape your notice.

CHAPTER 6

Of indifference

The hypothetical proposition is indifferent: the judgment about it is not indifferent, but it is either knowledge or opinion or error. Thus life is indifferent: the use is not indifferent. When any man then tells you that these things also are indifferent, do not become negligent; and when a man invites you to be careful, do not become abject and struck with admiration of material things. And it is good for you to know your own preparation and power, that in those matters where you have not been prepared, you may keep quiet, and not be vexed, if others have the advantage over you. For you, too, in syllogisms will claim to have the advantage over them; and if others should be vexed at this, you will console them by saying, "I have learned them, and you have not." Thus also where there is need of any practice, seek not that which is required from the need, but yield in that matter to those who have had practice, and be yourself content with firmness of mind.

Go and salute a certain person. "How?" Not meanly. "But I have been shut out, for I have not learned to make my way through the window; and when I have found the door shut, I must either come back or enter through the window." But still speak to him. "In what way?" Not meanly. But suppose that you have not got what you wanted. Was this your business, and not his? Why then do you claim that which belongs to another? Always remember what is your own, and what belongs to another; and you will not be disturbed. Chrysippus therefore said well, "So long as future things are uncertain, I always cling to those which are more adapted to the conservation of that which is according to nature; for God himself has given me the faculty of such choice." But if I knew that it was fated for me to be sick, I would even move toward it; for the foot also, if it had intelligence, would move to go into the mud. For why are ears of corn produced? Is it not that they may become dry? And do they not become dry that they may be reaped? for they are not separated from communion with other things. If then they had perception, ought they to wish never to be reaped? But this is a curse upon ears of corn, never to be reaped. So we must know that in the case of men too it is a curse not to die, just the same as not to be ripened and not to be reaped. But since we must be reaped, and we also know that we are reaped, we are vexed at it; for we neither know what we are nor have we studied what belongs to man, as those who have studied horses know what belongs to horses. But Chrysantas, when he was going to strike the enemy, checked himself when he heard the trumpet sounding a retreat: so it seemed better to him to obey the general's command than to follow his own inclination. But not one of us chooses, even when necessity summons, readily to obey it, but weeping and groaning we suffer what we do suffer, and we call them "circumstances." What kind of circumstances, man? If you give the name of circumstances to the things which are around you, all things are circumstances; but if you call hardships by this name, what hardship is there in the dying of that which has been produced? But that which destroys is either a sword, or a wheel, or the sea, or a tile, or a tyrant. Why do you care about the way of going down to Hades? All ways are equal. But if you will listen to the truth, the way which the tyrant sends you is shorter. A tyrant never killed a man in six months: but a fever is often a year about it. All these things are only sound and the noise of empty names.

"I am in danger of my life from Caesar." And am not I in danger who dwell in Nicopolis, where there are so many earthquakes: and when you are crossing the Hadriatic, what hazard do you run? Is it not the hazard of your life? "But I am in danger also as to opinion." Do you mean your own? how? For who can compel you to have any opinion which you do not choose? But is it as to another man's opinion? and what kind of danger is yours, if others have false opinions? "But I am in danger of being banished." What is it to be banished? To be somewhere else than at Rome? "Yes: what then if I should be sent to Gyara?" If that suits you, you will go there; but if it does not, you can go to another place instead of Gyara, whither he also will go, who sends you to Gyara, whether he choose or not. Why then do you go up to Rome as if it were something great? It is not worth all this preparation, that an ingenuous youth should say, "It was not worth while to have heard so much and to have written so much and to have sat so long by the side of an old man who is not worth much." Only remember that division by which your own and not your own are distinguished: never claim anything which belongs to others. A tribunal and a prison are each a place, one high and the other low; but the will can be maintained equal, if you choose to maintain it equal in each. And we shall then be imitators of Socrates, when we are able to write paeans in prison. But in our present disposition, consider if we could endure in prison another person saying to us. "Would you like me to read Paeans to you?" "Why do you trouble me? do you not know the evils which hold me? Can I in such circumstances?" What circumstances? "I am going to die." And will other men be immortal?

CHAPTER 7

How we ought to use divination

Through an unreasonable regard to divination many of us omit many duties. For what more can the diviner see than death or danger or disease, generally things of that kind? If then I must expose myself to danger for a friend, and if it is my duty even to die for him, what need have I then for divination? Have I not within me a diviner who has told me the nature of good and of evil, and has explained to me the signs of both? What need have I then to consult the viscera of victims or the flight of birds, and why do I submit when he says, "It is for your interest"? For does he know what is for my interest, does he know what is good; and as he has learned the signs of the viscera, has he also learned the signs of good and evil? For if he knows the signs of these, he knows the signs both of the beautiful and of the ugly, and of the just and of the unjust. Do you tell me, man, what is the thing which is signified for me: is it life or death, poverty or wealth? But whether these things are for my interest or whether they are not, I do not intend to ask you. Why don't you give your opinion on matters of grammar, and why do you give it here about things on which we are all in error and disputing with one another? The woman, therefore, who intended to send by a vessel a month's provisions to Gratilla in her banishment, made a good answer to him who said that Domitian would seize what she sent. "I would rather," she replied, "that Domitian should seize all than that I should not send it."

What then leads us to frequent use of divination? Cowardice, the dread of what will happen. This is the reason why we flatter the diviners. "Pray, master, shall I succeed to the property of my father?" "Let us see: let us sacrifice on the occasion." "Yes, master, as fortune chooses." When he has said, "You shall succeed to the inheritance," we thank him as if we received the inheritance from him. The consequence is that they play upon us.

What then should we do? We ought to come without desire or aversion, as the wayfarer asks of the man whom he meets which of two roads leads (to his journey's end), without any desire for that which leads to the right rather than to the left, for he has no wish to go by any road except the road which leads (to his end). In the same way ought we to come to God also as a guide; as we use our eyes, not asking them to show us rather such things as we wish, but receiving the appearances of things such as the eyes present them to us. But now we trembling take the augur by the hand, and, while we invoke God, we entreat the augur, and say, "Master have mercy on me; suffer me to come safe out of this difficulty." Wretch would you have, then, anything other than what is best? Is there then anything better than what pleases God? Why do you, so far as in your power, corrupt your judge and lead astray your adviser?

CHAPTER 8

What is the nature of the good

God is beneficial. But the Good also is beneficial. It is consistent then that where the nature of God is, there also the nature of the good should be. What then is the nature of God? Flesh? Certainly not. An estate in land? By no means. Fame? No. Is it intelligence, knowledge, right reason? Yes. Herein then simply seek the nature of the good; for I suppose that you do not seek it in a plant. No. Do you seek it in an irrational animal? No. If then you seek it in a rational animal, why do you still seek it anywhere except in the superiority of rational over irrational animals? Now plants have not even the power of using appearances, and for this reason you do not apply the term good to them. The good then requires the use of appearances. Does it require this use only? For if you say that it requires this use only, say that the good, and that happiness and unhappiness are in irrational animals also. But you do not say this, and you do right; for if they possess even in the highest degree the use of appearances, yet they have not the faculty of understanding the use of appearances; and there is good reason for this, for they exist for the purpose of serving others, and they exercise no superiority. For the ass, I suppose, does not exist for any superiority over others. No; but because we had need of a back which is able to bear something; and in truth we had need also of his being able to walk, and for this reason he received also the faculty of making use of appearances, for otherwise he would not have been able to walk. And here then the matter stopped. For if he had also received the faculty of comprehending the use of appearances, it is plain that consistently with reason he would not then have been subjected to us, nor would he have done us these services, but he would have been equal to us and like to us.

Will you not then seek the nature of good in the rational animal? for if it is not there, you not choose to say that it exists in any other thing. "What then? are not plants and animals also the works of God?" They are; but they are not superior things, nor yet parts of the Gods. But you are a superior thing; you are a portion separated from the deity; you have in yourself a certain portion of him. Why then are you ignorant of your own noble descent? Why do you not know whence you came? will you not remember when you are eating, who you are who eat and whom you feed? When you are in conjunction with a woman, will you not remember who you are who do this thing? When you are in social intercourse, when you are exercising yourself, when you are engaged in discussion, know you not that you are nourishing a god, that you are exercising a god? Wretch, you are carrying about a god with you, and you know it not. Do you think that I mean some God of silver or of gold, and external? You carry him within yourself, and you perceive not that you are polluting him by impure thoughts and dirty deeds. And if an image of

God were present, you would not dare to do any of the things which you are doing: but when God himself is present within and sees all and hears all, you are not ashamed of thinking such things and doing such things, ignorant as you are of your own nature and subject to the anger of God. Then why do we fear when we are sending a young man from the school into active life, lest he should do anything improperly, eat improperly, have improper intercourse with women; and lest the rags in which he is wrapped should debase him, lest fine garments should make him proud? This youth does not know his own God: he knows not with whom he sets out. But can we endure when he says, "I wish I had you with me." Have you not God with you? and do you seek for any other, when you have him? or will God tell you anything else than this? If you were a statue of Phidias, either Athena or Zeus you would think broth of yourself and of the artist, and if you had any understanding you would try to do nothing unworthy of him who made you or of yourself, and try not to appear in an unbecoming dress to those who look on you. But now because Zeus has made you, for this reason do you care not how you shall appear? And yet is the artist like the artist in the other? or the work in the one case like the other? And what work of an artist, for instance, has in itself the faculties, which the artist shows in making it? Is it not marble or bronze, or gold or ivory? and the Athena of Phidias when she has once extended the hand and received in it the figure of Victory stands in that attitude forever. But the works of God have power of motion, they breathe, they have the faculty of using the appearances of things, and the power of examining them. Being the work of such an artist, do you dishonor him? And what shall I say, not only that he made you, but also entrusted you to yourself and made you a deposit to yourself? Will you not think of this too, but do you also dishonor your guardianship? But if God had entrusted an orphan to you, would you thus neglect him? He has delivered yourself to your care, and says, "I had no one fitter to entrust him to than yourself: keep him for me such as he is by nature, modest, faithful, erect, unterrified, free from passion and perturbation." And then you do not keep him such.

But some will say, "Whence has this fellow got the arrogance which he displays and these supercilious looks?" I have not yet so much gravity as befits a philosopher; for I do not yet feel confidence in what I have learned and what I have assented to: I still fear my own weakness. Let me get confidence and the, you shall see a countenance such as I ought to have and an attitude such as I ought to have: then I will show to you the statue, when it is perfected, when it is polished. What do you expect? a supercilious countenance? Does the Zeus at Olympia lift up his brow? No, his look is fixed as becomes him who is ready to say

Irrevocable is my word and shall not fail.

Such will I show myself to you, faithful, modest, noble, free from perturbation. "What, and immortal too, exempt from old age, and from sickness?" No, but dying as becomes a god, sickening as becomes a god. This power I possess; this I can do. But the rest I do not possess, nor can I do. I will show the nerves of a philosopher. "What nerves are these?" A desire never disappointed, an aversion which never falls on that which it would avoid, a proper pursuit, a diligent purpose, an assent which is not rash. These you shall see.

CHAPTER 9

That when we cannot fulfill that which the character of a man promises, we assume the character of a philosopher

It is no common thing to do this only, to fulfill the promise of a man's nature. For what is a man? The answer is: "A rational and mortal being." Then, by the rational faculty, from whom are we separated? From wild beasts. And from what others? From sheep and like animals. Take care then to do nothing like a wild beast; but if you do, you have lost the character of a man; you have not fulfilled your promise. See that you do nothing like a sheep; but if you do, in this case the man is lost. What then do we do as sheep? When we act gluttonously, when we act lewdly, when we act rashly, filthily, inconsiderately, to what have we declined? To sheep. What have we lost? The rational faculty. When we act contentiously and harmfully and passionately, and violently, to what have we declined? To wild beasts. Consequently some of us are great wild beasts, and others little beasts, of a bad disposition and small, whence we may say, "Let me be eaten by a lion." But in all these ways the promise of a man acting as a man is destroyed. For when is a conjunctive proposition maintained? When it fulfills what its nature promises; so that the preservation of a complex proposition is when it is a conjunction of truths. When is a disjunctive maintained? When it fulfills what it promises. When are flutes, a lyre, a horse, a dog, preserved? What is the wonder then if man also in like manner is preserved, and in like manner is lost? Each man is improved and preserved by corresponding acts, the carpenter by acts of carpentry, the grammarian by acts of grammar. But if a man accustoms himself to write ungrammatically, of necessity his art will be corrupted and destroyed. Thus modest actions preserve the modest man, and immodest actions destroy him: and actions of fidelity preserve the faithful man, and the contrary actions destroy him. And on the other hand contrary actions strengthen contrary characters: shamelessness strengthens the shameless man, faithlessness the faithless man, abusive words the abusive man, anger the man of an angry temper, and unequal receiving and giving make the avaricious man more avaricious.

For this reason philosophers admonish us not to be satisfied with learning only, but also to add study, and then practice. For we have long been accustomed to do contrary things, and we put in practice opinions which are contrary to true opinions. If then we shall not also put in practice right opinions, we shall be nothing more than the expositors of the opinions of others. For now who among us is not able to discuss according to the rules of art about good and evil things? "That of things some are good, and some are bad, and some are indifferent: the good then are virtues, and the things which participate in virtues; and the bad are the contrary; and the indifferent are wealth, health, reputation."

Then, if in the midst of our talk there should happen some greater noise than usual, or some of those who are present should laugh at us, we are disturbed. Philosopher, where are the things which you were talking about? Whence did you produce and utter them? From the lips, and thence only. Why then do you corrupt the aids provided by others? Why do you treat the weightiest matters as if you were playing a game of dice? For it is one thing to lay up bread and wine as in a storehouse, and another thing to eat. That which has been eaten, is digested, distributed, and is become sinews, flesh, bones, blood, healthy color, healthy breath. Whatever is stored up, when you choose you can readily take and show it; but you have no other advantage from it except so far as to appear to possess it. For what is the difference between explaining these doctrines and those of men who have different opinions? Sit down now and explain according to the rules of art the opinions of Epicurus, and perhaps you will explain his opinions in a more useful manner than Epicurus himself. Why then do you call yourself a Stoic? Why do you deceive the many? Why do you deceive the many? Why do you act the part of a Jew, when you are a Greek? Do you not see how each is called a Jew, or a Syrian or an Egyptian? and when we see a man inclining to two sides, we are accustomed to say, "This man is not a Jew, but he acts as one." But when he has assumed the affects of one who has been imbued with Jewish doctrine and has adopted that sect, then he is in fact and he is named a Jew. Thus we too being falsely imbued, are in name Jews, but in fact we are something else. Our affects are inconsistent with our words; we are far from practicing what we say, and that of which we are proud, as if we knew it. Thus being, unable to fulfill even what the character of a man promises, we even add to it the profession of a philosopher, which is as heavy a burden, as if a man who is unable to bear ten pounds should attempt to raise the stone which Ajax lifted.

CHAPTER 10

How we may discover the duties of life from names

Consider who you are. In the first place, you are a man; and this is one who has nothing superior to the faculty of the will, but all other things subjected to it; and the faculty itself he possesses unenslaved and free from subjection. Consider then from what things you have been separated by reason. You have been separated from wild beasts: you have been separated from domestic animals. Further, you are a citizen of the world, and a part of it, not one of the subservient, but one of the principal parts, for you are capable of comprehending the divine administration and of considering the connection of things. What then does the character of a citizen promise? To hold nothing as profitable to himself; to deliberate about nothing as if he were detached from the community, but to act as the hand or foot would do, if they had reason and understood the constitution of nature, for they would never put themselves in motion nor desire anything, otherwise than with reference to the whole. Therefore the philosophers say well, that if the good man had foreknowledge of what would happen, he would cooperate toward his own sickness and death and mutilation, since he knows that these things are assigned to him according to the universal arrangement, and that the whole is superior to the part and the state to the citizen. But now, because we do not know the future, it is our duty to stick to the things which are in their nature more suitable for our choice, for we were made among other things for this.

After this, remember that you are a son. What does this character promise? To consider that everything which is the son's belongs to the father, to obey him in all things, never to blame him to another, nor to say or do anything which does him injury, to yield to him in all things and give way, cooperating with him as far as you can. After this know that you are a brother also, and that to this character it is due to make concessions; to be easily persuaded, to speak good of your brother, never to claim in opposition to him any of the things which are independent of the will, but readily to give them up, that you may have the larger share in what is dependent on the will. For see what a thing it is, in place of a lettuce, if it should so happen, or a seat, to gain for yourself goodness of disposition. How great is the advantage.

Next to this, if you are senator of any state, remember that you are a senator: if a youth, that you are a youth: if an old man, that you are an old man; for each of such names, if it comes to be examined, marks out the proper duties. But if you go and blame your brother, I say to you, "You have forgotten who you are and what is your name." In the next place, if you were a smith and made a wrong use of the hammer, you would have forgotten the smith; and if you have forgotten the brother and instead of a brother have become an enemy, would you appear not to have changed one thing for another in that case? And if instead of a man, who is a tame animal and social, you are become a mischievous wild beast, treacherous, and biting, have you lost nothing? But, you must lose a bit of money that you may suffer damage? And does the loss of nothing else do a man damage? If you had lost the art of grammar or music, would you think the loss of it a damage? and if you shall lose modesty, moderation and gentleness, do you think the loss nothing? And yet the things first mentioned are lost by some cause external and independent of the will, and the second by our own fault; and as to the first neither to have them nor to lose them is shameful; but as to the second, not to have them and to lose them is shameful and matter of reproach and a misfortune. What does the pathic lose? He loses the man. What does he lose who makes the pathic what he is? Many other things; and he also loses the man no less than the other. What does he lose who commits adultery? He loses the modest, the temperate, the decent, the citizen, the neighbor. What does he lose who is angry? Something else. What does the coward lose? Something else. No man is bad without suffering some loss and damage. If then you look for the damage in the loss of money only, all these men receive no harm or damage; it may be, they have even profit and gain, when they acquire a bit of money by any of these deeds. But consider that if you refer everything to a small coin, not even he who loses his nose is in your opinion damaged. "Yes," you say, "for he is mutilated in his body." Well; but does he who has lost his smell only lose nothing? Is there, then, no energy of the soul which is an advantage to him who possesses it, and a damage to him who has lost it? "Tell me what sort you mean." Have we not a natural modesty? "We have." Does he who loses this sustain no damage? is he deprived of nothing, does he part with nothing of the things which belong to him? Have we not naturally fidelity? natural affection, a natural disposition to help others, a natural disposition to forbearance? The man then who allows himself to be damaged in these matters, can he be free from harm and uninjured? "What then? shall I not hurt him, who has hurt me?" In the first place consider what hurt is, and remember what you have heard from the philosophers. For if the good consists in the will, and the evil also in the will, see if what you say is not this: "What then, since that man has hurt himself by doing an unjust act to me, shall I not hurt myself by doing some unjust act to him?" Why do we not imagine to something of this kind? But where there is any detriment to the body or to our possession, there is harm there; and where the same thing happens to the faculty of the will, there is no harm; for he who has been deceived or he who has done an unjust act neither suffers in the head nor in the eye nor in the hip, nor does he lose his estate; and we wish for nothing else than these things. But whether we shall have the will modest and faithful or shameless and faithless, we care not the least, except only in the school so far as a few words are concerned. Therefore our proficiency is limited to these few words; but beyond them it does not exist even in the slightest degree.

CHAPTER 11

What the beginning of philosophy is

The beginning of philosophy to him at least who enters on it in the right way and by the door, is a consciousness of his own weakness and inability about necessary things. For we come into the world with no natural notion of a right-angled triangle, or of a diesis, or of a half tone; but we learn each of these things by a certain transmission according to art; and for this reason those who do not know them, do not think that they know them. But as to good and evil, and beautiful and ugly, and becoming and unbecoming, and happiness and misfortune, and proper and improper, and what we ought to do and what we ought not to do, whoever came into the world without having an innate idea of them? Wherefore we all use these names, and we endeavor to fit the preconceptions to the several cases thus: "He has done well, he has not done well; he has done as he ought, not as he ought; he has been unfortunate, he has been fortunate; he is unjust, he is just": who does not use these names? who among us defers the use of them till he has learned them, as he defers the use of the words about lines or sounds? And the cause of this is that we come into the world already taught as it were by nature some things on this matter, and proceeding from these we have added to them self-conceit. "For why," a man says, "do I not know the beautiful and the ugly? Have I not the notion of it?" You have. "Do I not adapt it to particulars?" You do. "Do I not then adapt it properly?" In that lies the whole question; and conceit is added here. For, beginning from these things which are admitted, men proceed to that which is matter of dispute by means of unsuitable adaptation; for if they possessed this power of adaptation in addition to those things, what would hinder them from being perfect? But now since you think that you properly adapt the preconceptions to the particulars, tell me whence you derive this. Because I think so. But it does not seem so to another, and he thinks that he also makes a proper adaptation; or does he not think so? He does think so. Is it possible then that both of you can properly apply the preconceptions to things about which you have contrary opinions? It is not possible. Can you then show us anything better toward adapting the preconceptions beyond your thinking that you do? Does the madman do any other things than the things as in which seem to him right? Is then this criterion for him also? It is not sufficient. Come then to something which is superior to seeming. What is this?

Observe, this is the beginning of philosophy, a perception of the disagreement of men with one another, and an inquiry into the cause of the disagreement, and a condemnation and distrust of that which only "seems," and a certain investigation of that which "seems" whether it "seems" rightly, and a discovery of some rule, as we have discovered a balance in the determination of weights, and a carpenter's rule in the case of straight and crooked things. This is the beginning of philosophy. "Must we say that all thins are right which seem so to all?" And how is it possible that contradictions can be right? "Not all then, but all which seem to us to be right." How more to you than those which seem right to the Syrians? why more than what seem right to the Egyptians? why more than what seems right to me or to any other man? "Not at all more." What then "seems" to every man is not sufficient for determining what "is"; for neither in the case of weights or measures are we satisfied with the bare appearance, but in each case we have discovered a certain rule. In this matter then is there no rule certain to what "seems?" And how is it possible that the most necessary things among men should have no sign, and be incapable of being discovered? There is then some rule. And why then do we not seek the rule and discover it, and afterward use it without varying from it, not even stretching out the finger without it? For this, I think, is that which when it is discovered cures of their madness those who use mere "seeming" as a measure, and misuse it; so that for the future proceeding from certain things known and made clear we may use in the case of particular things the preconceptions which are distinctly fixed.

What is the matter presented to us about which we are inquiring? "Pleasure." Subject it to the rule, throw it into the balance. Ought the good to be such a thing that it is fit that we have confidence in it? "Yes." And in which we ought to confide? "It ought to be." Is it fit to trust to anything which is insecure? "No." Is then pleasure anything secure? "No." Take it then and throw it out of the scale, and drive it far away from the place of good things. But if you are not sharp-sighted, and one balance is not enough for you, bring another. Is it fit to be elated over what is good? "Yes." Is it proper then to be elated over present pleasure? See that you do not say that it is proper; but if you do, I shall then not think you are worthy even of the balance. Thus things are tested and weighed when the rules are ready. And to philosophize is this, to examine and confirm the rules; and then to use them when they are known is the act of a wise and good man.

CHAPTER 12

Of disputation or discussion

What things a man must learn in order to be able to apply the art of disputation, has been accurately shown by our philosophers; but with respect to the proper use of the things, we are entirely without practice. Only give to any of us, whom you please, an illiterate man to discuss with,, and he cannot discover how to deal with the man. But when he has moved the man a little, if he answers beside the purpose, he does not know how to treat him, but he then either abuses or ridicules him, and says, "He is an illiterate man; it is not possible to do anything with him." Now a guide, when he has found a man out of the road leads him into the right way: he does not ridicule or abuse him and then leave him. Do you also show this illiterate man the truth, and you will see that he follows. But so long as you do not show him the truth, do not ridicule him, but rather feel your own incapacity.

How then did Socrates act? He used to compel his adversary in disputation to bear testimony to him, and he wanted no other witness. Therefore he could say, "I care not for other witnesses, but I am always satisfied with the evidence of my adversary, and I do not ask the opinion of others, but only the opinion of him who is disputing with me." For he used to make the conclusions drawn from natural notions so plain that every man saw the contradiction and withdrew from it: "Does the envious man rejoice?" "By no means, but he is rather pained." Well, "Do you think that envy is pain over evils? and what envy is there of evils?" Therefore he made his adversary say that envy is pain over good things. "Well then, would any man envy those who are nothing to him?" "By no means." Thus having completed the notion and distinctly fixed it he would go away without saying to his adversary, "Define to me envy"; and if the adversary had defined envy, he did not say, "You have defined it badly, for the terms of the definition do not correspond to the thing defined." These are technical terms, and for this reason disagreeable and hardly intelligible to illiterate men, which terms we cannot lay aside. But that the illiterate man himself, who follows the appearances presented to him, should be able to concede anything or reject it, we can never by the use of these terms move him to do. Accordingly, being conscious of our own inability, we do not attempt the thing; at least such of us as have any caution do not. But the greater part and the rash, when they enter into such disputations, confuse themselves and confuse others; and finally abusing their adversaries and abused by them, they walk away.

Now this was the first and chief peculiarity of Socrates, never to be irritated in argument, never to utter anything abusive, anything insulting, but to bear with abusive persons and to put an end to the quarrel. If you would know what great power he had in this way, read the Symposium of Xenophon, and you will see how many quarrels he put an end to. Hence with good reason in the poets also this power is most highly praised,

Quickly with the skill he settles great disputes.

Well then; the matter is not now very safe, and particularly at Rome; for he who attempts to do it, must not do it in a corner, you may be sure, but must go to a man of consular rank, if it so happen, or to a rich man, and ask him, "Can you tell me, Sir, to whose care you have entrusted your horses?" "I can tell you." Here you entrusted them to a person indifferently and to one who has no experience of horses? "By no means." Well then; can you tell me to whom you entrust your gold or silver things or your vestments? "I don't entrust even these to anyone indifferently." Well; your own body, have you already considered about entrusting the care of it to any person? "Certainly." To a man of experience, I suppose, and one acquainted with the aliptic, or with the healing art? "Without a doubt." Are these the best things that you have, or do you also possess something else which is better than all these? "What kind of thing do you mean?" That I mean which makes use of these things, and tests each of these things and deliberates. "Is it the soul that you mean?" You think right, for it is the soul that I mean. "In truth I do think the soul is a much better thing than all the others which I possess." Can you then show us in what way you have taken care of the soul? for it is not likely that you, who are so wise a man and have a reputation in the city, inconsiderately and carelessly allow the most valuable thing that you possess to be neglected and to perish? "Certainly not." But have you taken care of the soul yourself; and have you learned from another to do this, or have you discovered the means yourself? Here comes the danger that in the first place he may say, "What is this to you, my good man, who are you?" Next, if you persist in troubling him, there is a danger that he may raise his hands and give you blows. I was once myself also an admirer of this mode of instruction until I fell into these dangers.

CHAPTER 13

On anxiety

When I see a man anxious, I say, "What does this man want? If he did not want something which is not in his power, how could he be anxious?" For this reason a lute player when he is singing by himself has no anxiety, but when he enters the theatre, he is anxious even if he has a good voice and plays well on the lute; for he not only wishes to sing well, but also to obtain applause: but this is not in his power. Accordingly, where he has skill, there he has confidence. Bring any single person who knows nothing of music, and the musician does not care for him. But in the matter where a man knows nothing and has not been practiced, there he is anxious. What matter is this? He knows not what a crowd is or what the praise of a crowd is. However he has learned to strike the lowest chord and the highest; but what the praise of the many is, and what power it has in life he neither knows nor has he thought about it. Hence he must of necessity tremble and grow pale. I cannot then say that a man is not a lute player when I see him afraid, but I can say something else, and not one thing, but many. And first of all I call him a stranger and say, "This man does not know in what part of the world he is, but though he has been here so long, he is ignorant of the laws of the State and the customs, and what is permitted and what is not; and he has never employed any lawyer to tell him and to explain the laws." But a man does not write a will, if he does not does not know how it ought to be written, or he employs a person who does know; nor does he rashly seal a bond or write a security. But he uses his desire without a lawyer's advice, and aversion, and pursuit, and attempt and purpose. "How do you mean without a lawyer?" He does not know that he wills what is not allowed, and does not will that which is of necessity; and he does not know either what is his own or what is or what is another man's; but if he did know, he could never be impeded, he would never be hindered, he would not be anxious. "How so?" Is any man then afraid about things which are not evil? "No." Is he afraid about things which are evils, but still so far within his power that they may not happen? "Certainly he is not." If, then, the things which are independent of the will are neither good nor bad, and all things which do depend on the will are within our power, and no man can either take them from us or give them to us, if we do not choose, where is room left for anxiety? But we are anxious about our poor body, our little property, about the will of Caesar; but not anxious about things internal. Are we anxious about not forming a false opinion? No, for this is in my power. About not exerting our movements contrary to nature? No, not even about this. When then you see a man pale, as the physician says, judging from the complexion, this man's spleen is disordered, that man's liver; so also say, this man's desire and aversion are disordered, he is not in the right way, he is in a fever. For nothing else changes the color, or causes trembling or chattering of the teeth, or causes a man to

Sink in his knees and shift from foot to foot.

For this reason when Zeno was going to meet Antigonus, he was not anxious, for Antigonus had no power over any of the things which Zeno admired; and Zeno did not care for those things over which Antigonus had power. But Antigonus was anxious when he was going to meet Zeno, for he wished to please Zeno; but this was a thing external. But Zeno did not want to please Antigonus; for no man who is skilled in any art wishes to please one who has no such skill.

Should I try to please you? Why? I suppose, you know the measure by which one man is estimated by another. Have you taken pains to learn what is a good man and what is a bad man, and how a man becomes one or the other? Why, then, are you not good yourself? "How," he replies, "am I not good?" Because no good man laments or roans or weeps, no good man is pale and trembles, or says, "How will he receive me, how will he listen to me?" Slave, just as it pleases him. Why do you care about what belongs to others? Is it now his fault if he receives badly what proceeds from you? "Certainly." And is it possible that a fault should be one man's, and the evil in another? "No." Why then are you anxious about that which belongs to others? "Your question is reasonable; but I am anxious how I shall speak to him." Cannot you then speak to him as you choose? "But I fear that I may be disconcerted?" If you are going to write the name of Dion, are you afraid that you would be disconcerted? "By no means." Why? is it not because you have practiced writing the name? "Certainly." Well, if you were going to read the name, would you not feel the same? and why? Because every art has a certain strength and confidence in the things which belong to it. Have you then not practiced speaking? and what else did you learn in the school? Syllogisms and sophistical propositions? For what purpose? was it not for the purpose of discoursing skillfully? and is not discoursing skillfully the same as discoursing seasonably and cautiously and with intelligence, and also without making mistakes and without hindrance, and besides all this with confidence? "Yes." When, then, you are mounted on a horse and go into a plain, are you anxious at being matched against a man who is on foot, and anxious in a matter in which you are practiced, and he is not? "Yes, but that person has power to kill me." Speak the truth then, unhappy man, and do not brag, nor claim to be a philosopher, nor refuse to acknowledge your masters, but so long as you present this handle in your body, follow every man who is stronger than yourself. Socrates used to practice speaking, he who talked as he did to the tyrants, to the dicasts, he who talked in his prison. Diogenes had practiced speaking, he who spoke as he did to Alexander, to the pirates, to the person who bought him. These men were confident in the things which they practiced. But do you walk off to your own affairs and never leave them: go and sit in a corner, and weave syllogisms, and propose them to another. There is not in you the man who can rule a state.

CHAPTER 14

To Naso

When a certain Roman entered with his son and listened to one reading, Epictetus said, "This is the method of instruction"; and he stopped. When the Roman asked him to go on, Epictetus said: Every art, when it is taught, causes labor to him who is unacquainted with it and is unskilled in it, and indeed the things which proceed from the arts immediately show their use in the purpose for which they were made; and most of them contain something attractive and pleasing. For indeed to be present and to observe how a shoemaker learns is not a pleasant thing; but the shoe is useful and also not disagreeable to look at. And the discipline of a smith when he is learning is very disagreeable to one who chances to be present and is a stranger to the art: but the work shows the use of the art. But you will see this much more in music; for if you are present while a person is learning, the discipline will appear most disagreeable; and yet the results of music are pleasing and delightful to those who know nothing of music. And here we conceive the work of a philosopher to be something of this kind: he must adapt his wish to what is going on, so that neither any of the things which are taking place shall take place contrary to our wish, nor any of the things which do not take place shall not take place when we wish that they should. From this the result is to those who have so arranged the work of philosophy, not to fall in the desire, nor to fall in with that which they would avoid; without uneasiness, without fear, without perturbation to pass through life themselves, together with their associates maintaining the relations both natural and acquired, as the relation of son, of father, of brother, of citizen, of man, of wife, of neighbor, of fellow-traveler, of ruler, of ruled. The work of a philosopher we conceive to be something like this. It remains next to inquire how this must be accomplished.

We see then that the carpenter when he has learned certain things becomes a carpenter; the pilot by learning certain things becomes a pilot. May it not, then, in philosophy also not be sufficient to wish to be wise and good, and that there is also a necessity to learn certain things? We inquire then what these things are. The philosophers say that we ought first to learn that there is a God and that he provides for all things; also that it is not possible to conceal from him our acts, or even our intentions and thoughts. The next thing, is to learn what is the nature of the Gods; for such as they are discovered to be, he, who would please and obey them, must try with all his power to be like them. If the divine is faithful, man also must be faithful; if it is free, man also must be free; if beneficent, man also must be beneficent; if magnanimous, man also must be magnanimous; as being, then an imitator of God, he must do and say everything consistently with this fact.

"With what then must we begin?" If you will enter on the discussion, I will tell you that you must first understand names. "So, then, you say that I do not now understand names?" You do not understand them. "How, then, do I use them?" Just as the illiterate use written language, as cattle use appearances: for use is one thing, understanding is another. But if you think that you understand them, produce whatever word you please, and let us try whether we understand it. But it is a disagreeable thing for a man to be confuted who is now old and, it may be, has now served his three campaigns. I too know this: for now you are come to me as if you were in want of nothing: and what could you even imagine to be wanting to you? You are rich, you have children, and a wife, perhaps and many slaves: Caesar knows you, in Rome you have many friends, you render their dues to all, you know how to requite him who does you a favor, and to repay in the same kind him who does a wrong. What do you lack? If, then, I shall show you that you lack the things most necessary and the chief things for happiness, and that hitherto you have looked after everything rather than what you ought, and, to crown all, that you neither know what God is nor what man is, nor what is good nor what is bad; and as to what I have said about your ignorance of other matters, that may perhaps be endured, but if I say that you know nothing about yourself, how is it possible that you should endure me and bear the proof and stay here? It is not possible; but you immediately go off in bad humor. And yet what harm have I done you? unless the mirror also injures the ugly man because it shows him to himself such as he is; unless the physician also is supposed to insult the sick man, when he says to him, "Man, do you think that you ail nothing? But you have a fever: go without food to-day; drink water." And no one says, "What an insult!" But if you say to a man, "Your desires are inflamed, your aversions are low, your intentions are inconsistent, your pursuits are not comfortable to nature, your opinions are rash and false," the man immediately goes away and says, "he has insulted me."

Our way of dealing is like that of a crowded assembly. Beasts are brought to be sold and oxen; and the greater part of the men come to buy and sell, and there are some few who come to look at the market and to inquire how it is carried on, and why, and who fixes the meeting and for what purpose. So it is here also in this assembly: some like cattle trouble themselves about nothing except their fodder. For to all of you who are busy about possessions and lands and slaves and magisterial offices, these are nothing except fodder. But there are a few who attend the assembly, men who love to look on and consider what is the world, who governs it. Has it no governor? And how is it possible that a city or a family cannot continue to exist, not even the shortest time without an administrator and guardian, and that so great and beautiful a system should be administered with such order and yet without a purpose and by chance? There is then an administrator. What kind of administrator and how does he govern? And who are we, who were produced by him, and for what purpose? Have we some connection with him and some relation toward him, or none? This is the way in which these few are affected, and then they apply themselves only to this one thing, to examine the meeting and then to go away. What then? They are ridiculed by the many, as the spectators at the fair are by the traders; and if the beasts had any understanding, they would ridicule those who admired anything else than fodder.

CHAPTER 15

To or against those who obstinately persist in what they have determined

When some persons have heard these words, that a man ought to be constant, and that the will is naturally free and not subject to compulsion, but that all other things are subject to hindrance, to slavery, and are in the power of others, they suppose that they ought without deviation to abide by everything which they have determined. But in the first place that which has been determined ought to be sound. I require tone in the body, but such as exists in a healthy body, in an athletic body; but if it is plain to me that you have the tone of a frenzied man and you boast of it, I shall say to you, "Man, seek the physician": this is not tone, but atony. In a different way something of the same kind is felt by those who listen to these discourses in a wrong manner; which was the case with one of my companions who for no reason resolved to starve himself to death. I heard of it when it was the third day of his abstinence from food and I went to inquire what had happened. "I have resolved," he said. But still tell me what it was which induced you to resolve; for if you have resolved rightly, we shall sit with you and assist you to depart; but if you have made an unreasonable resolution, change your mind. "We ought to keep to our determinations." What are you doing, man? We ought to keep not to all our determinations, but to those which are right; for if you are now persuaded that it is right, do not change your mind, if you think fit, but persist and say, "We ought to abide by our determinations." Will you not make the beginning and lay the foundation in an inquiry whether the determination is sound or not sound, and so then build on it firmness and security? But if you lay a rotten and ruinous foundation, will not your miserable little building fall down the sooner, the more and the stronger are the materials which you shall lay on it? Without any reason would you withdraw from us out of life a man who is a friend, and a companion, a citizen of the same city, both the great and the small city? Then, while you are committing murder and destroying a man who has done no wrong, do you say that you ought to abide by your determinations? And if it ever in any way came into your head to kill me, ought you to abide by your determinations?

Now this man was with difficulty persuaded to change his mind. But it is impossible to convince some persons at present; so that I seem now to know, what I did not know, before, the meaning of the common saying, "That you can neither persuade nor break a fool." May it never be my lot to have a wise fool for my friend: nothing is more intractable. "I am determined," the man says. Madmen are also; but the more firmly they form a judgment on things which do not exist, the more ellebore they require. Will you not act like a sick man and call in the physician? "I am sick, master, help me; consider what I must do: it is my duty to obey you." So it is here also: "I know not what I ought to do, but I am come to learn." Not so; but, "Speak to me about other things: upon this I have determined." What other things? for what is greater and more useful than for you to be persuaded that it is not sufficient to have made your determination and not to change it. This is the tone of madness, not of health. "I will die, if you compel me to this." Why, man? What has happened? "I have determined." I have had a lucky escape that you have not determined to kill me. "I take no money." Why? "I have determined." Be assured that with the very tone which you now use in refusing to take, there is nothing to hinder you at some time from inclining without reason to take money and then saying, "I have determined." As in a distempered body, subject to defluxions, the humor inclines sometimes to these parts and then to those, so too a sickly soul knows not which way to incline: but if to this inclination and movement there is added a tone, then the evil becomes past help and cure.

CHAPTER 16

That we do not strive to use our opinions about good and evil

Where is the good? In the will. Where is the evil? In the will. Where is neither of them? In those things which are independent of the will. Well then? Does any one among us think of these lessons out of the schools? Does any one meditate by himself to give an answer to things as in the case of questions? Is it day? "Yes." Is it night? "No." Well, is the number of stars even? "I cannot say." When money is shown to you, have you studied to make the proper answer, that money is not a good thing? Have you practiced yourself in these answers, or only against sophisms? Why do you wonder then if in the cases which you have studied, in those you have improved; but in those which you have not studied, in those you remain the same? When the rhetorician knows that he has written well, that he has committed to memory what he has written, and brings an agreeable voice, why is he still anxious? Because he is not satisfied with having studied. What then does he want? To be praised by the audience? For the purpose, then, of being able to practice declamation, he has been disciplined: but with respect to praise and blame he has not been disciplined. For when did he hear from any one what praise is, what blame is, what the nature of each is, what kind of praise should be sought, or what kind of blame should be shunned? And when did he practice this discipline which follows these words? Why then do you still wonder if, in the matters which a man has learned, there he surpasses others, and in those in which he has not been disciplined, there he is the same with the many. So the lute player knows how to play, sings well, and has a fine dress, and yet he trembles when he enters on the stage; for these matters he understands, but he does not know what a crowd is, nor the shouts of a crowd, nor what ridicule is. Neither does he know what anxiety is, whether it is our work or the work of another, whether it is possible to stop it or not. For this reason, if he has been praised, he leaves the theatre puffed up, but if he has been ridiculed, the swollen bladder has been punctured and subsides.

This is the case also with ourselves. What do we admire? Externals. About what things are we busy? Externals. And have we any doubt then why we fear or why we are anxious? What, then, happens when we think the things which are coming on us to be evils? It is not in our power not to be afraid, it is not in our power not to be anxious. Then we say, "Lord God, how shall I not be anxious?" Fool, have you not hands, did not God make them for you, Sit down now and pray that your nose may not run. Wipe yourself rather and do not blame him. Well then, has he given to you nothing in the present case? Has he not given to you endurance? has he not given to you magnanimity? has he not given to you manliness? When you have such hands, do you look for one who shall wipe your nose? But we neither study these things nor care for them. Give me a man who cares how he shall do anything, not for the obtaining of a thing but who cares about his own energy. What man, when he is walking about, cares for his own energy? who, when he is deliberating, cares about his own deliberation, and not about obtaining that about which he deliberates? And if he succeeds, he is elated and says, "How well we have deliberated; did I not tell you, brother, that it is impossible, when we have thought about anything, that it should not turn out thus?" But if the thing should turn out otherwise, the wretched man is humbled; he knows not even what to say about what has taken place. Who among us for the sake of this matter has consulted a seer? Who among us as to his actions has not slept in indifference? Who? Give to me one that I may see the man whom I have long been looking for, who is truly noble and ingenuous, whether young or old; name him.

Why then are we still surprised, if we are well practiced in thinking about matters, but in our acts are low, without decency, worthless, cowardly, impatient of labor, altogether bad? For we do not care about things, nor do we study them. But if we had feared not death or banishment, but fear itself, we should have studied not to fall into those things which appear to us evils. Now in the school we are irritable and wordy; and if any little question arises about any of these things, we are able to examine them fully. But drag us to practice, and you will find us miserably shipwrecked. Let some disturbing appearance come on us, and you will know what we have been studying and in what we have been exercising ourselves. Consequently, through want of discipline, we are always adding something to the appearance and representing things to be greater than what they are. For instance as to myself, when I am on a voyage and look down on the deep sea, or look round on it and see no land, I am out of my mind and imagine that I must drink up all this water if I am wrecked, and it does not occur to me that three pints are enough. What then disturbs me? The sea? No, but my opinion. Again, when an earthquake shall happen, I imagine that the city is going to fall on me; is not one little stone enough to knock my brains out?

What then are the things which are heavy on us and disturb us? What else than opinions? What else than opinions lies heavy upon him who goes away and leaves his companions and friends and places and habits of life? Now little children, for instance, when they cry on the nurse leaving them for a short time, forget their sorrow if they receive a small cake. Do you choose then that we should compare you to little children? No, by Zeus, for I do not wish to be pacified by a small cake, but by right opinions. And what are these? Such as a man ought to study all day, and not to be affected by anything that is not his own, neither by companion nor place nor gymnasia, and not even by his own body, but to remember the law and to have it before his eyes. And what is the divine law? To keep a man's own, not to claim that which belongs to others, but to use what is given, and when it is not given, not to desire it; and when a thing is taken away, to give it up readily and immediately, and to be thankful for the time that a man has had the use of it, if you would not cry for your nurse and mamma. For what matter does it make by what thing a man is subdued, and on what he depends? In what respect are you better than he who cries for a girl, if you grieve for a little gymnasium, and little porticoes and young men and such places of amusement? Another comes and laments that he shall no longer drink the water of Dirce. Is the Marcian water worse than that of Dirce? "But I was used to the water of Dirce?" And you in turn will be used to the other. Then if you become attached to this also, cry for this too, and try to make a verse like the verse of Euripides,

The hot baths of Nero and the Marcian water.

See how tragedy is made when common things happen to silly men.

"When then shall I see Athens again and the Acropolis?" Wretch, are you not content with what you see daily? have you anything better or greater to see than the sun, the moon, the stars, the whole earth, the sea? But if indeed you comprehend him who administers the Whole, and carry him about in yourself, do you still desire small stones, and a beautiful rock? When, then, you are going to leave the sun itself and the moon, what will you do? will you sit and weep like children? Well, what have you been doing in the school? what did you hear, what did you learn? why did you write yourself a philosopher, when you might have written the truth; as, "I made certain introductions, and I read Chrysippus, but I did not even approach the door of a philosopher." For how should I possess anything of the kind which Socrates possessed, who died as he did, who lived as he did, or anything such as Diogenes possessed? Do you think that any one of such men wept or grieved, because he was not going to see a certain man, or a certain woman, nor to be in Athens or in Corinth, but, if it should so happen, in Susa or in Ecbatana? For if a man can quit the banquet when he chooses, and no longer amuse himself, does he still stay and complain, and does he not stay, as at any amusement, only so long as he is pleased? Such a man, I suppose, would endure perpetual exile or to be condemned to death. Will you not be weaned now, like children, and take more solid food, and not cry after mammas and nurses, which are the lamentations of old women? "But if I go away, I shall cause them sorrow." You cause them sorrow? By no means; but that will cause them sorrow which also causes you sorrow, opinion. What have you to do then? Take away your own opinion, and if these women are wise, they will take away their own: if they do not, they will lament through their own fault.

My man, as the proverb says, make a desperate effort on behalf of tranquility of mind, freedom and magnanimity. Lift up your head at last as released from slavery. Dare to look up to God and say, "Deal with me for the future as thou wilt; I am of the same mind as thou art; I am thine: I refuse nothing that pleases thee: lead me where thou wilt: clothe me in any dress thou choosest: is it thy will that I should hold the office of a magistrate, that I should be in the condition of a private man, stay there or be an exile, be poor, be rich? I will make thy defense to men in behalf of all these conditions. I will show the nature of each thing what it is." You will not do so; but sit in an ox's belly, and wait for your mamma till she shall feed you. Who would Hercules have been, if he had sat at home? He would have been Eurystheus and not Hercules. Well, and in his travels through the world how many intimates and how many friends had he? But nothing more dear to him than God. For this reason it was believed that he was the son of God, and he was. In obedience to God, then, he went about purging away injustice and lawlessness. But you are not Hercules and you are not able to purge away the wickedness of others; nor yet are you Theseus, able to pure away the evil things of Attica. Clear away your own. From yourself, from your thoughts cast away, instead of Procrustes and Sciron, sadness, fear, desire, envy, malevolence, avarice, effeminacy, intemperance. But it is not possible to eject these things otherwise than by looking to God only, by fixing your affections on him only, by being consecrated to his commands. But if you choose anything else, you will with sighs and groans be compelled to follow what is stronger than yourself, always seeking tranquility and never able to find it; for you seek tranquility there where it is not, and you neglect to seek it where it is.

CHAPTER 17

How we must adapt preconceptions to particular cases

What is the first business of him who philosophizes? To throw away self-conceit. For it is impossible for a man to begin to learn that which he thinks that he knows. As to things then which ought to be done and ought not to be done, and good and bad, and beautiful and ugly, all of us talking of them at random go to the philosophers; and on these matters we praise, we censure, we accuse, we blame, we judge and determine about principles honorable and dishonorable. But why do we go to the philosophers? Because we wish to learn what we do not think we know. And what is this? Theorems. For we wish to learn what philosophers say as being something elegant and acute; and some wish to learn that they may get profit what they learn. It is ridiculous then to think that a person wishes to learn one thing, and will learn another; or further, that a man will make proficiency in that which he does not learn. But the many are deceived by this which deceived also the rhetorician Theopompus, when he blames even Plato for wishing everything to be defined. For what does he say? "Did none of us before you use the words 'good' or 'just,' or do we utter the sounds in an unmeaning and empty way without understanding what they severally signify?" Now who tells you, Theopompus, that we had not natural notions of each of these things and preconceptions? But it is not possible to adapt preconceptions to their correspondent objects if we have not distinguished them, and inquired what object must be subjected to each preconception. You may make the same charge against physicians also. For who among us did not use the words "healthy" and "unhealthy" before Hippocrates lived, or did we utter these words as empty sounds? For we have also a certain preconception of health, but we are not able to adapt it. For this reason one says, "Abstain from food"; another says, "Give food"; another says, "Bleed"; and another says, "Use cupping." What is the reason? is it any other than that a man cannot properly adapt the preconception of health to particulars?

So it is in this matter also, in the things which concern life. Who among us does not speak of good and bad, of useful and not useful; for who among us has not a preconception of each of these things? Is it then a distinct and perfect preconception? Show this. How shall I show this? Adapt the preconception properly to the particular things. Plato, for instance, subjects definitions to the preconception of the useful, but you to the preconception of the useless. Is it possible then that both of you are right? How is it possible? Does not one man adapt the preconception of good to the matter of wealth, and another not to wealth, but to the matter of pleasure and to that of health? For, generally, if all of us who use those words know sufficiently each of them, and need no diligence in resolving, the notions of the preconceptions, why do we differ, why do we quarrel, why do we blame one another?

And why do I now allege this contention with one another and speak of it? If you yourself properly adapt your preconceptions, why are you unhappy, why are you hindered? Let us omit at present the second topic about the pursuits and the study of the duties which relate to them. Let us omit also the third topic, which relates to the assents: I give up to you these two topics. Let us insist upon the first, which presents an almost obvious demonstration that we do not properly adapt the preconceptions. Do you now desire that which is possible and that which is possible to you? Why then are you hindered? why are you unhappy? Do you not now try to avoid the unavoidable? Why then do you fall in with anything which you would avoid? Why are you unfortunate? Why, when you desire a thing, does it not happen, and, when you do not desire it, does it happen? For this is the greatest proof of unhappiness and misery: "I wish for something, and it does not happen." And what is more wretched than I?

It was because she could not endure this that Medea came to murder her children: an act of a noble spirit in this view at least, for she had a just opinion what it is for a thing not to succeed which a person wishes. Then she says, "Thus I shall be avenged on him who has wronged and insulted me; and what shall I gain if he is punished thus? how then shall it be done? I shall kill my children, but I shall punish myself also: and what do I care?" This is the aberration of soul which possesses great energy. For she did not know wherein lies the doing of that which we wish; that you cannot get this from without, nor yet by the alteration and new adaptation of things. Do not desire the man, and nothing which you desire will fall to happen: do not obstinately desire that he shall live with you: do not desire to remain in Corinth; and, in a word, desire nothing than that which God wills. And who shall hinder you? who shall compel you? No man shall compel you any more than he shall compel Zeus.

When you have such a guide, and your wishes and desires are the same as his, why do you fear disappointment? Give up your desire to wealth and your aversion to poverty, and you will be disappointed in the one, you will fall into the other. Well, give them up to health, and you will be unfortunate: give them up to magistracies, honors, country, friends, children, in a word to any of the things which are not in man's power. But give them up to Zeus and to the rest of the gods; surrender them to the gods, let the gods govern, let your desire and aversion be ranged on the side of the gods, and wherein will you be any longer unhappy? But if, lazy wretch, you envy, and complain, and are jealous, and fear, and never cease for a single day complaining both of yourself and of the gods, why do you still speak of being educated? What kind of an education, man? Do you mean that you have been employed about sophistical syllogisms? Will you not, if it is possible, unlearn all these things and begin from the beginning, and see at the same time that hitherto you have not even touched the matter; and then, commencing from this foundation, will you not build up all that comes after, so that nothing, may happen which you do not choose, and nothing shall fail to happen which you do choose?

Give me one young man who has come to the school with this intention, who is become a champion for this matter and says, "I give up everything else, and it is enough for me if "t shall ever be in my power to pass my life free from hindrance and free from trouble, and to stretch out my neck to all things like a free man, and to look up to heaven as a friend of God, and fear nothing that can happen." Let any of you point out such a man that I may "Come, young man, into the possession of that which is your own, it is your destiny to adorn philosophy: yours are these possessions, yours these books, yours these discourses." Then when he shall have labored sufficiently and exercised himself in this of the matter, let him come to me again and say, "I desire to be free from passion and free from perturbation; and I wish as a pious man and a philosopher and a diligent person to know what is my duty to the gods, what to my parents, what to my brothers, what to my country, what to strangers." Come also to the second matter: this also is yours. "But I have now sufficiently studied the second part also, and I would gladly be secure and unshaken, and not only when I am awake, but also when I am asleep, and when I am filled with wine, and when I am melancholy." Man, you are a god, you have great designs.

"No: but I wish to understand what Chrysippus says in his treatise of the Pseudomenos." Will you not hang yourself, wretch, with such your intention? And what good will it do you? You will read the whole with sorrow, and you will speak to others trembling, Thus you also do. "Do you wish me, brother, to read to you, and you to me?" "You write excellently, my man; and you also excellently in the style of Xenophon, and you in the style of Plato, and you in the style of Antisthenes." Then, having told your dreams to one another, you return to the same things: your desires are the same, your aversions the same, your pursuits are the same, and your designs and purposes, you wish for the same things and work for the same. In the next place you do not even seek for one to give you advice, but you are vexed if you hear such things. Then you say, "An ill-natured old fellow: when I was going away, he did not weep nor did he say, 'Into what danger you are going: if you come off safe, my child, I will burn lights.' This is what a good-natured man would do." It will be a great thing for you if you do return safe, and it will be worth while to burn lights for such a person: for you ought to be immortal and exempt from disease.

Casting away then, as I say, this conceit of thinking that we know something useful, we I must come to philosophy as we apply to geometry, and to music: but if we do not, we shall not even approach to proficiency, though we read all the collections and commentaries of Chrysippus and those of Antipater and Archedemus.

CHAPTER 18

How we should struggle against appearances

Every habit and faculty is maintained and increased by the corresponding actions: the habit of walking by walking, the habit of running by running. If you would be a good reader, read; if a writer, write. But when you shall not have read thirty days in succession, but have done something else, you will know the consequence. In the same way, if you shall have lain down ten days, get up and attempt to make a long walk, and you will see how your legs are weakened. Generally, then, if you would make anything a habit, do it; if you would not make it a habit, do not do it, but accustom yourself to do something else in place of it.

So it is with respect to the affections of the soul: when you have been angry, you must know that not only has this evil befallen you, but that you have also increased the habit, and in a manner thrown fuel upon fire. When you have been overcome in sexual intercourse with a person, do not reckon this single defeat only, but reckon that you have also nurtured, increased your incontinence. For it is impossible for habits and faculties, some of them not to be produced, when they did not exist before, and others not be increased and strengthened by corresponding acts.

In this manner certainly, as philosophers say, also diseases of the mind grow up. For when you have once desired money, if reason be applied to lead to a perception of the evil, the desire is stopped, and the ruling faculty of our mind is restored to the original authority. But if you apply no means of cure, it no longer returns to the same state, but, being again excited by the corresponding appearance, it is inflamed to desire quicker than before: and when this takes place continually, it is henceforth hardened, and the disease of the mind confirms the love of money. For he who has had a fever, and has been relieved from it, is not in the same state that he was before, unless he has been completely cured. Something of the kind happens also in diseases of the soul. Certain traces and blisters are left in it, and unless a man shall completely efface them, when he is again lashed on the same places, the lash will produce not blisters but sores. If then you wish not to be of an angry temper, do not feed the habit; throw nothing on it which will increase it: at first keep quiet, and count the days on which you have not been angry. I used to be in passion every day; now every second day; then every third, then every fourth. But if you have intermitted thirty days, make a sacrifice to God. For the habit at first begins to be weakened, and then is completely destroyed. "I have not been vexed to-day, nor the day after, nor yet on any succeeding day during two or three months; but I took care when some exciting things happened." Be assured that you are in a good way.

To-day when I saw a handsome person, I did not say to myself, "I wish I could lie with her," and "Happy is her husband"; for he who says this says, "Happy is her adulterer also." Nor do I picture the rest to my mind; the woman present, and stripping herself and lying down by my side. I stroke my head and say, "Well done, Epictetus, you have solved a fine little sophism, much finer than that which is called the master sophism." And if even the woman is willing, and gives signs, and sends messages, and if she also fondle me and come close to me, and I should abstain and be victorious, that would be a sophism beyond that which is named "The Liar," and "The Quiescent." Over such a victory as this a man may justly be proud; not for proposing, the master sophism.

How then shall this be done? Be willing at length to be approved by yourself, be willing to appear beautiful to God, desire to be in purity with your own pure self and with God. Then when any such appearance visits you, Plato says, "Have recourse to expiations, go a suppliant to the temples of the averting deities." It is even sufficient if "you resort to the society of noble and just men," and compare yourself with them, whether you find one who is living or dead. Go to Socrates and see him lying down with Alcibiades, and mocking his beauty: consider what a victory he at last found that he had gained over himself; what an Olympian victory; in what number he stood from Hercules; so that, by the Gods, one may justly salute him, "Hail, wondrous man, you who have conquered not less these sorry boxers and pancratiasts nor yet those who are like them, the gladiators." By placing these objects on the other side you will conquer the appearance: you will not be drawn away by it. But, in the first place, be not hurried away by the rapidity of the appearance, but say, "Appearances, wait for me a little: let me see who you are, and what you are about: let me put you to the test." And then do not allow the appearance to lead you on and draw lively pictures of the things which will follow; for if you do, it will carry you off wherever it pleases. But rather bring in to oppose it some other beautiful and noble appearance and cast out this base appearance. And if you are accustomed to be exercised in this way, you will see what shoulders, what sinews, what strength you have. But now it is only trifling words, and nothing more.

This is the true athlete, the man who exercises himself against such appearances. Stay, wretch, do not be carried away. Great is the combat, divine is the work; it is for kingship, for freedom, for happiness, for freedom from perturbation. Remember God: call on him as a helper and protector, as men at sea call on the Dioscuri in a storm. For what is a greater storm than that which comes from appearances which are violent and drive away the reason? For the storm itself, what else is it but an appearance? For take away the fear of death, and suppose as many thunders and lightnings as you please, and you will know what calm and serenity there is in the ruling faculty. But if you have once been defeated and say that you will conquer hereafter, then say the same again, be assured that you at last be in so wretched a condition and so weak that you will not even know afterward that you are doing wrong, but you will even begin to make apologies for your wrongdoing, and then you will confirm the saying of Hesiod to be true,

With constant ills the dilatory strives.

CHAPTER 19

Against those who embrace, philosophical opinions only in words

The argument called the "ruling argument" appears to have been proposed from such principles as these: there is in fact a common contradiction between one another in these three positions, each two being in contradiction to the third. The propositions are, that everything past must of necessity be true; that an impossibility does not follow a possibility; and that thing is possible which neither is nor t at a t will be true. Diodorus observing this contradiction employed the probative force of the first two for the demonstration of this proposition, "That nothing is possible which is not true and never will be." Now another will hold these two: "That something is possible, which is neither true nor ever will be": and "That an impossibility does not follow a possibility," But he will not allow that everything which is past is necessarily true, as the followers of Cleanthes seem to think, and Antipater copiously defended them. But others maintain the other two propositions, "That a thing is possible which is neither true nor will he true": and "That everything which is past is necessarily true"; but then they will maintain that an impossibility can follow a possibility. But it is impossible to maintain these three propositions, because of their common contradiction.

If then any man should ask me which of these propositions do I maintain? I will answer him that I do not know; but I have received this story, that Diodorus maintained one opinion, the followers of Panthoides, I think, and Cleanthes maintained another opinion, and those of Chrysippus a third. "What then is your opinion?" I was not made for this purpose, to examine the appearances that occur to me and to compare what others say and to form an opinion of my own on the thing. Therefore I differ not at all from the grammarian. "Who was Hector's father?" Priam. "Who were his brothers?" Alexander and Deiphobus. "Who was their mother?" Hecuba. I have heard this story. "From whom?" From Homer. And Hellanicus also, I think, writes about the same things, and perhaps others like him. And what further have I about the ruling argument? Nothing. But, if I am a vain man, especially at a banquet, I surprise the guests by enumerating those who have written on these matters. Both Chrysippus has written wonderfully in his first book about "Possibilities," and Cleanthes has written specially on the subject, and Archedemus. Antipater also has written not only in his work about "Possibilities," but also separately in his work on the ruling argument. Have you not read the work? "I have not read it." Read. And what profit will a man have from it? he will be more trifling and impertinent than he is now; for what else have you rained by reading it? What opinion have you formed on this subject? none; but you will tell us of Helen and Priam, and the island of Calypso which never was and never will be. And in this matter indeed it is of no great importance if you retain the story, but have formed no opinion of your own. But in matters of morality this happens to us much more than in these things of which we are speaking.

"Speak to me about good and evil." Listen:

The wind from Ilium to Ciconian shores
Brought me.

"Of things some are good, some are bad, and others are indifferent. The good then are the virtues and the things which partake of the virtues; the bad are the vices, and the things which partake of them; and the indifferent are the things which lie between the virtues and the vices, wealth, health, life, death, pleasure, pain." Whence do you know this? "Hellanicus says it in his Egyptian history"; for what difference does it make to say this, or to say that "Diogenes has it in his Ethic," or Chrysippus or Cleanthes? Have you then examined any of these things and formed an opinion of your own? Show how you are used to behave in a storm on shipboard? Do you remember this division, when the sail rattles and a man, who knows nothing of times and seasons, stands by you when you are screaming and says, "Tell me, I ask you by the Gods, what you were saying just now. Is it a vice to suffer shipwreck: does it participate in vice?" Will you not take up a stick and lay it on his head? What have we to do with you, man? we are perishing and you come to mock us? But if Caesar sent for you to answer a charge, do you remember the distinction? If, when you are going in, pale and trembling, a person should come up to you and say, "Why do you tremble, man? what is the matter about which you are engaged? Does Caesar who sits within give virtue and vice to those who go in to him?" You reply, "Why do you also mock me and add to my present sorrows?" Still tell me, philosopher, tell me why you tremble? Is it not death of which you run the risk, or a prison, or pain of the body, or banishment, or disgrace? What else is there? Is there any vice or anything which partakes of vice? What then did you use to say of these things? "What have you to do with me, man? my own evils are enough for me." And you say right. Your own evils are enough for you, your baseness, your cowardice, your boasting which you showed when you sat in the school. Why did you decorate yourself with what belonged to others? Why did you call yourself a Stoic?

Observe yourselves thus in your actions, and you will find to what sect you belong. You will find that most of you are Epicureans, a few Peripatetics, and those feeble. For wherein will you show that you really consider virtue equal to everything else or even superior? But show me a Stoic, if you can. Where or how? But you can show me an endless number who utter small arguments of the Stoics. For do the same persons repeat the Epicurean opinions any worse? And the Peripatetic, do they not handle them also with equal accuracy? who then is a Stoic? As we call a statue Phidiac which is fashioned according to the art of Phidias; so show me a man who is fashioned according to the doctrines which he utters. Show me a man who is sick and happy, in danger and happy, dying and happy, in exile and happy, in disgrace and happy. Show him: I desire, by the gods, to see a Stoic. You cannot show me one fashioned so; but show me at least one who is forming, who has shown a tendency to be a Stoic. Do me this favor: do not grudge an old man seeing a sight which I have not seen yet. Do you think that you must show me the Zeus of Phidias or the Athena, a work of ivory and gold? Let any of you show me a human soul ready to think as God does, and not to blame either God or man, ready not to be disappointed about anything, not to consider himself damaged by anything, not to be angry, not to be envious, not to be jealous; and why should I not say it direct? desirous from a man to become a god, and in this poor mortal body thinking of his fellowship with Zeus. Show me the man. But you cannot. Why then do you delude yourselves and cheat others? and why do you put on a guise which does not belong to you, and walk about being thieves and pilferers of these names and things which do not belong to you?

And now I am your teacher, and you are instructed in my school. And I have this purpose, to make you free from restraint, compulsion, hindrance, to make you free, prosperous, happy, looking to God in everything small and great. And you are here to learn and practice these things. Why, then, do you not finish the work, if you also have such a purpose as you ought to have, and if I, in addition to the purpose, also have such qualification as I ought to have? What is that which is wanting? When I see an artificer and material by him, I expect the work. Here, then, is the artificer, here the material; what is it that we want? Is not the thing, one that can be taught? It is. Is it not then in our power? The only thing of all that is in our power. Neither wealth is in our power, nor health, nor reputation, nor in a word anything else except the right use of appearances. This is by nature free from restraint, this alone is free from impediment. Why then do you not finish the work? Tell me the reason. For it is either through my fault that you do not finish it, or through your own fault, or through the nature of the thing. The thing itself is possible, and the only thing in our power. It remains then that the fault is either in me or in you, or, what is nearer the truth, in both. Well then, are you willing that we begin at last to bring such a purpose into this school, and to take no notice of the past? Let us only make a beginning. Trust to me, and you will see.

CHAPTER 20

Against the Epicureans and Academics

The propositions which are true and evident are of necessity used even by those who contradict them: and a man might perhaps consider it to be the greatest proof of a thing being evident that it is found to be necessary even for him who denies it to make use of it at the same time. For instance, if a man should deny that there is anything universally true, it is plain that he must make the contradictory negation, that nothing is universally true. What, wretch, do you not admit even this? For what else is this than to affirm that whatever is universally affirmed is false? Again, if a man should come forward and say: "Know that there is nothing that can be known, but all things are incapable of sure evidence"; or if another say, "Believe me and you will be the better for it, that a man ought not to believe anything"; or again, if another should say, "Learn from me, man, that it is not possible to learn anything; I tell you this and will teach you, if you choose." Now in what respect do these differ from those? Whom shall I name? Those who call themselves Academics? "Men, agree that no man agrees: believe us that no man believes anybody."

Thus Epicurus also, when he designs to destroy the natural fellowship of mankind, at the same time makes use of that which he destroys. For what does he say? "Be not deceived men, nor be led astray, nor be mistaken: there is no natural fellowship among rational animals; believe me. But those who say otherwise, deceive you and seduce you by false reasons." What is this to you? Permit us to be deceived. Will you fare worse, if all the rest of us are persuaded that there is a natural fellowship among us, and that it ought by all means to be preserved? Nay, it will be much better and safer for you. Man, why do you trouble yourself about us? Why do you keep awake for us? Why do you light your lamp? Why do you rise early? Why do you write so many books, that no one of us may be deceived about the gods and believe that they take care of men; or that no one may suppose the nature of good to be other than pleasure? For if this is so, lie down and sleep, and lead the life of a worm, of which you judged yourself worthy: eat and drink, and enjoy women, and ease yourself, and snore. And what is it to you, how the rest shall think about these things, whether right or wrong? For what have we to do with you? You take care of sheep because they supply us with wool, and milk, and, last of all, with their flesh. Would it not be a desirable thing if men could be lulled and enchanted by the Stoics, and sleep and present themselves to you and to those like you to be shorn and milked? For this you ought to say to your brother Epicureans: but ought you not to conceal it from others, and particularly before everything to persuade them that we are by nature adapted for fellowship, that temperance is a good thing; in order that all things may be secured for you? Or ought we to maintain this fellowship with some and not with others? With whom, then, ought we to maintain it? With such as on their part also maintain it, or with such as violate this fellowship? And who violate it more than you who establish such doctrines?

What then was it that waked Epicurus from his sleepiness, and compelled him to write what he did write? What else was it than that which is the strongest thing in men, nature, which draws a man to her own will though he be unwilling and complaining? "For since," she says, "you think that there is no community among mankind, write this opinion and leave it for others, and break your sleep to do this, and by your own practice condemn your own opinions." Shall we then say that Orestes was agitated by the Erinyes and roused from his deep sleep, and did not more savage Erinyes and Pains rouse Epicurus from his sleep and not allow him to rest, but compelled him to make known his own evils, as madness and wine did the Galli? So strong and invincible is man's nature. For how can a vine be moved not in the mariner of a vine, but in the manner of an olive tree? or on the other hand how can an olive tree be moved not in the manner of an olive tree, but in the manner of a vine? It is impossible: it cannot be conceived. Neither then is it possible for a man completely to lose the movements of a man; and even those who are deprived of their genital members are not able to deprive themselves of man's desires. Thus Epicurus also mutilated all the offices of a man, and of a father of a family, and of a citizen and of a friend, but he did not mutilate human desires, for he could not; not more than the lazy Academics can cast away or blind their own senses, though they have tried with all their might to do it. What a shame is this? when a man has received from nature measures and rules for the knowing of truth, and does not strive to add to these measures and rules and to improve them, but, just the contrary, endeavors to take away and destroy whatever enables us to discern the truth?

What say you philosopher? piety and sanctity, what do you think that they are? "If you like, I will demonstrate that they are good things." Well, demonstrate it, that our citizens may be turned and honor the deity and may no longer be negligent about things of the highest value. "Have you then the demonstrations?" I have, and I am thankful. "Since then you are well pleased with them, hear the contrary: 'That there are no Gods, and, if there are, they take no care of men, nor is there any fellowship between us and them; and that this piety and sanctity which is talked of among most men is the lying of boasters and sophists, or certainly of legislators for the purpose of terrifying and checking wrong-doers.'" Well done, philosopher, you have done something for our citizens, you have brought back all the young men to contempt of things divine. "What then, does not this satisfy you? Learn now, that justice is nothing, that modesty is folly, that a father is nothing, a son nothing." Well done, philosopher, persist, persuade the young men, that we may have more with the same opinions as you who say the same as you. From such you an principles as those have grown our well-constituted states; by these was Sparta founded: Lycurgus fixed these opinions in the Spartans by his laws and education, that neither is the servile condition more base than honorable, nor the condition of free men more honorable than base, and that those who died at Thermopylae died from these opinions; and through what other opinions did the Athenians leave their city? Then those who talk thus, marry and beget children, and employ themselves in public affairs and make themselves priests and interpreters. Of whom? of gods who do not exist: and they consult the Pythian priestess that they may hear lies, and they repeat the oracles to others. Monstrous impudence and imposture.

Man what are you doing? are you refuting yourself every day; and will you not give up these frigid attempts? When you eat, where do you carry your hand to? to your mouth or to your eye? when you wash yourself, what do you go into? do you ever call a pot a dish, or a ladle a spit? If I were a slave of any of these men, even if I must be flayed by him dally, I would rack him. If he said, "Boy, throw some olive-oil into the bath," I would take pickle sauce and pour it down on his head. "What is this?" he would say. An appearance was presented to me, I swear by your genius, which could not be distinguished from oil and was exactly like it. "Here give me the barley drink," he says. I would fill and carry him a dish of sharp sauce. "Did I not ask for the barley drink?" Yes, master; this is the barley drink. "Take it and smell; take it and taste." How do you know then if our senses deceive us? If I had three or four fellow-slaves of the same opinion, I should force him to hang himself through passion or to change his mind. But now they mock us by using all the things which nature gives, and in words destroying them.

Grateful indeed are men and modest, who, if they do nothing else, are daily eating bread and yet are shameless enough to say, we do not know if there is a Demeter or her daughter Persephone or a Pluto; not to mention that they are enjoying the night and the day, the seasons of the year, and the stars, and the sea, and the land, and the co-operation of mankind, and yet they are not moved in any degree by these things to turn their attention to them; but they only seek to belch out their little problem, and when they have exercised their stomach to go off to the bath. But what they shall say, and about what things or to what persons, and what their hearers shall learn from this talk, they care not even in the least degree, nor do they care if any generous youth after hearing such talk should suffer any harm from it, nor after he has suffered harm should lose all the seeds of his generous nature: nor if we should give an adulterer help toward being shameless in his acts; nor if a public peculator should lay hold of some cunning excuse from these doctrines; nor if another who neglects his parents should be confirmed in his audacity by this teaching. What then in your opinion is good or bad? This or that? Why then should a man say any more in reply to such persons as these, or give them any reason or listen to any reasons from them, or try to convince them? By Zeus one might much sooner expect to make certainties change their mind than those who are become so deaf and blind to their own evils.

CHAPTER 21

Of inconsistency

Some things men readily confess, and other things they do not. No one then will confess that he is a fool or without understanding; but, quite the contrary, you will hear all men saying, "I wish that I had fortune equal to my understanding." But readily confess that they are timid, and they say: "I am rather timid, I confess; but to other respects you will not find me to foolish." A man will not readily confess that he is intemperate; and that he is unjust he will not confess at all. He will by no means confess that be is envious or a busybody. Most men will confess that they are compassionate. What then is the reason? The chief thing is inconsistency and confusion in the things which relate to good and evil. But different men have different reasons; and generally what they imagine to be base, they do not confess at all. But they suppose timidity to be a characteristic of a good disposition, and compassion also; but silliness to be the absolute characteristic of a slave. And they do not at all admit the things which are offenses against society. But in the case of most errors, for this reason chiefly, they are induced to confess them, because they that there is something involuntary in them as in timidity and compassion; and if a man confess that he is in any respect intemperate, he alleges love as an excuse for what is involuntary. But men do not imagine injustice to be at all There is also in jealousy, as they suppose, something involuntary; and for this reason they confess to jealousy also.

Living among such men, who are so confused so ignorant of what they say, and of evils which they have or have not, and why they have them, or how they shall be relieved of them, I think it is worth the trouble for a man to watch constantly "Whether I also am one of them, what imagination I have about myself, how I conduct myself, whether I conduct myself as a prudent man, whether I conduct myself as a temperate man, whether I ever say this, that I have been taught to be prepared for everything that may happen. Have I the consciousness, which a man who knows nothing ought to have, that I know nothing? Do I go to my teacher as men go to oracles, prepared to obey? or do I like a sniveling boy go to my school to learn history and understand the books which I did not understand before, and, if it should happen so, to explain them also to others?" Man, you have had a fight in the house with a poor slave, you have turned the family upside down, you have frightened the neighbors, and you come to me as if you were a wise man, and you take your seat and judge how I have explained some word, and how I have babbled whatever came into my head. You come full of envy, and humbled, because you bring nothing from home; and you sit during, the discussion thinking of nothing else than how your father is disposed toward you and your brother. "What are they saying about me there? now they think that I am improving, and are saying, 'He will return with all knowledge.'

I wish I could learn everything before I return: but much labor is necessary, and no one sends me anything, and the baths at Nicopolis are dirty; everything is bad at home, and bad here."

Then they say, "No one gains any profit from the school." Why, who comes to the school, who comes for the purpose of being improved? who comes to present his opinions to be purified? who comes to learn what he is in want of? Why do you wonder then if you carry back from the school the very things which you bring into it? For you come not to lay aside or to correct them or to receive other principles in place of them. By no means, nor anything like it. You rather look to this, whether you possess already that for which you come. You wish to prattle about theorems? What then? Do you not become greater triflers? Do not your little theorems give you some opportunity of display? You solve sophistical syllogisms. Do you not examine the assumptions of the syllogism named "The Liar"? Do you not examine hypothetical syllogisms? Why, then, are you still vexed if you receive the things for which you come to the school? "Yes; but if my child die or my brother, or if I must die or be racked, what good will these things do me?" Well, did you come for this? for this do you sit by my side? did you ever for this light your lamp or keep awake? or, when you went out to the walking-place, did you ever propose any appearance that had been presented to you instead of a syllogism, and did you and your friends discuss it together? Where and when? Then you say, "Theorems are useless." To whom? To such as make a bad use of them. For eyesalves are not useless to those who use them as they ought and when they ought. Fomentations are not useless. Dumb-bells are not useless; but they are useless to some, useful to others. If you ask me now if syllogisms are useful, I will tell you that they are useful, and if you choose, I will prove it. "How then will they in any way be useful to me?" Man, did you ask if they are useful to you, or did you ask generally? Let him who is suffering from dysentery ask me if vinegar is useful: I will say that it is useful. "Will it then be useful to me?" I will say, "No." Seek first for the discharge to be stopped and the ulcers to be closed. And do you, O men, first cure the ulcers and stop the discharge; be tranquil in your mind, bring it free from distraction into the school, and you will know what power reason has.

CHAPTER 22

On friendship

What a man applies himself to earnestly, that he naturally loves. Do men then apply themselves earnestly to the things which are bad? By no means. Well, do they apply themselves to things which in no way concern themselves? Not to these either. It remains, then, that they employ themselves earnestly only about things which are good; and if they are earnestly employed about things, they love such things also. Whoever, then, understands what is good, can also know how to love; but he who cannot distinguish good from bad, and things which are neither good nor bad from both, can he possess the power of loving? To love, then, is only in the power of the wise.

"How is this?" a man may say; am foolish, and yet love my child." I am surprised indeed that you have begun by making the admission that you are foolish. For what are you deficient in? Can you not make use of your senses? do you not distinguish appearances? do you not use food which is suitable for your body, and clothing and habitation? Why then do you admit that you are foolish? It is in truth because you are often disturbed by appearances and perplexed, and their power of persuasion often conquers you; and sometimes you think these things to be good, and then the same things to be bad, and lastly neither good nor bad; and in short you grieve, fear, envy, are disturbed, you are changed. This is the reason why you confess that you are foolish. And are you not changeable in love? But wealth, and pleasure and, in a word, things themselves, do you sometimes think them to he good and sometimes bad? and do you not think the same men at one time to be good, at another time bad? and have you not at one time a friendly feeling toward them and at another time the feeling of an enemy? and do you not at one time praise them and at another time blame them? "Yes; I have these feelings also." Well then, do you think that he who has been deceived about a man is his friend? "Certainly not." And he who has selected a man as his friend and is of a changeable disposition, has he good-will toward him? "He has not." And he who now abuses a man, and afterward admires him? "This man also has no good-will to the other." Well then, did you never see little dogs caressing and playing with one another, so that you might say there is nothing more friendly? but, that you may know what friendship is, throw a bit of flesh among them, and you will learn. Throw between yourself and your son a little estate, and you will know how soon he will wish to bury you and how soon you wish your son to die. Then you will change your tone and say, "What a son I have brought up! He has long been wishing to bury me." Throw a smart girl between you; and do you, the old man, love her, and the young one will love her too, If a little fame intervene, or dangers, it will be just the same. You will utter the words of the father of Admetus!

Life gives you pleasure: and why not your father.

Do you think that Admetus did not love his own child when he was little? that he was not in agony when the child had a fever? that he did not often say, "I wish I had the fever instead of the child?" then when the test (the thing) came and was near, see what words they utter. Were not Eteocles and Polynices from the same mother and from the same father? Were they not brought up together, had they not lived together, drunk together, slept together, and often kissed one another? So that, if any man, I think, had seen them, he would have ridiculed the philosophers for the paradoxes which they utter about friendship. But when a quarrel rose between them about the royal power, as between dogs about a bit of meat, see what they say,

Polynices: Where will you take your station before the towers?
Eteocles: Why do you ask me this?
Pol. I place myself opposite and try to kill you.
Et. I also wish to do the same.

Such are the wishes that they utter.

For universally, be not deceived, every animal is attached to nothing so much as to its own interest. Whatever then appears to it an impediment to this interest, whether this be a brother, or a father, or a child, or beloved, or lover, it hates, spurns, curses: for its nature is to love nothing so much as its own interest; this is father, and brother and kinsman, and country, and God. When, then, the gods appear to us to be an impediment to this, we abuse them and throw down their statues and burn their temples, as Alexander ordered the temples of Aesculapius to be burned when his dear friend died.

For this reason if a man put in the same place his interest, sanctity, goodness, and country, and parents, and friends, all these are secured: but if he puts in one place his interest, in another his friends, and his country and his kinsmen and justice itself, all these give way being borne down by the weight of interest. For where the "I" and the "Mine" are placed, to that place of necessity the animal inclines: if in the flesh, there is the ruling power: if in the will, it is there: and if it is in externals, it is there. If then I am there where my will is, then only shall I be a friend such as I ought to be, and son, and father; for this will he my interest, to maintain the character of fidelity, of modesty, of patience, of abstinence, of active cooperation, of observing my relations. But if I put myself in one place, and honesty in another, then the doctrine of Epicurus becomes strong, which asserts either that there is no honesty or it is that which opinion holds to be honest.

It was through this ignorance that the Athenians and the Lacedaemonians quarreled, and the Thebans with both; and the great king quarreled with Hellas, and the Macedonians with both; and the Romans with the Getae. And still earlier the Trojan war happened for these reasons. Alexander was the guest of Menelaus; and if any man had seen their friendly disposition, he would not have believed any one who said that they were not friends. But there was cast between them a bit of meat, a handsome woman, and about her war arose. And now when you see brothers to be friends appearing to have one mind, do not conclude from this anything about their friendship, not even if they say it and swear that it is impossible for them to be separated from one another. For the ruling principle of a bad man cannot be trusted, it is insecure, has no certain rule by which it is directed, and is overpowered at different times by different appearances. But examine, not what other men examine, if they are born of the same parents and brought up together, and under the same pedagogue; but examine this only, wherein they place their interest, whether in externals or in the will. If in externals, do not name them friends, no more than name them trustworthy or constant, or brave or free: do not name them even men, if you have any judgment. For that is not a principle of human nature which makes them bite one another, and abuse one another, and occupy deserted places or public places, as if they were mountains, and in the courts of justice display the acts of robbers; nor yet that which makes them intemperate and adulterers and corrupters, nor that which makes them do whatever else men do against one another through this one opinion only, that of placing themselves and their interests in the things which are not within the power of their will. But if you hear that in truth these men think the good to be only there, where will is, and where there is a right use of appearances, no longer trouble yourself whether they are father or son, or brothers, or have associated a long time and are companions, but when you have ascertained this only, confidently declare that they are friends, as you declare that they are faithful, that they are just. For where else is friendship than where there is fidelity, and modesty, where there is a communion of honest things and of nothing else?

"But," you may say, "such a one treated me with regard so long; and did he not love me?" How do you know, slave, if he did not regard you in the same way as he wipes his shoes with a sponge, or as he takes care of his beast? How do you know, when you have ceased to be useful as a vessel, he will not throw you away like a broken platter? "But this woman is my wife, and we have lived together so long." And how long did Eriphyle live with Amphiaraus, and was the mother of children and of many? But a necklace came between them. "And what is a necklace?" It is the opinion about such things. That was the bestial principle, that was the thing which broke asunder the friendship between husband and wife, that which did not allow the woman to be a wife nor the mother to be a mother. And let every man among you who has seriously resolved either to be a friend himself or to have another for his friend, cut out these opinions, hate them, drive them from his soul. And thus, first of all, he will not reproach himself, he will not be at variance with himself, will not change his mind, he will not torture himself. In the next place, to another also, who is like himself, he will be altogether and completely a friend. But he will bear with the man who is unlike himself, he will be kind to him, gentle, ready to pardon on account of his ignorance, on account of his being mistaken in things of the greatest importance; but he will be harsh to no man, being well convinced of Plato's doctrine that every mind is deprived of truth unwillingly. If you cannot do this, yet you can do in all other respects as friends do, drink together, and lodge together, and sail together, and you may be born of the same parents; for snakes also are: but neither will they be friends nor you, so long as you retain these bestial and cursed opinions.

CHAPTER 23

On the power of speaking

Every man will read a book with more pleasure or even with more case, if it is written in fairer characters. Therefore every man will also listen more readily to what is spoken, if it is signified by appropriate and becoming words. We must not say, then, that there is no faculty of expression: for this affirmation is the characteristic of an impious and also of a timid man. Of an impious man, because he undervalues the gifts which come from God, just as if he would take away the commodity of the power of vision, or of hearing, or of seeing. Has, then, God given you eyes to no purpose? and to no purpose has he infused into them a spirit so strong and of such skillful contrivance as to reach a long way and to fashion the forms of things which are seen? What messenger is so swift and vigilant? And to no purpose has he made the interjacent atmosphere so efficacious and elastic that the vision penetrates through the atmosphere which is in a manner moved? And to no purpose has he made light, without the presence of which there would be no use in any other thing?

Man, be neither ungrateful for these gifts nor yet forget the things which are superior to them. But indeed for the power of seeing and hearing, and indeed for life itself, and for the things which contribute to support it, for the fruits which are dry, and for wine and oil give thanks to God: but remember that he has given you something else better than all these, I mean the power of using them, proving them and estimating the value of each. For what is that which gives information about each of these powers, what each of them is worth? Is it each faculty itself? Did you ever hear the faculty of vision saying anything about itself? or the faculty of hearing? or wheat, or barley, or a horse or a dog? No; but they are appointed as ministers and slaves to serve the faculty which has the power of making use of the appearances of things. And if you inquire what is the value of each thing, of whom do you inquire? who answers you? How then can any other faculty be more powerful than this, which uses the rest as ministers and itself proves each and pronounces about them? for which of them knows what itself is, and what is its own value? which of them knows when it ought to employ itself and when not? what faculty is it which opens and closes the eyes, and turns them away from objects to which it ought not to apply them and does apply them to other objects? Is it the faculty of vision? No; but it is the faculty of the will. What is that faculty which closes and opens the ears? what is that by which they are curious and inquisitive, or, on the contrary, unmoved by what is said? is it the faculty of hearing? It is no other than the faculty of the will. Will this faculty then, seeing that it is amid all the other faculties which are blind and dumb and unable to see anything else except the very acts for which they are appointed in order to minister to this and serve it, but this faculty alone sees sharp and sees what is the value of each of the rest; will this faculty declare to us that anything else is the best, or that itself is? And what else does the do when it is opened than see? But whether we ought to look on the wife of a certain person, and in what manner, who tells us? The faculty of the will. And whether we ought to believe what is said or not to believe it, and if we do believe, whether we ought to be moved by it or not, who tells us? Is it not the faculty of the will? But this faculty of speaking and of ornamenting words, if there is indeed any such peculiar faculty, what else does it do, when there happens to be discourse about a thing, than to ornament the words and arrange them as hairdressers do the hair? But whether it is better to speak or to be silent, and better to speak in this way or that way, and whether this is becoming or not becoming and the season for each and the and the use, what else tells us than the faculty of the will? Would you have it then to come forward and condemn itself?

"What then," it says, "if the fact is so, can that which ministers be superior to that to which it ministers, can the horse be superior to the rider, or the do, to the huntsman, or the instrument to the musician, or the servants to the king?" What is that which makes use of the rest? The will. What takes care of all? The will. What destroys the whole man, at one time by hunger, at another time by hanging, and at another time by a precipice? The will. Then is anything stronger in men than this? and how is it possible that the things which are subject to restraint are stronger than that which is not What things are naturally formed to hinder the faculty of vision? Both will and things which do not depend on the faculty of the will. It is the same with the faculty of hearing, with the faculty of speaking in like manner. But what has a natural power of hindering the will? Nothing which is independent of the will; but only the will itself, when it is perverted. Therefore this is alone vice or alone virtue.

Then being so great a faculty and set over all the rest, let it come forward and tell us that the most excellent of all things is the flesh. Not even if the flesh itself declared that it is the most excellent, would any person bear that it should say this. But what is it, Epicurus, which pronounces this, which wrote about "The End of our Being," which wrote on "The Nature of Things," which wrote about the Canon, which led you to wear a beard, which wrote when it was dying that it was spending the last and a happy day? Was this the flesh or the will? Then do you admit that you possess anything superior to this? and are you not mad? are you in fact so blind and deaf?

What then? Does any man despise the other faculties I hope not. Does any man say that there is no use or excellence in the speaking faculty? I hope not. That would be foolish, impious, ungrateful toward God. But a man renders to each thing its due value. For there is some use even in an ass, but not so much as in an ox: there is also use in a dog, but not so much as in a slave: there is also some use in a slave, but not so much as in citizens: there is also some use in citizens, but riot so much as in magistrates. Not, indeed, because some things are superior, must we undervalue the use which other things have. There is a certain value in the power of speaking, but it is not so great as the power of the will. When, then, I speak thus, let no man think that I ask you to neglect the power of speaking, for neither do I ask you to neglect the eyes, nor the ears nor the hands nor the feet nor clothing nor shoes. But if you ask me, "What, then, is the most excellent of all things?" what must I say? I cannot say the power of speaking, but the power of the will, when it is right. For it is this which uses the other, and all the other faculties both small and great. For when this faculty of the will is set right, a man who is not good becomes good: but when it falls, a man becomes bad. It is through this that we are unfortunate, that we are fortunate, that we blame one another, are pleased with one another. In a word, it is this which if neglect it makes unhappiness, and if we carefully look after it makes happiness.

But to take away the faculty of speaking, and to say that there is no such faculty in reality, is the act not only of an ungrateful man toward those who gave it, but also of a cowardly man: for such a person seems to me to fear if there is any faculty of this kind, that we shall not be able to despise it. Such also are those who say that there is no difference between beauty and ugliness. Then it would happen that a man would be affected in the same way if he saw Thersites and if he saw Achilles; in the same way, if he saw Helen and any other woman. But these are foolish and clownish notions, and the notions of men who know not the nature of each thing, but are afraid, if a man shall see the difference, that he shall immediately be seized and carried off vanquished. But this is the great matter; to leave to each thing the power which it has, and leaving to it this power to see what is the worth of the power, and to learn what is the most excellent of all things, and to pursue this always, to be diligent about this, considering t all other things of secondary value compared with this, but yet, as far as we can, not neglecting all those other things. For we must take care of the eyes also, not as if they were the most excellent thing, but we must take care of them on account of the most excellent thing, because it will not be in its true natural condition, if it does not rightly use the other faculties, and prefer some things to others.

What then is usually done? Men generally act as a traveler would do on his way to his own country, when he enters a good inn, and being pleased with it should remain there. Man, you have forgotten your purpose: you were not traveling to this inn, but you were pass through it. "But this is a pleasant inn." And how many other inns are pleasant? and how many meadows are pleasant? yet only passing through. But your purpose is this, return to your country, to relieve your kinsmen of anxiety, to discharge the duties of a citizen, to marry, to beget children, to fill the usual magistracies. For you are not come to select more pleasant places, but to live in these where you were born and of which you were made a citizen. Something of the kind takes place in the matter which we are considering. Since, by the aid of speech and such communication as you receive here, you must advance to perfection, and purge your will, and correct the faculty which makes use of the appearances of things; and since it is necessary also for the teaching of theorems to be effected by a certain mode of expression and with a certain variety and sharpness, some persons captivated by these very things abide in them, one captivated by the expression, another by syllogisms, another again by sophisms, and still another by some other inn of the kind; and there they stay and waste away as if they were among Sirens.

Man, your purpose was to make yourself capable of using conformably to nature the appearances presented to you, in your desires not to be frustrated, in your aversion from things not to fall into that which you would avoid, never to have no luck, nor ever to have bad luck, to be free, not hindered, not compelled, conforming yourself to the administration of Zeus, obeying it, well satisfied with this, blaming no one, charging no one with fault, able from your whole soul to utter these verses:

"Lead me, O Zeus, and thou, too, Destiny."

Then having this purpose before you, if some little form of expression pleases you, if some theorems please you, do you abide among them and choose t dwell o well there, forgetting the things at home, and do you say, "These things are fine"? Who says that they are not fine? but only as being a way home, as inns are. For what hinders you from being an unfortunate man, even if you speak like Demosthenes? and what prevents you, if you can resolve syllogisms like Chrysippus, from being wretched, from sorrowing, from envying, in a word, from being disturbed, from being unhappy? Nothing. You see then that these were inns, worth nothing; and that the purpose before you was something else. When I speak thus to some persons, they think that I am rejecting care about speaking, or care about theorems. I am not rejecting this care, but I am rejecting the abiding about these things incessantly and putting our hopes in them. If a man by this teaching does harm to those who listen to him, reckon me too among those who do this harm: for I am not able, when I see one thing which is most excellent and supreme, to say that another is so, in order to please you.

CHAPTER 24

To a person who was one of those who was not valued by him

A certain person said to him: "Frequently I desired to hear you and came to you, and you never gave me any answer: and now, if it is possible, I entreat you to say something to me." Do you think, said Epictetus, that as there is an art in anything else, so there is also an art in speaking, and that he who has the art, will speak skillfully, and he who has not, will speak unskillfully? "I do think so." He, then, who by speaking receives benefit himself and is able to benefit others, will speak skillfully: but he who is rather damaged by speaking and does damage to others, will he be unskilled in this art of speaking? And you may find that some are damaged and others benefited by speaking. And are all who hear benefited by what they hear? Or will you find that among them also some are benefited and some damaged? "There are both among these also," he said. In this case also, then, those who hear skillfully are benefited, and those who hear unskillfully are damaged? He admitted this. Is there then a skill in hearing also, as there is in speaking? "It seems so." If you choose, consider the matter in this way also. The practice of music, to whom does it belong? "To a musician." And the proper making of a statue, to whom do you think that it belongs? "To a statuary." And the looking at a statue skillfully, does this appear to you to require the aid of no art? "This also requires the aid of art." Then if speaking properly is the business of the skillful man, do you see that to hear also with benefit is the business of the skillful man? Now as to speaking and hearing perfectly, and usefully, let us for the present, if you please, say no more, for both of us are a long way from everything of the kind. But I think that every man will allow this, that he who is going to hear philosophers requires some amount of practice in hearing. Is it not so?

Tell me then about what I should talk to you: about what matter are you able to listen? "About good and evil." Good and evil in what? In a horse? "No." Well, in an ox? "No." What then? In a man? "Yes." Do know then what a man is, what the notion is that we have of him, or have we our ears in any degree practiced about this matter? But do you understand what nature is? or can you even in any degree understand me when I say, "I shall use demonstration to you?" How? Do you understand this very thing, what demonstration is, or how anything is demonstrated, or by what means; or what things are like demonstration, but are not demonstration? Do you know what is true or what is false? What is consequent on a thing, what is repugnant to a thing, or not consistent, or inconsistent? But must I excite you to philosophy, and how? Shall I show to you the repugnance in the opinions of most men, through which they differ about things good and evil, and about things which are profitable and unprofitable, when you know not this very thing, what repugnance is? Show me then what I shall accomplish by discoursing with you; excite my inclination to do this. As the grass which is suitable, when it is presented to a sheep, moves its inclination to eat, but if you present to it a stone or bread, it will not be moved to eat; so there are in us certain natural inclinations also to speak, when the hearer shall appear to be somebody, when he himself shall excite us: but when he shall sit by us like a stone or like grass, how can he excite a man's desire? Does the vine say to the husbandman, "Take care of me?" No, but the vine by showing in itself that it will be profitable to the husbandman, if he does take care of it, invites him to exercise care. When children are attractive and lively, whom do they not invite to play with them, and crawl with them, and lisp with them? But who is eager to play with an ass or to bray with it? for though it is small, it is still a little ass.

"Why then do you say nothing to me?" I can only say this to you, that he who knows not who he is, and for what purpose he exists, and what is this world, and with whom he is associated, and what things are the good and the bad, and the beautiful and the ugly, and who neither understands discourse nor demonstration, nor what is true nor what is false, and who is not able to distinguish them, will neither desire according to nature, nor turn away, nor move upward, nor intend, nor assent, nor dissent, nor suspend his judgment: to say all in a few words, he will go about dumb and blind, thinking that he is somebody, but being nobody. Is this so now for the first time? Is it not the fact that, ever since the human race existed, all errors and misfortunes have arisen through this ignorance? Why did Agamemnon and Achilles quarrel with one another? Was it not through not knowing what things are profitable and not profitable? Does not the one say it is profitable to restore Chryseis to her father, and does not the other say that it is not profitable? does not the one say that he ought to take the prize of another, and does not the other say that he ought not? Did they not for these reasons forget both who they were and for what purpose they had come there? Oh, man, for what purpose did you come? to gain mistresses or to fight? "To fight." With whom? the Trojans or the Hellenes? "With the Trojans." Do you then leave Hector alone and draw your sword against your own king? And do you, most excellent Sir, neglect the duties of the king, you who are the people's guardian and have such cares; and are you quarreling about a little girl with the most warlike of your allies, whom you ought by every means to take care of and protect? and do you become worse than a well-behaved priest who treats you these fine gladiators with all respect? Do you see what kind of things ignorance of what is profitable does?

"But I also am rich." Are you then richer than Agamemnon? "But I am also handsome." Are you then more handsome than Achilles? "But I have also beautiful hair." But had not Achilles more beautiful hair and gold-colored? and he did not comb it elegantly nor dress it. "But I am also strong." Can you then lift so great a stone as Hector or Ajax? "But I am also of noble birth." Are you the son of a goddess mother? are you the son of a father sprung from Zeus? What good then do these things do to him, when he sits and weeps for a girl? "But I am an orator." And was he not? Do you not see how he handled the most skillful of the Hellenes in oratory, Odysseus and Phoenix? how he stopped their mouths?

This is all that I have to say to you; and I say even this not willingly. "Why?" Because you have not roused me. For what must I look to in order to be roused, as men who are expert in are roused by generous horses? Must I look to your body? You treat it disgracefully. To your dress? That is luxurious. To your behavior to your look? That is the same as nothing. When you would listen to a philosopher, do not say to him, "You tell me nothing"; but only show yourself worthy of hearing or fit for hearing; and you will see how you will move the speaker.

CHAPTER 25

That logic is necessary

When one of those who were present said, "Persuade me that logic is necessary," he replied: Do you wish me to prove this to you? The answer was, "Yes." Then I must use a demonstrative form of speech. This was granted. How then will you know if I am cheating you by argument? The man was silent. Do you see, said Epictetus, that you yourself are admitting that logic is necessary, if without it you cannot know so much as this, whether logic is necessary or not necessary

CHAPTER 26

What is the property of error

Every error comprehends contradiction: for since he who errs does not wish to err, but to he right, it is plain that he does not do what he wishes. For what does the thief wish to do? That which is for his own interest. If, then, the theft is not for his interest, he does not do that which he wishes. But every rational: soul is by nature offended at contradiction, and so long as it does not understand this contradiction, it is not hindered from doing contradictory things: but when it does understand the contradiction, it must of necessity avoid the contradiction and avoid it as much as a man must dissent from the false when he sees that a thing is false; but so long as this falsehood does not appear to him, he assents to it as to truth.

He, then, is strong in argument and has the faculty of exhorting and confuting, who is able to show to each man the contradiction through which he errs and clearly to prove how he does not do that which he wishes and does that which he does not wish. For if any one shall show this, a man will himself withdraw from that which he does; but so long as you do not show this, do not be surprised if a man persists in his practice; for having the appearance of doing right, he does what he does. For this reason Socrates, also trusting to this power, used to say, "I am used to call no other witness of what I say, but I am always satisfied with him with whom I am discussing, and I ask him to give his opinion and call him as a witness, and through he is only one, he is sufficient in the place of all." For Socrates knew by what the rational soul is moved, just like a pair of scales, and that it must incline, whether it chooses or not. Show the rational governing faculty a contradiction, and it will withdraw from it; but if you do not show it, rather blame yourself than him who is not persuaded.

BOOK THREE

CHAPTER 1

Of finery in dress

A certain young man a rhetorician came to see Epictetus, with his hair dressed more carefully than was usual and his attire in an ornamental style; whereupon Epictetus said: Tell me you do not think that some dogs are beautiful and some horses, and so of all other animals. "I do think so," the youth replied. Are not then some men also beautiful and others ugly? "Certainly." Do we, then, for the same reason call each of them in the same kind beautiful, or each beautiful for something peculiar? And you will judge of this matter thus. Since we see a dog naturally formed for one thing, and a horse for another, and for another still, as an example, a nightingale, we may generally and not improperly declare each of them to be beautiful then when it is most excellent according to its nature; but since the nature of each is different, each of them seems to me to be beautiful in a different way. Is it not so? He admitted that it was. That then which makes a dog beautiful, makes a horse ugly; and that which makes a horse beautiful, makes a dog ugly, if it is true that their natures are different. "It seems to be so." For I think that what makes a pancratiast beautiful, makes a wrestler to be not good, and a runner to be most ridiculous; and he who is beautiful for the Pentathlon, is very ugly for wrestling. "It is so," said he. What, then, makes a man beautiful? Is that which in its kind makes both a dog and a horse beautiful? "It is," he said. What then makes a dog beautiful? The possession of the excellence of a dog. And what makes a horse beautiful? The possession of the excellence of a horse. What then makes a man beautiful? Is it not the possession of the excellence of a man? And do you, then, if you wish to be beautiful, young man, labor at this, the acquisition of human excellence. But what is this? Observe whom you yourself praise, when you praise many persons without partiality: do you praise the just or the unjust? "The just." Whether do you praise the moderate or the immoderate? "The moderate." And the temperate or the intemperate? "The temperate." If, then, you make yourself such a person, you will know that you will make yourself beautiful: but so long as you neglect these things, you must be ugly, even though you contrive all you can to appear beautiful.

Further I do not know what to say to you: for if I say to you what I think, I shall offend you, and you will perhaps leave the school and not return to it: and if I do not say what I think, see how I shall be acting, if you come to me to be improved, and I shall not improve you at all, and if you come to me as to a philosopher, and I shall say nothing to you as a philosopher. And how cruel it is to you to leave you uncorrected. If at any time afterward you shall acquire sense, you will with good reason blame me and say, "What did Epictetus observe in me that, when he saw me in such a plight coming to him in such a scandalous condition, he neglected me and never said a word? did he so much despair of me? was I not young? was I not able to listen to reason? and how many other young men at this age commit many like errors? I hear that a certain Polemon from being a most dissolute youth underwent such a great change. Well, suppose that he did not think that I should be a Polemon; yet he might have set my hair right, he might have stripped off my decorations, he might have stopped me from plucking the hair out of my body; but when he saw me dressed like—what shall I say?—he kept silent." I do not say like what; but you will say, when you come to your senses and shall know what it is and what persons use such a dress.

If you bring this charge against me hereafter, what defense shall I make? Why, shall I say that the man will not be persuaded by me? Was Laius persuaded by Apollo? Did he and get drunk and show no care for the oracle? Well then, for this reason did Apollo refuse to tell him the truth? I indeed do not know, whether you will be persuaded by me or not; but Apollo knew most certainly that Laius would not be persuaded and yet he spoke. But why did he speak? I say in reply: But why is he Apollo, and why does he deliver oracles, and why has he fixed himself in this place as a prophet and source of truth and for the inhabitants of the world to resort to him? and why are the words "Know yourself" written in front of the temple, though no person takes any notice of them?

Did Socrates persuade all his hearers to take care of themselves? Not the thousandth part. But, however, after he had been placed in this position by the deity, as he himself says, he never left it. But what does he say even to his judges? "If you acquit me on these conditions that I no longer do that which I do now, I will not consent and I will not desist; but I will go up both to young and to old, and, to speak plainly, to every man whom I meet, and I will ask the questions which I ask now; and most particularly will I do this to you my fellow-citizens, because you are more nearly related to me." Are you so curious, Socrates, and such a busybody? and how does it concern you how we act? and what is it that you say? "Being of the same community and of the same kin, you neglect yourself, and show yourself a bad citizen to the state, and a bad kinsman to your kinsmen, and a bad neighbor to your neighbors." "Who, then are you?" Here it is a great thing to say, "I am he whose duty it is to take care of men; for it is not every little heifer which dares to resist a lion; but if the bull comes up and resists him, say to the bull, if you choose, 'And who are you, and what business have you here?'" Man, in every kind there is produced something which excels; in oxen, in dogs, in bees, in horses. Do not then say to that which excels, "Who, then, are you?" If you do, it will find a voice in some way and say, "I am such a thing as the purple in a garment: do not expect me to be like the others, or blame my nature that it has made me different from the rest of men."

What then? am I such a man? Certainly not. And are you such a man as can listen to the truth? I wish you were. But however since in a manner I have been condemned to wear a white beard and a cloak, and you come to me as to a philosopher, I will not treat you in a cruel way nor yet as if I despaired of you, but I will say: Young man, whom do you wish to make beautiful? In the first place, know who you are and then adorn yourself appropriately. You are a human being; and this is a mortal animal which has the power of using appearances rationally. But what is meant by "rationally?" Conformably to nature and completely. What, then, do you possess which is peculiar? Is it the animal part? No. Is it the condition of mortality? No. Is it the power of using appearances? No. You possess the rational faculty as a peculiar thing: adorn and beautify this; but leave your hair to him who made it as he chose. Come, what other appellations have you? Are you man or woman? "Man." Adorn yourself then as man, not as woman. Woman is naturally smooth and delicate; and if she has much hair (on her body), she is a monster and is exhibited at Rome among monsters. And in a man it is monstrous not to have hair; and if he has no hair, he is a monster; but if he cuts off his hairs and plucks them out, what shall we do with him? where shall we exhibit him? and under what name shall we show him? "I will exhibit to you a man who chooses to be a woman rather than a man." What a terrible sight! There is no man who will not wonder at such a notice. Indeed I think that the men who pluck out their hairs do what they do without knowing what they do. Man what fault have you to find with your nature? That it made you a man? What then? was it fit that nature should make all human creatures women? and what advantage in that case would you have had in being adorned? for whom would you have adorned yourself, if all human creatures were women? But you are not pleased with the matter: set to work then upon the whole business. Take away—what is its name?—that which is the cause of the hairs: make yourself a woman in all respects, that we may not be mistaken: do not make one half man, and the other half woman. Whom do you wish to please? The women?, Please them as a man. "Well; but they like smooth men." Will you not hang yourself? and if women took delight in catamites, would you become one? Is this your business? were you born for this purpose, that dissolute women should delight in you? Shall we make such a one as you a citizen of Corinth and perchance a prefect of the city, or chief of the youth, or general or superintendent of the games? Well, and when you have taken a wife, do you intend to have your hairs plucked out? To please whom and for what purpose? And when you have begotten children, will you introduce them also into the state with the habit of plucking their hairs? A beautiful citizen, and senator and rhetorician. We ought to pray that such young men be born among us and brought up.

Do not so, I entreat you by the Gods, young man: but when you have once heard these words, go away and say to yourself, "Epictetus has not said this to me; for how could he? but some propitious good through him: for it would never have come into his thoughts to say this, since he is not accustomed to talk thus with any person. Come then let us obey God, that we may not be subject to his anger." You say, "No." But, if a crow by his croaking signifies anything to you, it is not the crow which signifies, but God through the crow; and if he signifies anything through a human voice, will he not cause the man to say this to you, that you may know the power of the divinity, that he signifies to some in this way, and to others in that way, and concerning the greatest things and the chief he signifies through the noblest messenger? What else is it which the poet says:

For we ourselves have warned him, and have sent
Hermes the careful watcher, Argus' slayer,
The husband not to kill nor wed the wife.

Was Hermes going to descend from heaven to say this to him? And now the Gods say this to you and send the messenger, the slayer of Argus, to warn you not to pervert that which is well arranged, nor to busy yourself about it, but to allow a man to be a man, and a woman to be a woman, a beautiful man to be as a beautiful man, and an ugly man as an ugly man, for you are not flesh and hair, but you are will; and if your will beautiful, then you will be beautiful. But up the present time I dare not tell you that you are ugly, for I think that you are readier to hear anything than this. But see what Socrates says to the most beautiful and blooming of men Alcibiades: "Try, then, to be beautiful." What does he say to him? "Dress your hair and pluck the hairs from your legs." Nothing of that kind. But "Adorn your will, take away bad opinions." "How with the body?" Leave it as it is by nature. Another has looked after these things: entrust them to him. "What then, must a man be uncleaned?" Certainly not; but what you are and are made by nature, cleanse this. A man should be cleanly as a man, a woman as a woman, a child as a child. You say no: but let us also pluck out the lion's mane, that he may not be uncleaned, and the cock's comb for he also ought to he cleaned. Granted, but as a cock, and the lion as a lion, and the hunting dog as a hunting dog.

CHAPTER 2

In what a man ought to be exercised who has made proficiency; and that we neglect the chief things

There are three things in which a man ought to exercise himself who would be wise and good. The first concerns the desires and the aversions, that a man may not fail to get what he desires, and that he may not fall into that which he does not desire. The second concerns the movements (toward) and the movements from an object, and generally in doing what a man ought to do, that he may act according to order, to reason, and not carelessly. The third thing concerns freedom from deception and rashness in judgment, and generally it concerns the assents. Of these topics the chief and the most urgent is that which relates to the affects; for an affect is produced in no other way than by a failing to obtain that which a man desires or a falling into that which a man would wish to avoid. This is that which brings in perturbations, disorders, bad fortune, misfortunes, sorrows, lamentations and envy; that which makes men envious and jealous; and by these causes we are unable even to listen to the precepts of reason. The second topic concerns the duties of a man; for I ought not to be free from affects like a statue, but I ought to maintain the relations natural and acquired, as a pious man, as a son, as a father, as a citizen.

The third topic is that which immediately concerns those who are making proficiency, that which concerns the security of the other two, so that not even in sleep any appearance unexamined may surprise us, nor in intoxication, nor in melancholy. "This," it may be said, "is above our power." But the present philosophers neglecting the first topic and the second, employ themselves on the third, using sophistical arguments, making conclusions from questioning, employing hypotheses, lying. "For a man must," as it is said, "when employed on these matters, take care that he is not deceived." Who must? The wise and good man. This then is all that is wanting to you. Have you successfully worked out the rest? Are you free from deception in the matter of money? If you see a beautiful girl, do you resist the appearance? If your neighbor obtains an estate by will, are you not vexed? Now is there nothing else wanting to you except unchangeable firmness of mind? Wretch, you hear these very things with fear and anxiety that some person may despise you, and with inquiries about what any person may say about you. And if a man come and tell you that in a certain conversation in which the question was, "Who is the best philosopher," a man who was present said that a certain person was the chief philosopher, your little soul which was only a finger's length stretches out to two cubits. But if another who is present "You are mistaken; it is not worthwhile to listen to a certain person, for what does he know? he has only the first principles, and no more?" then you are confounded, you grow pale, you cry out immediately, "I will show him who I am, that I am a great philosopher." It is seen by these very things: why do you wish to show it by others? Do you not know that Diogenes pointed out one of the sophists in this way by stretching out his middle finger? And then when the man was wild with rage, "This," he said, "is the certain person: I pointed him out to you." For a man is not shown by the finger, as a stone or a piece of wood: but when any person shows the man's principles, then he shows him as a man.

Let us look at your principles also. For is it not plain that you value not at all your own will, but you look externally to things which are independent of your will? For instance, what will a certain person say? and what will people think of you? will you be considered a man of learning; have you read Chrysippus or Antipater? for if you have read Archedemus also, you have everything. Why are you still uneasy lest you should not show us who you are? Would you let me tell you what manner of man you have shown us that you are? You have exhibited yourself to us as a mean fellow, querulous, passionate, cowardly, finding fault with everything, blaming everybody, never quiet, vain: this is what you have exhibited to us. Go away now and read Archedemus; then, if a mouse should leap down and make a noise, you are a dead man. For such a death awaits you as it did—what was the man's name?—Crinis; and he too was proud, because he understood Archedemus.

Wretch, will you not dismiss these things that do not concern you at all? These things are suitable to those who are able to learn them without perturbation, to those who can say: "I am not subject to anger, to grief, to envy: I am not hindered, I am not restrained. What remains for me? I have leisure, I am tranquil: let us see how we must deal with sophistical arguments; let us see how when a man has accepted an hypothesis he shall not be led away to anything absurd." To them such things belong. To those who are happy it is appropriate to light a fire, to dine; if they choose, both to sing and to dance. But when the vessel is sinking, you come to me and hoist the sails.

CHAPTER 3

What is the matter on which a good man should he employed, and in what we ought chiefly to practice ourselves

The material for the wise and good man is his own ruling faculty: and the body is the material for the physician and the aliptes; the land is the matter for the husbandman. The business of the wise and good man is to use appearances conformably to nature: and as it is the nature of every soul to assent to the truth, to dissent from the false, and to remain in suspense as to that which is uncertain; so it is its nature to be moved toward the desire of the good, and to aversion from the evil; and with respect to that which is neither good nor bad it feels indifferent. For as the money-changer is not allowed to reject Caesar's coin, nor the seller of herbs, but if you show the coin, whether he chooses or not, he must give up what is sold for the coin; so it is also in the matter of the soul. When the good appears, it immediately attracts to itself; the evil repels from itself. But the soul will never reject the manifest appearance of the good, any more than persons will reject Caesar's coin. On this principle depends every movement both of man and God.

For this reason the good is preferred to every intimate relationship. There is no intimate relationship between me and my father, but there is between me and the good. "Are you so hard-hearted?" Yes, for such is my nature; and this is the coin which God has given me. For this reason, if the good is something different from the beautiful and the just, both father is gone, and brother and country, and everything. But shall I overlook my own good, in order that you may have it, and shall I give it up to you? Why? "I am your father." But you are not my good. "I am your brother." But you are not my good. But if we place the good in a right determination of the will, the very observance of the relations of life is good, and accordingly he who gives up any external things obtains that which is good. Your father takes away your property. But he does not injure you. Your brother will have the greater part of the estate in land. Let him have as much as he chooses. Will he then have a greater share of modesty, of fidelity, of brotherly affection? For who will eject you from this possession? Not even Zeus, for neither has he chosen to do so; but he has made this in my own power, and he has given it to me just as he possessed it himself, free from hindrance, compulsion, and impediment. When then the coin which another uses is a different coin, if a man presents this coin, he receives that which is sold for it. Suppose that there comes into the province a thievish proconsul, what coin does he use? Silver coin. Show it to him, and carry off what you please. Suppose one comes who is an adulterer: what coin does he use? Little girls. "Take," a man says, "the coin, and sell me the small thing." "Give," says the seller, "and buy." Another is eager to possess boys. Give him the coin, and receive what you wish. Another is fond of hunting: give him a fine nag or a dog. Though he groans and laments, he will sell for it that which you want. For another compels him from within, he who has fixed this coin.

Against this kind of thing chiefly a man should exercise himself. As soon as you go out in the morning, examine every man whom you see, every man whom you hear; answer as to a question, "What have you seen?" A handsome man or woman? Apply the rule: Is this independent of the will, or dependent? Independent. Take it away. What have you seen? A man lamenting over the death of a child. Apply the rule. Death is a thing independent of the will. Take it away. Has the proconsul met you? Apply the rule. What kind of thing is a proconsul's office? Independent of the will, or dependent on it? Independent. Take this away also: it does not stand examination: cast it away: it is nothing to you.

If we practiced this and exercised ourselves in it daily from morning to night, something indeed would be done. But now we are forthwith caught half-asleep by every appearance, and it is only, if ever, that in the school we are roused a little. Then when we go out, if we see a man lamenting, we say, "He is undone." If we see a consul, we say, "He is happy." If we see an exiled man, we say, "He is miserable." If we see a poor man, we say, "He is wretched: he has nothing to eat."

We ought then to eradicate these bad opinions, and to this end we should direct all our efforts. For what is weeping and lamenting? Opinion. What is bad fortune? Opinion. What is civil sedition, what is divided opinion, what is blame, what is accusation, what is impiety, what is trifling? All these things are opinions, and nothing more, and opinions about things independent of the will, as if they were good and bad. Let a man transfer these opinions to things dependent on the will, and I engage for him that he will be firm and constant, whatever may be the state of things around him. Such as is a dish of water, such is the soul. Such as is the ray of light which falls on the water, such are the appearances. When the water is moved, the ray also seems to be moved, yet it is not moved. And when, then, a man is seized with giddiness, it is not the arts and the virtues which are confounded, but the spirit on which they are impressed; but if the spirit be restored to its settled state, those things also are restored.

CHAPTER 4

Against a person who showed his partisanship in an unseemly way in a theatre

The governor of Epirus having shown his favor to an actor in an unseemly way and being publicly blamed on this account, and afterward having reported to Epictetus that he was blamed and that he was vexed at those who blamed him, Epictetus said: What harm have they been doing? These men also were acting, as partisans, as you were doing. The governor replied, "Does, then, any person show his partisanship in this way?" When they see you, said Epictetus, who are their governor, a friend of Caesar and his deputy, showing partisanship in this way, was it not to be expected that they also should show their partisanship in the same way? for if it is not right to show partisanship in this way, do not do so yourself; and if it is right, why are you angry if they followed your example? For whom have the many to imitate except you, who are their superiors, to whose example should they look when they go to the theatre except yours? "See how the deputy of Caesar looks on: he has cried out, and I too, then, will cry out. He springs up from his seat, and I will spring up. His slaves sit in various parts of the theatre and call out. I have no slaves, but I will myself cry out as much as I can and as loud as all of them together." You ought then to know when you enter the theatre that you enter as a rule and example to the rest how they ought to look at the acting. Why then did they blame you? Because every man hates that which is a hindrance to him. They wished one person to be crowned; you wished another. They were a hindrance to you, and you were a hindrance to them. You were found to be the stronger; and they did what they could; they blamed that which hindered them. What, then, would you have? That you should do what you please, and they should not even say what they please? And what is the wonder? Do not the husbandmen abuse Zeus when they are hindered by him? do not the sailors abuse him? do they ever cease abusing Caesar? What then does not Zeus know? is not what is said reported to Caesar? What, then, does he do? he knows that, if he punished all who abuse him, he would have nobody to rule over. What then? when you enter the theatre, you ought to say not, "Let Sophron be crowned", but you ought to say this, "Come let me maintain my will in this matter so that it shall be conformable to nature: no man is dearer to me than myself. It would be ridiculous, then, for me to be hurt (injured) in order that another who is an actor may be crowned." Whom then do I wish to gain the prize? Why the actor who does gain the prize; and so he will always gain the prize whom I wish to gain it. "But I wish Sophron to be crowned." Celebrate as many games as you choose in your own house, Nemean, Pythian, Isthmian, Olympian, and proclaim him victor. But in public do not claim more than your due, nor attempt to appropriate to yourself what belongs to all. If you do not consent to this, bear being abused: for when you do the same as the many, you put yourself on the same level with them.

CHAPTER 5

Against those who on account of sickness go away home

"I am sick here," said one of the pupils, "and I wish to return home." At home, I suppose, you free from sickness. Do you not consider whether you are doing, anything here which may be useful to the exercise of your will, that it may be corrected? For if you are doing nothing toward this end, it was to no purpose that you came. Go away. Look after your affairs at home. For if your ruling power cannot be maintained in a state conformable to nature, it is possible that your land can, that you will he able to increase your money, you will take care of your father in his old age, frequent the public place, hold magisterial office: being bad you will do badly anything else that you have to do. But if you understand yourself, and know that you are casting away certain bad opinions and adopting others in their place, and if you have changed your state of life from things which are not within your will to things which are within your will, and if you ever say, "Alas!" you are not saying what you say on account of your father, or your brother, but on account of yourself, do you still allege your sickness? Do you not know that both disease and death must surprise us while we are doing something? the husbandman while he is tilling the ground, the sailor while he is on his voyage? what would you be doing when death surprises you, for you must be surprised when you are doing something? If you can be doing anything better than this when you are surprised, do it. For I wish to be surprised by disease or death when I am looking after nothing else than my that may be free from perturbation, own will that I may be free from hindrance, free from compulsion, and in a state of liberty. I wish to be found practicing these things that I may be able to say to God, "Have I in any respect transgressed thy commands? have I in any respect wrongly used the powers which Thou gavest me? have I misused my perceptions or my preconceptions? have I ever blamed Thee? have I ever found fault with Thy administration? I have been sick, because it was Thy will, and so have others, but I was content to be sick. I have been poor because it was Thy will, but I was content also. I have not filled a magisterial office, because it was not Thy pleasure that I should: I have never desired it. Hast Thou ever seen me for this reason discontented? have I not always approached Thee with a cheerful countenance, ready to do Thy commands and to obey Thy signals? Is it now Thy will that I should depart from the assemblage of men? I depart. I give Thee all thanks that Thou hast allowed me to join in this Thy assemblage of men and to see Thy works, and to comprehend this Thy administration." May death surprise me while I am thinking of these things, while I am thus writing and reading.

"But my mother will not hold my head when I am sick." Go to your mother then; for you are a fit person to have your head held when you are sick. "But at home I used to lie down on a delicious bed." Go away to your bed: indeed you are fit to lie on such a bed even when you are in health: do not, then, lose what you can do there.

But what does Socrates say? "As one man," he says, "is pleased with improving his land, another with improving his horse, so I am daily pleased in observing that I am growing better." "Better in what? in using nice little words?" Man, do not say that. "In little matters of speculation?" What are you saying? "And indeed I do not see what else there is on which philosophers employ their time." Does it seem nothing to you to have never found fault with any person, neither with God nor man? to have blamed nobody? to carry the same face always in going out and coming in? This is what Socrates knew, and yet he never said that he knew anything or taught anything. But if any man asked for nice little words or little speculations, he would carry him to Protagoras or to Hippias; and if any man came to ask for pot-herbs, he would carry him to the gardener. Who then among you has this purpose? for if indeed you had it, you would both be content in sickness, and in hunger, and in death. If any among you has been in love with a charming girl, he knows that I say what is true.

CHAPTER 6

Miscellaneous

When some person asked him how it happened that since reason has been more cultivated by the men of the present age, the progress made in former times was greater. In what respect, he answered, has it been more cultivated now, and in what respect was the progress greater then? For in that in which it has now been more cultivated, in that also the progress will now be found. At present it has been cultivated for the purpose of resolving syllogisms, and progress is made. But in former times it was cultivated for the purpose of maintaining the governing faculty in a condition conformable to nature, and progress was made. Do not, then, mix things which are different and do not expect, when you are laboring at one thing, to make progress in another. But see if any man among us when he is intent see I upon this, the keeping himself in a state conformable to nature and living so always, does not make progress. For you will not find such a man.

The good man is invincible, for he does not enter the contest where he is not stronger. If you want to have his land and all that is on it, take the land; take his slaves, take his magisterial office, take his poor body. But you will not make his desire fail in that which it seeks, nor his aversion fall into that which he would avoid. The only contest into which he enters is that about things which are within the power of his will; how then will he not be invincible?

Some person having asked him what is Common sense, Epictetus replied: As that may be called a certain Common hearing which only distinguishes vocal sounds, and that which distinguishes musical sounds is not Common, but artificial; so there are certain things which men, who are not altogether perverted, see by the common notions which all possess. Such a constitution of the mind is named Common sense.

It is not easy to exhort weak young men; for neither is it easy to hold cheese with a hook. But those who have a good natural disposition, even if you try to turn them aside, cling still more to reason. Wherefore Rufus generally attempted to discourage, and he used this method as a test of those who had a good natural disposition and those who had not. "For," it was his habit to say, "as a stone, if you cast it upward, will be brought down to the earth by its own nature, so the man whose mind is naturally good, the more you repel him, the more he turns toward that to which he is naturally inclined."

CHAPTER 7

To the administrator of the free cities who was an Epicurean

When the administrator came to visit him, and the man was an Epicurean, Epictetus said: It is proper for us who are not philosophers to inquire of you who are philosophers, as those who come to a strange city inquire of the citizens and those who are acquainted with it, what is the best thing in the world, in order that we also, after inquiry, may go in quest of that which is best and look at it, as strangers do with the things in cities. For that there are three things which relate to man, soul, body, and things external, scarcely any man denies. It remains for you philosophers to answer what is the best. What shall we say to men? Is the flesh the best? and was it for this that Maximus sailed as far as Cassiope in winter with his son, and accompanied him that he might be gratified in the flesh? Then the man said that it was not, and added, "Far be that from him." Is it not fit then, Epictetus said, to be actively employed about the best? "It is certainly of all things the most fit." What, then, do we possess which is better than the flesh? "The soul," he replied. And the good things of the best, are they better, or the good things of the worse? "The good things of the best." And are the good things of the best within the power of the will or not within the power of the will? "They are within the power of the will." Is, then, the pleasure of the soul a thing within the power of the will? "It is," he replied. And on what shall this pleasure depend? On itself? But that cannot be conceived: for there must first exist a certain substance or nature of good, by obtaining which we shall have pleasure in the soul. He assented to this also. On what, then, shall we depend for this pleasure of the soul? for if it shall depend on things of the soul, the substance of the good is discovered; for good cannot be one thing, and that at which we are rationally delighted another thing; nor if that which precedes is not good, can that which comes after be good, for in order that the thing which comes after may be good, that which precedes must be good. But you would not affirm this, if you are in your right mind, for you would then say what is inconsistent both with Epicurus and the rest of your doctrines. It remains, then, that the pleasure of the soul is in the pleasure from things of the body: and again that those bodily things must be the things which precede and the substance of the good.

For this reason Maximus acted foolishly if he made the voyage for any other reason than for the sake of the flesh, that is, for the sake of the best. And also a man acts foolishly if he abstains from that which belongs to others, when he is a judge and able to take it. But, if you please, let us consider this only, how this thing may be done secretly, and safely, and so that no man will know it. For not even does Epicurus himself declare stealing to be bad, but he admits that detection is; and because it is impossible to have security against detection, for this reason he says, "Do not steal." But I say to you that if stealing is done cleverly and cautiously, we shall not be detected: further also we have powerful friends in Rome both men and women, and the Hellenes are weak, and no man will venture to go up to Rome for the purpose. Why do you refrain from your own good? This is senseless, foolish. But even if you tell me that you do refrain, I will not believe you. For as it is impossible to assent to that which appears false, and to turn away from that which is true, so it is impossible to abstain from that which appears good. But wealth is a good thing, and certainly most efficient in producing pleasure. Why will you not acquire wealth? And why should we not corrupt our neighbor's wife, if we can do it without detection? and if the husband foolishly prates about the matter, why not pitch him out of the house? If you would be a philosopher such as you ought to be, if a perfect philosopher, if consistent with your own doctrines. If you would not, you will not differ at all from us who are called Stoics; for we also say one thing, but we do another: we talk of the things which are beautiful, but we do what is base. But you will be perverse in the contrary way, teaching what is bad, practicing what is good.

In the name of God, are you thinking of a city of Epicureans? "I do not marry." "Nor I, for a man ought not to marry; nor ought we to beget children, nor engage in public matters." What then will happen? whence will the citizens come? who will bring them up? who will be governor of the youth, who preside wi over gymnastic exercises? and in what also will the teacher instruct them? will he teach them what the Lacedaemonians were taught, or what the Athenians were taught? Come take a young man, bring him up according to your doctrines. The doctrines are bad, subversive of a state, pernicious to families, and not becoming to women. Dismiss them, man. You live in a chief city: it is your duty to be a magistrate, to judge justly, to abstain from that which belongs to others; no woman ought to seem beautiful to you except your own wife, and no youth, no vessel of silver, no vessel of gold. Seek for doctrines which are consistent with what I say, and, by making them your guide, you will with pleasure abstain from things which have such persuasive power to lead us and overpower us. But if to the persuasive power of these things, we also devise such a philosophy as this which helps to push us on toward them and strengthens us to this end, what will be the consequence? In a piece of toreutic art which is the best part? the silver or the workmanship? The substance of the hand is the flesh; but the work of the hand is the principal part. The duties then are also three; those which are directed toward the existence of a thing; those which are directed toward its existence in a particular kind; and third, the chief or leading things themselves. So also in man we ought not to value the material, the poor flesh, but the principal. What are these? Engaging in public business, marrying, begetting children, venerating God, taking care of parents, and, generally, having desires, aversions, pursuits of things and avoidances, in the way in which we ought to do these things, and according to our nature. And how are we constituted by nature? Free, noble, modest: for what other animal blushes? what other is capable of receiving the appearance of shame? and we are so constituted by nature as to subject pleasure to these things, as a minister, a servant, in order that it may call forth our activity, in order that it may keep us constant in acts which are conformable to nature.

"But I am rich and I want nothing." Why, then, do you pretend to be a philosopher? Your golden and your silver vessels are enough for you. What need have you of principles? "But I am also a judge of the Greeks." Do you know how to judge? Who taught you to know? "Caesar wrote to me a codicil." Let him write and give you a commission to judge of music; and what will be the use of it to you? Still how did you become a judge? whose hand did you kiss? the hand of Symphorus or Numenius? Before whose bedchamber have you slept? To whom have you sent gifts? Then do you not see that to be a judge is just of the same value as Numenius is? "But I can throw into prison any man whom I please." So you can do with a stone. "But I can beat with sticks whom I please." So you may an ass. This is not a governing of men. Govern us as rational animals: show us what is profitable to us, and we will follow it: show us what is unprofitable, and we will turn away from it. Make us imitators of yourself, as Socrates made men imitators of himself. For he was like a governor of men, who made them subject to him their desires, their aversion, their movements toward an object and their turning away from it. "Do this: do not do this: if you do not obey, I will throw you into prison." This is not governing men like rational animals. But I: As Zeus has ordained, so act: if you do not act so, you will feel the penalty, you will be punished. What will be the punishment? Nothing else than not having done your duty: you will lose the character of fidelity, modesty, propriety. Do not look for greater penalties than these.

CHAPTER 8

How we must exercise ourselves against appearances

As we exercise ourselves against sophistical questions, so we ought to exercise ourselves daily against appearances; for these appearances also propose questions to us. "A certain person son is dead." Answer: the thing is not within the power of the will: it is not an evil. "A father has disinherited a certain son. What do you think of it?" It is a thing beyond the power of the will, not an evil. "Caesar has condemned a person." It is a thing beyond the power of the will, not an evil. "The man is afflicted at this." Affliction is a thing which depends on the will: it is an evil. He has borne the condemnation bravely." That is a thing within the power of the will: it is a good. If we train ourselves in this manner, we shall make progress; for we shall never assent to anything of which there is not an appearance capable of being comprehended. Your son is dead. What has happened? Your son is dead. Nothing more? Nothing. Your ship is lost. What has happened? Your ship is lost. A man has been led to prison. What has happened? He has been led to prison. But that herein he has fared badly, every man adds from his own opinion. "But Zeus," you say, "does not do right in these matters." Why? because he has made you capable of endurance? because he has made you magnanimous? because he has taken from that which befalls you the power of being evil? because it is in your power to be happy while you are suffering what you suffer; because he has opened the door to you, when things do not please you? Man, go out and do not complain.

Hear how the Romans feel toward philosophers, if you would like to know. Italicus, who was the most in repute of the philosophers, once when I was present being, vexed with his own friends and as if he was suffering something intolerable said, "I cannot bear it, you are killing me: you will make me such as that man is"; pointing to me.

CHAPTER 9

To a certain rhetorician who was going up to Rome on a suit

When a certain person came to him, who was going up to Rome on account of a suit which had regard to his rank, Epictetus inquired the reason of his going to Rome, and the man then asked what he thought about the matter. Epictetus replied: If you ask me what you will do in Rome, whether you will succeed or fall, I have no rule about this. But if you ask me how you will fare, I can tell you: if you have right opinions, you will fare well; if they are false, you will fare ill. For to every man the cause of his acting is opinion. For what is the reason why you desired to be elected governor of the Cnossians? Your opinion. What is the reason that you are now going up to Rome? Your opinion. And going in winter, and with danger and expense. "I must go." What tells you this? Your opinion. Then if opinions are the causes of all actions, and a man has bad opinions, such as the cause may be, such also is the effect. Have we then all sound opinions, both you and your adversary? And how do you differ? But have you sounder opinions than your adversary? Why? You think so. And so does he think that his opinions are better; and so do madmen. This is a bad criterion. But show to me that you have made some inquiry into your opinions and have taken some pains about them. And as now you are sailing to Rome in order to become governor of the Cnossians, and you are not content to stay at home with the honors which you had, but you desire something greater and more conspicuous, so when did you ever make a voyage for the purpose of examining your own opinions, and casting them out, if you have any that are bad? Whom have you approached for this purpose? What time have you fixed for it? What age? Go over the times of your life by yourself, if you are ashamed of me. When you were a boy, did you examine your own opinions? and did you not then, as you do all things now, do as you did do? and when you were become a youth and attended the rhetoricians, and yourself practiced rhetoric, what did you imagine that you were deficient in? And when you were a young man and engaged in public matters, and pleaded causes yourself, and were gaining reputation, who then seemed your equal? And when would you have submitted to any man examining and show that your opinions are bad? What, then, do you wish me to say to you? "Help me in this matter." I have no theorem (rule) for this. Nor have you, if you came to me for this purpose, come to me as a philosopher, but as to a seller of vegetables or a shoemaker. "For what purpose then have philosophers theorems?" For this purpose, that whatever may happen, our ruling faculty may be and continue to be conformable to nature. Does this seem to you a small thing? "No; but the greatest." What then? does it need only a short time? and is it possible to seize it as you pass by? If you can, seize it.

Then you will say, "I met with Epictetus as I should meet with a stone or a statue": for you saw me, and nothing more. But he meets with a man as a man, who learns his opinions, and in his turn shows his own. Learn my opinions: show me yours; and then say that you have visited me. Let us examine one another: if I have any bad opinion, take it away; if you have any, show it. This is the meaning of meeting with a philosopher. "Not so, but this is only a passing visit, and while we are hiring the vessel, we can also see Epictetus. Let us see what he says." Then you go away and say: "Epictetus was nothing: he used solecisms and spoke in a barbarous way." For of what else do you come as judges? "Well, but a man may say to me, "If I attend to such matters, I shall have no land, as you have none; I shall have no silver cups as you have none, nor fine beasts as you have none." In answer to this it is perhaps sufficient to say: I have no need of such things: but if you possess many things you have need of others: whether you choose or not, you are poorer than I am. "What then have I need of?" Of that which you have not: of firmness, of a mind which is conformable to nature, of being free from perturbation. Whether I have a patron or not, what is that to me? but it is something to you. I am richer than you: I am not anxious what Caesar will think of me: for this reason, I flatter no man. This is what I possess instead of vessels of silver and gold. You have utensils of gold; but your discourse, your opinions, your assents, your movements, your desires are of earthen ware. But when I have these things conformable to nature, why should I not employ my studies also upon reason? for I have leisure: my mind is not distracted. What shall I do, since I have no distraction? What more suitable to a man have I than this? When you have nothing to do, you are disturbed, you go to the theatre or you wander about without a purpose. Why should not the philosopher labor to improve his reason? You employ yourself about crystal vessels: I employ myself about the syllogism named "The Living": you about myrrhine vessels; I employ myself about the syllogism named "The Denying." To you everything appears small that you possess: to me all that I have appears great. Your desire is insatiable: mine is satisfied. To (children) who put their hand into a narrow necked earthen vessel and bring out figs and nuts, this happens; if they fill the hand, they cannot take it out, and then they cry. Drop a few of them and you will draw things out. And do you part with your desires: do not desire many things and you will have what you want.

CHAPTER 10

In what manner we ought to bear sickness

When the need of each opinion comes, we ought to have it in readiness: on the occasion of breakfast, such as relate to breakfast; in the bath, those that concern the bath; in bed, those that concern bed.

Let sleep not come upon thy languid eyes
Before each daily action thou hast scann'd;
What's done amiss, what done, what left undone;
From first to last examine all, and then
Blame what is wrong in what is right rejoice.

And we ought to retain these verses in such way that we may use them, not that we may utter them aloud, as when we exclaim "Paean Apollo." Again in fever we should have ready such opinions as concern a fever; and we ought not, as soon as the fever begins, to lose and forget all. (A man who has a fever) may "If I philosophize any longer, may I be hanged: wherever I go, I must take care of the poor body, that a fever may not come." But what is philosophizing? Is it not a preparation against events which may happen? Do you not understand that you are saying something of this kind? "If I shall still prepare myself to bear with patience what happens, may I be hanged." But this is just as if a man after receiving blows should give up the Pancratium. In the Pancratium it is in our power to desist and not to receive blows. But in the other matter, we give up philosophy, what shall we gain I gain? What then should a man say on the occasion of each painful thing? "It was for this that I exercised myself, for this I disciplined myself." God says to you, "Give me a proof that you have duly practiced athletics, that you have eaten what you ought, that you have been exercised, that you have obeyed the aliptes." Then do you show yourself weak when the time for action comes? Now is the time for the fever. Let it be borne well. Now is the time for thirst, well; now is the time for hunger, bear it well. Is it not in your power? who shall hinder you? The physician will hinder you from drinking; but he cannot prevent you from bearing thirst well: and he will hinder you from eating; but he cannot prevent you from bearing hunger well.

"But I cannot attend to my philosophical studies." And for what purpose do you follow them? Slave, is it not that you may be happy, that you may be constant, is it not that you may be in a state conformable to nature and live so? What hinders you when you have a fever from having your ruling faculty conformable to nature? Here is the proof of the thing, here is the test of the philosopher. For this also is a part of life, like walking, like sailing, like journeying by land, so also is fever. Do you read when you are walking? No. Nor do you when you have a fever. if you walk about well, you have all that belongs to a man who walks. If you bear fever well, you have all that belongs to a man in a fever. What is it to bear a fever well? Not to blame God or man; not to be afflicted it that which happens, to expect death well and nobly, to do what must be done: when the physician comes in, not to be frightened at what he says; nor if he says, "You are doing well," to be overjoyed. For what good has he told you? and when you were in health, what good was that to you? And even if he says, "You are in a bad way," do not despond. For what is it to be ill? is it that you are near the severance of the soul and the body? what harm is there in this? If you are not near now, will you not afterward be near? Is the world going to be turned upside down when you are dead? Why then do you flatter the physician? Why do you say, "If you please, master, I shall be well"? Why do you give him an opportunity of raising his eyebrows? Do you not value a physician, as you do a shoemaker when he is measuring your foot, or a carpenter when he is building your house, and so treat the physician as to the body which is not yours, but by nature dead? He who has a fever has an opportunity of doing this: if he does these things, he has what belongs to him. For it is not the business of a philosopher to look after these externals, neither his wine nor his oil nor his poor body, but his own ruling power. But as to externals how must he act? so far as not to be careless about them. Where then is there reason for fear? where is there, then, still reason for anger, and of fear about what belongs to others, about things which are of no value? For we ought to have these two principles in readiness: that except the will nothing is good nor bad; and that we ought not to lead events, but to follow them. "My brother ought not to have behaved thus to me." No; but he will see to that: and, however he may behave, I will conduct myself toward him as I ought. For this is my own business: that belongs to another; no man can prevent this, the other thing can be hindered.

CHAPTER 11

Certain miscellaneous matters

There are certain penalties fixed as by law for those who disobey the divine administration. Whoever thinks any other thing to be good except those things which depend on the will, let him envy, let him desire, let him flatter, let him be perturbed: whoever considers anything else to be evil, let him grieve, let him lament, let him weep, let him be unhappy. And yet, though so severely punished, we cannot desist.

Remember what the poet says about the stranger:

Stranger, I must not, e'en if a worse man come.

This, then, may be applied even to a father: "I must not, even if a worse man than you should come, treat a father unworthily-, for all are from paternal Zeus." And of a brother, "For all are from the Zeus who presides over kindred." And so in the other relations of life we shall find Zeus to be an inspector.

CHAPTER 12

About exercise

We ought not to make our exercises consist in means contrary to nature and adapted to cause admiration, for, if we do so, we, who call ourselves philosophers, shall not differ at all from jugglers. For it is difficult even to walk on a rope; and not only difficult, but it is also dangerous. Ought we for this reason to practice walking on a rope, or setting up a palm tree, or embracing statues? By no means. Everything, which is difficult and dangerous is not suitable for practice; but that is suitable which conduces to the working out of that which is proposed to us as a thing to be worked out. To live with desire and aversion, free from restraint. And what is this? Neither to be disappointed in that which you desire, nor to fall into anything which you would avoid. Toward this object, then, exercise ought to tend. For, since it is not possible to have your desire not disappointed and your aversion free from falling into that which you would avoid, great and constant practice you must know that if you allow your desire and aversion to turn to things which are not within the power of the will, you will neither have your desire capable of attaining your object, nor your aversion free from the power of avoiding that which you would avoid. And since strong habit leads, and we are accustomed to employ desire and aversion only to things which are not within the power of our will, we ought to oppose to this habit a contrary habit, and where there is great slipperiness in the appearances, there to oppose the habit of exercise.

I am rather inclined to pleasure: I will incline to the contrary side above measure for the sake of exercise. I am averse to pain: I will rub and exercise against this the appearances which are presented to me for the purpose of withdrawing my aversion from every such thing. For who is a practitioner in exercise? He who practices not using his desire, and applies his aversion only to things which are within the power of his will, and practices most in the things which are difficult to conquer. For this reason one man must practice himself more against one thing and another against another thing. What, then, is it to the purpose to set up a palm tree, or to carry about a tent of skins, or a mortar and a pestle? Practice, man, if you are irritable, to endure if you are abused, not to be vexed if you are treated with dishonor. Then you will make so much progress that, even if a man strikes you, you will say to yourself, "Imagine that you have embraced a statue": then also exercise yourself to use wine properly so as not to drink much, for in this also there are men who foolishly practice themselves; but first of all you should abstain from it, and abstain from a young girl and dainty cakes. Then at last, if occasion presents itself, for the purpose of trying yourself at a proper time, you will descend into the arena to know if appearances overpower you as they did formerly. But at first fly far from that which is stronger than yourself: the contest is unequal between a charming young girl and a beginner in philosophy. "The earthen pitcher," as the saying is, "and the rock do not agree."

After the desire and the aversion comes the second topic of the movements toward action and the withdrawals from it; that you may be obedient to reason, that you do nothing out of season or place, or contrary to any propriety of the kind. The third topic concerns the assents, which is related to the things which are persuasive and attractive. For as Socrates said, "we ought not to live a life without examination," so we ought not to accept an appearance without examination, but we should say, "Wait, let me see what you are and whence you come"; like the watch at night, "Show me the pass." "Have you the signal from nature which the appearance that may be accepted ought to have?" And finally whatever means are applied to the body by those who exercise it, if they tend in any way toward desire and it, aversion, they also may be fit means of exercise; but if they are for display, they are the indications of one who has turned himself toward something external, and who is hunting for something else, and who looks for spectators who will say, "Oh the great man." For this reason, Apollonius said well, "When you intend to exercise yourself for your own advantage, and you are thirsty from heat, take in a mouthful of cold water, and spit it out, and tell nobody."

CHAPTER 13

What solitude is, and what kind of person a solitary man is

Solitude is a certain condition of a helpless man. For because a man is alone, he is not for that reason also solitary; just as though a man is among numbers, he is not therefore not solitary. When then we have lost either a brother, or a son, or a friend on whom we were accustomed to repose, we say that we are left solitary, though we are often in Rome, though such a crowd meet us, though so many live in the same place, and sometimes we have a great number of slaves. For the man who is solitary, as it is conceived, is considered to be a helpless person and exposed to those who wish to harm him. For this reason when we travel, then especially do we say that we are lonely when we fall among robbers, for it is not the sight of a human creature which removes us from solitude, but the sight of one who is faithful and modest and helpful to us. For if being alone is enough to make solitude, you may say that even Zeus is solitary in the conflagration and bewails himself saying, "Unhappy that I am who have neither Hera, nor Athena, nor Apollo, nor brother, nor son, nor descendant nor kinsman." This is what some say that he does when he is alone at the conflagration. For they do not understand how a man passes his life when he is alone, because they set out from a certain natural principle, from the natural desire of community and mutual love and from the pleasure of conversation among men. But none the less a man ought to be prepared in a manner for this also, to be able to be sufficient for himself and to be his own companion. For as Zeus dwells with himself, and is tranquil by himself, and thinks of his own administration and of its nature, and is employed in thoughts suitable to himself; so ought we also to be able to talk with ourselves, not to feel the want of others also, not to be unprovided with the means of passing our time; to observe the divine administration and the relation of ourselves to everything else; to consider how we formerly were affected toward things that happen and how at present; what are still the things which give us pain; how these also can be cured and how removed; if any things require improvement, to improve them according to reason.

For you see that Caesar appears to furnish us with great peace, that there are no longer enemies nor battles nor great associations of robbers nor of pirates, but we can travel at every hour and sail from east to west. But can Caesar give us security from fever also, can he from shipwreck, from fire, from earthquake or from lightning? well, I will say, can he give us security against love? He cannot. From sorrow? He cannot. From envy? He cannot. In a word then he cannot protect us from any of these things. But the doctrine of philosophers promises to give us security even against these things. And what does it say? "Men, if you will attend to me, wherever you are, whatever you are doing, you will not feel sorrow, nor anger, nor compulsion, nor hindrance, but you will pass your time without perturbations and free from everything." When a man has this peace, not proclaimed by Caesar (for how should he be able to proclaim it?), but by God through reason, is he not content when he is alone? when he sees and reflects, "Now no evil can happen to me; for me there is no robber, no earthquake, everything is full of peace, full of tranquility: every way, every city, every meeting, neighbor, companion is harmless. One person whose business it is, supplies me with food; another with raiment; another with perceptions, and preconceptions. And if he does not supply what is necessary, He gives the signal for retreat, opens the door, and says to you, 'Go.' Go whither? To nothing terrible, but to the place from which you came, to your friends and kinsmen, to the elements: what there was in you of fire goes to fire; of earth, to earth; of air, to air; of water to water: no Hades, nor Acheron, nor Cocytus, nor Pyriphlegethon, but all is full of Gods and Demons." When a man has such things to think on, and sees the sun, the moon and stars, and enjoys earth and sea, he is not solitary nor even helpless. "Well then, if some man should come upon me when I am alone and murder me?" Fool, not murder you, but your poor body.

What kind of solitude then remains? what want? why do we make ourselves worse than children? and what do children do when they are left alone? They take up shells and ashes, and they build something, then pull it down, and build something else, and so they never want the means of passing the time. Shall I, then, if you sail away, sit down and weep, because I have been left alone and solitary? Shall I then have no shells, no ashes? But children do what they do through want of thought, and we through knowledge are unhappy.

Every great power is dangerous to beginners. You must then bear such things as you are able, but conformably to nature: but not... Practice sometimes a way of living like a man in health. Abstain from food, drink water, abstain sometimes altogether from desire, in order that you may some time desire consistently with reason; and if consistently with reason, when you have anything good in you, you will desire well. "Not so; but we wish to live like wise men immediately and to be useful to men." Useful how? what are you doing? have you been useful to yourself? "But, I suppose, you wish to exhort them." You exhort them! You wish to be useful to them. Show to them in your own example what kind of men philosophy makes, and don't trifle. When you are eating, do good to those who eat with you; when you are drinking, to those who are drinking with you; by yielding to all, giving way, bearing with them, thus do them good, and do not spit on them your phlegm.

CHAPTER 14

Certain miscellaneous matters

As bad tragic actors cannot sing alone, but in company with many: so some persons cannot walk about alone. Man, if you are anything, both walk alone and talk to yourself, and do not hide yourself in the chorus. Examine a little at last, look around, stir yourself up, that you may know who you are.

When a man drinks water, or does anything for the sake of practice, whenever there is an opportunity he tells it to all: "I drink water." Is it for this that you drink water, for the purpose of drinking water? Man, if it is good for you to drink, drink; but if not, you are acting ridiculously. But if it is good for you and you do drink, say nothing about it to those who are displeased with water-drinkers. What then, do you wish to please these very men?

Of things that are done some are done with a final purpose, some according to occasion, others with a certain reference to circumstances, others for the purpose of complying with others. and some according to a fixed scheme of life.

You must root out of men these two things, arrogance and distrust. Arrogance, then, is the opinion that you want nothing: but distrust is the opinion that you cannot be happy when so many circumstances surround you. Arrogance is removed by confutation; and Socrates was the first who practiced this. And, that the thing is not impossible, inquire and seek. This search will do you no harm; and in a manner this is philosophizing, to seek how it is possible to employ desire and aversion without impediment.

"I am superior to you, for my father is a man of consular rank." Another says, "I have been a tribune, but you have not." If we were horses, would you say, "My father was swifter?" "I have much barley and fodder, or elegant neck ornaments." If, then, while you were saying this, I said, "Be it so: let us run then." Well, is there nothing in a man such as running in a horse, by which it will be known which is superior and inferior? Is there not modesty, fidelity, justice? Show yourself superior in these, that you may be superior as a man. If you tell me that you can kick violently, I also will say to you that you are proud of that which is the act of an ass.

CHAPTER 15

That we ought to proceed with circumspection to everything

In every act consider what precedes and what follows, and then proceed to the act. If you do not consider, you will at first begin with spirit, since you have not thought at all of the things which follow; but afterward, when some consequences have shown themselves, you will basely desist. "I wish to conquer at the Olympic games." "And I too, by the gods: for it is a fine thing." But consider here what precedes and what follows; and then, if it is for your good, undertake the thing. You must act according to rules, follow strict diet, abstain from delicacies, exercise yourself by compulsion at fixed times, in heat, in cold; drink no cold water, nor wine, when there is opportunity of drinking it. In a word you must surrender yourself to the trainer as you do to a physician. Next in the contest, you must be covered with sand, sometimes dislocate a hand, sprain an ankle, swallow a quantity of dust, be scourged with the whip; and after undergoing all this, you must sometimes be conquered. After reckoning all these things, if you have still an inclination, go to the athletic practice. If you do not reckon them, observe you behave like children who at one time you will play as wrestlers, then as gladiators, then blow a trumpet, then act a tragedy, when they have seen and admired such things. So you also do: you are at one time a wrestler, then a gladiator, then a philosopher, then a rhetorician; but with your whole soul you are nothing: like the ape, you imitate all that you see; and always one thing after another pleases you, but that which becomes familiar displeases you. For you have never undertaken anything after consideration, nor after having explored the whole matter and put it to a strict examination; but you have undertaken it at hazard and with a cold desire. Thus some persons having seen a philosopher and having heard one speak like Euphrates— yet who can speak like him?—wish to be philosophers themselves.

Man, consider first what the matter is, then your own nature also, what it is able to bear. If you are a wrestler, look at your shoulders, your thighs, your loins: for different men are naturally formed for different things. Do you think that, if you do, you can be a philosopher? Do you think that you can eat as you do now, drink as you do now, and in the same way be angry and out of humor? You must watch, labor, conquer certain desires, you must depart from your kinsmen, be despised by your slave, laughed at by those who meet you, in everything you must be in an inferior condition, as to magisterial office, in honors, in courts of justice. When you have considered all these things completely, then, if you think proper, approach to philosophy, if you would gain in exchange for these things freedom from perturbations, liberty, tranquility. If you have not considered these things, do not approach philosophy: do not act like children, at one time a philosopher, then a tax collector, then a rhetorician, then a procurator of Caesar These things are not consistent. You must be one man either good or bad: you must either labor at your own ruling faculty or at external things: you must either labor at things within or at external things: that is, you must either occupy the place of a philosopher or that of one of the vulgar.

A person said to Rufus when Galba was murdered, "Is the world now governed by Providence?" But Rufus replied, "Did I ever incidentally form an argument from Galba that the world is governed by Providence?"

CHAPTER 16

That we ought with caution to enter, into familiar intercourse with men

If a man has frequent intercourse with others, either for talk, or drinking together, or generally for social purposes, he must either become like them, or change them to his own fashion. For if a man places a piece of quenched charcoal close to a piece that is burning, either the quenched charcoal will quench the other, or the burning charcoal will light that which is quenched. Since, then, the danger is so great, we must cautiously enter into such intimacies with those of the common sort, and remember that it is impossible that a man can keep company with one who is covered with soot without being partaker of the soot himself. For what will you do if a man speaks about gladiators, about horses, about athletes, or, what is worse, about men? "Such a person is bad," "Such a person is good": "This was well done," "This was done badly." Further, if he scoff, or ridicule, or show an ill-natured disposition? Is any man among us prepared like a lute-player when he takes a lute, so that as soon as he has touched the strings, he discovers which are discordant, and tunes the instrument? such a power as Socrates had who in all his social intercourse could lead his companions to his own purpose? How should you have this power? It is therefore a necessary consequence that you are carried about by the common kind of people.

Why, then, are they more powerful than you? Because they utter these useless words from their real opinions: but you utter your elegant words only from your lips; for this reason they are without strength and dead, and it is nauseous to listen to your exhortations and your miserable virtue, which is talked of everywhere. In this way the vulgar have the advantage over you: for every opinion is strong and invincible. Until, then, the good sentiments are fixed in you, and you shall have acquired a certain power for your security, I advise you to be careful in your association with like wax in the sun there will be melted away whatever you inscribe on your minds in the school. Withdraw, then, yourselves far from the sun so long as you have these waxen sentiments. For this reason also philosophers advise men to leave their native country, because ancient habits distract them and do not allow a beginning to be made of a different habit; nor can we tolerate those who meet us and say: "See such a one is now a philosopher, who was once so-and-so." Thus also physicians send those who have lingering diseases to a different country and a different air; and they do right, Do you also introduce other habits than those which you have: fix your opinions and exercise yourselves in them. But you do not so: you go hence to a spectacle, to a show of gladiators, to a place of exercise, to a circus; then you come back hither, and again from this place you go to those places, and still the same persons. And there is no pleasing habit, nor attention, nor care about self and observation of this kind, "How shall I use the appearances presented to me? according to nature, or contrary to nature? how do I answer to them? as I ought, or as I ought not? Do I say to those things which are independent of the will, that they do not concern me?" For if you are not yet in this state, fly from your former habits, fly from the common sort, if you intend ever to begin to be something.

CHAPTER 17

On providence

When you make any charge against Providence, consider, and you will learn that the thing has happened according to reason. "Yes, but the unjust man has the advantage." In what? "In money." Yes, for he is superior to you in this, that he flatters, is free from shame, and is watchful. What is the wonder? But see if he has the advantage over you in being faithful, in being modest: for you will not find it to be so; but wherein you are superior, there you will find that you have the advantage. And I once said to a man who was vexed because Philostorgus was fortunate: "Would you choose to lie with Sura?" "May it never happen," he replied, "that this day should come?" "Why then are you vexed, if he receives something in return for that which he sells; or how can you consider him happy who acquires those things by such means as you abominate; or what wrong does Providence, if he gives the better things to the better men? Is it not better to be modest than to be rich?" He admitted this. Why are you vexed then, man, when you possess the better thing? Remember, then, always, and have in readiness, the truth that this is a law of nature, that the superior has an advantage over the inferior in that in which he is superior; and you will never be vexed.

"But my wife treats me badly." Well, if any man asks you what this is, say, "My wife treats me badly." "Is there, then, nothing more?" Nothing. "My father gives me nothing." But to say that this is an evil is something which must be added to it externally, and falsely added. For this reason we must not get rid of poverty, but of the opinion about poverty, and then we shall be happy.

CHAPTER 18

That we ought not to be disturbed by any news

When anything shall be reported to you which is of a nature to disturb, have this principle in readiness, that the news is about nothing which is within the power of your will. Can any man report to you that you have formed a bad opinion, or had a bad desire? By no means. But perhaps he will report that some person is dead. What then is that to you? He may report that some person speaks ill of you. What then is that to you? Or that your father is planning something or other. Against whom? Against your will? How can he? But is it against your poor body, against your little property? You are quite safe: it is not against you. But the judge declares that you have committed an act of impiety. And did not the judges make the same declaration against Socrates? Does it concern you that the judge has made this declaration? No. Why then do you trouble yourself any longer about it? Your father has a certain duty, and if he shall not fulfill it, he loses the character of a father, of a man of natural affection, of gentleness. Do not wish him to lose anything else on this account. For never does a man do wrong, in one thing, and suffer in another. On the other side it is your duty to make your defense firmly, modestly, without anger: but if you do not, you also lose the character of a son, of a man of modest behavior, of generous character. Well then, is the judge free from danger? No; but he also is in equal danger. Why then are you still afraid of his decision? What have you to do with that which is another man's evil? It is your own evil to make a bad defense: be on your guard against this only. But to be condemned or not to be condemned, as that is the act of another person, so it is the evil of another person. "A certain person threatens you." Me? No. "He blames you." Let him see how he manages his own affairs. "He is going to condemn you unjustly." He is a wretched man.

CHAPTER 19

What is the condition of a common kind of man and of a philosopher

The first difference between a common person and a philosopher is this: the common person says, "Woe to me for my little child, for my brother, for my father." The philosopher, if he shall ever be compelled to say, "Woe to me," stops and says, "but for myself." For nothing which is independent of the will can hinder or damage the will, and the will can only hinder or damage itself. If, then, we ourselves incline in this direction, so as, when we are unlucky, to blame ourselves and to remember that nothing else is the cause of perturbation or loss of tranquility except our own opinion, I swear to you by all the gods that we have made progress. But in the present state of affairs we have gone another way from the beginning. For example, while we were still children, the nurse, if we ever stumbled through want of care, did not chide us, but would beat the stone. But what did the stone do? Ought the stone to have moved on account of your child's folly? Again, if we find nothing to eat on coming out of the bath, the pedagogue never checks our appetite, but he flogs the cook. Man, did we make you the pedagogue of the cook and not of the child? Correct the child, improve him. In this way even when we are grown up we are like children. For he who is unmusical is a child in music; he who is without letters is a child in learning: he who is untaught, is a child in life.

CHAPTER 20

That we can derive advantage from all external things

In the case of appearances, which are objects of the vision, nearly all have allowed the good and the evil to be in ourselves, and not in externals. No one gives the name of good to the fact that it is day, nor bad to the fact that it is night, nor the name of the greatest evil to the opinion that three are four. But what do men say? They say that knowledge is good, and that error is bad; so that even in respect to falsehood itself there is a good result, the knowledge that it is falsehood. So it ought to be in life also. "Is health a good thing, and is sickness a bad thing" No, man. "But what is it?" To be healthy, and healthy in a right way, is good: to be healthy in a bad way is bad; so that it is possible to gain advantage even from sickness, I declare. For is it not possible to gain advantage even from death, and is it not possible to gain advantage from mutilation? Do you think that Menoeceus gained little by death? "Could a man who says so, gain so much as Menoeceus gained?" Come, man, did he not maintain the character of being a lover of his country, a man of great mind, faithful, generous? And if he had continued to live, would he not have lost all these things? would he not have gained the opposite? would he not have gained the name of coward, ignoble, a hater of his country, a man who feared death? Well, do you think that he gained little by dying? "I suppose not." But did the father of Admetus gain much by prolonging his life so ignobly and miserably? Did he not die afterward? Cease, I adjure you by the gods, to admire things. Cease to make yourselves slaves, first of things, then on account of things slaves of those who are able to give them or take them away.

"Can advantage then be derived from these things." From all; and from him who abuses you. Wherein does the man who exercises before the combat profit the athlete? Very greatly. This man becomes my exerciser before the combat: he exercises me in endurance, in keeping my temper, in mildness. You say no: but he, who lays hold of my neck and disciplines my loins and shoulders, does me good; and the exercise master does right when he says: "Raise him up with both hands, and the heavier he is, so much the more is my advantage." But if a man exercises me in keeping my, temper, does he not do good? This is not knowing how to gain an advantage from men. "Is my neighbor bad?" Bad to himself, but good to me: he exercises my good disposition, my moderation. "Is my father bad?" Bad to himself, but to me good. This is the rod of Hermes: "Touch with it what you please," as the saying is. "and it will be of gold." I say not so: but bring what you please, and I will make it good. Bring disease, bring death, bring poverty, bring abuse, bring trial on capital charges: all these things through the rod of Hermes shall be made profitable. "What will you do with death?" Why, what else than that it shall do you honor, or that it shall show you by act through it, what a man is who follows the will of nature? "What will you do with disease?" I will show its nature, I will be conspicuous in, it, I will be firm, I will be happy, I will not flatter the physician, I will not wish to die. What else do you seek? Whatever you shall give me, I will make it happy, fortunate, honored, a thing which a man shall seek.

You say No: but take care that you do not fall sick: it is a bad thing." This is the same as if you should say, "Take care that you never receive the impression that three are four: that is bad." Man, how is it bad? If I think about it as I ought, how shall it, then, do me any damage? and shall it not even do me good? If, then, I think about poverty as I ought to do, about disease, about not having office, is not that enough for me? will it not be an advantage? How, then, ought I any longer to look to seek evil and good in externals? What happens these doctrines are maintained here, but no man carries them away home; but immediately every one is at war with his slave, with his neighbors, with those who have sneered at him, with those who have ridiculed him. Good luck to Lesbius, who daily proves that I know nothing.

CHAPTER 21

Against those who readily come to the profession of sophists

They who have taken up bare theorems immediately wish to vomit them forth, as persons whose stomach is diseased do with food. First digest the thing, then do not vomit it up thus: f you do not digest it, the thing become truly an emetic, a crude food and unfit to eat. But after digestion show us some chance in your ruling faculty, as athletes show in their shoulders by what they have been exercised and what they have eaten; as those who have taken up certain arts show by what they have learned. The carpenter does not come and say, "Hear me talk about the carpenter's art"; but having undertaken to build a house, he makes it, and proves that he knows the art. You also ought to do something of the kind; eat like a man, drink like a man, dress, marry, beget children, do the office of a citizen, endure abuse, bear unreasonable brother, bear with your father, bear with your son, neighbor, compassion. Show us these things that we may see that you have in truth learned something from the philosophers. You say, "No, but come and hear me read commentaries." Go away, and seek somebody to vomit them on. "And indeed I will expound to you the writings of Chrysippus as no other man can: I will explain his text most clearly: I will add also, if I can, the vehemence of Antipater and Archedemus."

Is it, then, for this that young men shall leave their country and their parents, that they may come to this place, and hear you explain words? Ought they not to return with a capacity to endure, to be active in association with others, free from passions, free from perturbation, with such a provision for the journey of life with which they shall be able to bear well the things that happen and derive honor from them? And how can you give them any of these things which you do not possess? Have you done from the beginning anything else than employ yourself about the resolution of Syllogisms, of sophistical arguments, and in those which work by questions? "But such a man has a school; why should not I also have a school?" These things are not done, man, in a careless way, nor just as it may happen; but there must be a (fit) age and life and God as a guide. You say, "No." But no man sails from a port without having sacrificed to the Gods and invoked their help; nor do men sow without having called on Demeter; and shall a man who has undertaken so great a work undertake it safely without the Gods? and shall they who undertake this work come to it with success? What else are you doing, man, than divulging the mysteries? You say, "There is a temple at Eleusis, and one here also. There is an Hierophant at Eleusis, and I also will make an Hierophant: there is a herald, and I will establish a herald; there is a torch-bearer at Eleusis, and I also will establish a torch-bearer; there are torches at Eleusis, and I will have torches here. The words are the same:

how do the things done here differ from those done there?" Most impious man, is there no difference? these things are done both in due place and in due time; and when accompanied with sacrifice and prayers, when a man is first purified, and when he is disposed in his mind to the thought that he is going to approach sacred rites and ancient rites. In this way the mysteries are useful, in this way we come to the notion that all these things were established by the ancients for the instruction and correction of life. But you publish and divulge them out of time, out of place, without sacrifices, without purity; you have not the garments which the hierophant ought to have, nor the hair, nor the head-dress, nor the voice, nor the age; nor have you purified yourself as he has: but you have committed to memory the words only, and you say: "Sacred are the words by themselves."

You ought to approach these matters in another way; the thing is great, it is mystical, not a common thing, nor is it given to every man. But not even wisdom perhaps is enough to enable a man to take care of youths: a man must have also a certain readiness and fitness for this purpose, and a certain quality of body, and above all things he must have God to advise him to occupy this office, as God advised Socrates to occupy the place of one who confutes error, Diogenes the office of royalty and reproof, and the office of teaching precepts. But you open a doctor's shop, though you have nothing except physic: but where and how they should be applied, you know not nor have you taken any trouble about it. "See," that man says, "I too have salves for the eyes." Have you also the power of using them? Do you know both when and how they will do good, and to whom they will do good? Why then do you act at hazard in things of the greatest importance? why are you careless? why do you undertake a thing that is in no way fit for you? Leave it to those who are able to do it, and to do it well. Do not yourself bring disgrace on philosophy through your own acts, and be not one of those who load it with a bad reputation. But if theorems please you, sit still and turn them over by yourself; but never say that you are a philosopher, nor allow another to say it; but say: "He is mistaken, for neither are my desires different from what they were before, nor is my activity directed to other objects, nor do I assent to other things, nor in the use of appearances have I altered at all from my former condition." This you must think and say about yourself, if you would think as you ought: if not, act at hazard, and do what you are doing; for it becomes you.

CHAPTER 22

About cynicism

When one of his pupils inquired of Epictetus, and he was a person who appeared to be inclined to Cynism, what kind of person a Cynic ought to be and what was the notion of the thing, We will inquire, said Epictetus, at leisure: but I have so much to say to you that he who without God attempts so great a matter, is hateful to God, and has no other purpose than to act indecently in public. For in any well-managed house no man comes forward, and says to himself, "I ought to be manager of the house." If he does so, the master turns round and, seeing him insolently giving orders, drags him forth and flogs him. So it is also in this great city; for here also there is a master of the house who orders everything. "You are the sun; you can by going round make the year and seasons, and make the fruits grow and nourish them, and stir the winds and make them remit, and warm the bodies of men properly: go, travel round, and so administer things from the greatest to the least." "You are a calf; when a lion shall appear, do your proper business: if you do not, you will suffer." "You are a bull: advance and fight, for this is your business, and becomes you, and you can do it." "You can lead the army against Illium; be Agamemnon." "You can fight in single combat against Hector: be Achilles." But if Thersites came forward and claimed the command, he would either not have obtained it; or, if he did obtain it, he would have disgraced himself before many witnesses.

Do you also think about the matter carefully: it is not what it seems to you. "I wear a cloak now and I shall wear it then: I sleep hard now, and I shall sleep hard then: I will take in addition a little bag now and a staff, and I will go about and begin to beg and to abuse those whom I meet; and if I see any man plucking the hair out of his body, I will rebuke him, or if he has dressed his hair, or if he walks about in purple." If you imagine the thing to be such as this, keep far away from it: do not approach it: it is not at all for you. But if you imagine it to be what it is, and do not think yourself to be unfit for it, consider what a great thing you undertake.

In the first place in the things which relate to yourself, you must not be in any respect like what you do now: you must not blame God or man: you must take away desire altogether, you must transfer avoidance only to the things which are within the power of the will: you must not feel anger nor resentment nor envy nor pity; a girl must not appear handsome to you, nor must you love a little reputation, nor be pleased with a boy or a cake. For you ought to know that the rest of men throw walls around them and houses and darkness when they do any such things, and they have many means of concealment. A man shuts the door, he sets somebody before the chamber: if a person comes, say that he is out, he is not at leisure. But the Cynic instead of all these things must use modesty as his protection: if he does not, he will be indecent in his nakedness and under the open sky. This is his house, his door: this is the slave before his bedchamber: this is his darkness. For he ought not to wish to hide anything that he does: and if he does, he is gone, he has lost the character of a Cynic, of a man who lives under the open sky, of a free man: he has begun to fear some external thing, he has begun to have need of concealment, nor can he get concealment when he chooses. For where shall he hide himself and how? And if by chance this public instructor shall be detected, this pedagogue, what kind of things will he be compelled to suffer? when then a man fears these things, is it possible for him to be bold with his whole soul to superintend men? It cannot be: it is impossible.

In the first place, then, you must make your ruling faculty pure, and this mode of life also. "Now, to me the matter to work on is my understanding, as wood is to the carpenter, as hides to the shoemaker; and my business is the right use of appearances. But the body is nothing to me: the parts of it are nothing to me. Death? Let it come when it chooses, either death of the whole or of a part. Fly, you say. And whither; can any man eject me out of the world? He cannot. But wherever I ever I go, there is the sun, there is the moon, there are the stars, dreams, omens, and the conversation with Gods."

Then, if he is thus prepared, the true Cynic cannot be satisfied with this; but he must know that he is sent a messenger from Zeus to men about good and bad things, to show them that they have wandered and are seeking the substance of good and evil where it is not, but where it is, they never think; and that he is a spy, as Diogenes was carried off to Philip after the battle of Chaeroneia as a spy. For, in fact, a Cynic is a spy of the things which are good for men and which are evil, and it is his duty to examine carefully and to come and report truly, and not to be struck with terror so as to point out as enemies those who are not enemies, nor in any other way to be perturbed by appearances nor confounded.

It is his duty, then, to he able with a loud voice, if the occasion should arise, and appearing on the tragic stage to say like Socrates: "Men, whither are you hurrying, what are you doing, wretches? like blind people you are wandering up and down: you are going by another road, and have left the true road: you seek for prosperity and happiness where they are not, and if another shows you where they are, you do not believe him." Why do you seek it without? In the body? It is not there. If you doubt, look at Myro, look at Ophellius. In possessions? It is not there. But if you do not believe me, look at Croesus: look at those who are now rich, with what lamentations their life is filled. In power? It is not there. If it is, those must be happy who have been twice and thrice consuls; but they are not. Whom shall we believe in these matters? you who from without see their affairs and are dazzled by an appearance, or the men themselves? What do they say? Hear them when they groan, when they grieve, when on account of these very consulships and glory and splendor they think that they are more wretched and in greater danger. Is it in royal power? It is not: if it were, Nero would have been happy, and Sardanapalus. But neither was Agamemnon happy, though he was a better man than Sardanapalus and Nero; but while others are snoring what is he doing?

"Much from his head he tore his rooted hair."

And what does he say himself?

"I am perplexed," he says, "and
Disturb'd I am," and "my heart out of my bosom
Is leaping."

Wretch, which of your affairs goes badly? Your possessions? No. Your body? No. But you are rich in gold and copper. What then is the matter with you? That part of you, whatever it is, has been neglected by you and is corrupted, the part with which we desire, with which we avoid, with which we move toward and move from things. How neglected? He knows not the nature of good for which he is made by nature and the nature of evil; and what is his own, and what belongs to another; and when anything that belongs to others goes badly, he says, "Woe to me, for the Hellenes are in dancer." Wretched is his ruling faculty, and alone neglected and uncared for. "The Hellenes are going to die destroyed by the Trojans." And if the Trojans do not kill them, will they not die? "Yes; but not all at once." What difference, then, does it make? For if death is an evil, whether men die altogether, or if they die singly, it is equally an evil. Is anything else then going to happen than the separation of the soul and the body? Nothing. And if the Hellenes perish, is the door closed, and is it not in your power to die? "It is." Why then do you lament "Oh, you who are a king and have the sceptre of Zeus?" An unhappy king does not exist more than an unhappy god. What then art thou? In truth a shepherd: for you weep as shepherds do, when a wolf has carried off one of their sheep: and these who are governed by you are sheep. And why did you come hither? Was your desire in any danger? was your aversion? was your movement? was your avoidance of things? He replies, "No; but the wife of my brother was carried off." Was it not then a great gain to be deprived of an adulterous wife? "Shall we be despised, then, by the Trojans?" What kind of people are the Trojans, wise or foolish? If they are wise, why do you fight with them? If they are fools, why do you care about them.

In what, then, is the good, since it is not in these things? Tell us, you who are lord, messenger and spy. Where you do not think that it is, nor choose to seek it: for if you chose to seek it, you would have found it to he in yourselves; nor would you be wandering out of the way, nor seeking what belongs to others as if it were your own. Turn your thoughts into yourselves: observe the preconceptions which you have. What kind of a thing do you imagine the good to be? "That which flows easily, that which is happy, that which is not impeded." Come, and do you not naturally imagine it to be great, do you not imagine it to be valuable? do you not imagine it to be free from harm? In what material then ought you to seek for that which flows easily, for that which is not impeded? in that which serves or in that which is free? "In that which is free." Do you possess the body, then, free or is it in servile condition? "We do not know." Do you not know that it is the slave of fever, of gout, ophthalmia, dysentery, of a tyrant, of fire, of iron, of everything which is stronger? Yes, it is a slave." How, then, is it possible that anything which belongs to the body can be free from hindrance? and how is a thing great or valuable which is naturally dead, or earth, or mud? Well then, do you possess nothing which is free? "Perhaps nothing." And who is able to compel you to assent to that which appears false? "No man." And who can compel you not to assent to that which appears true? "No man." By this, then, you see that there is something in you naturally free. But to desire or to be averse from, or to move toward an object or to move from it, or to prepare yourself, or to propose to do anything, which of you can do this, unless he has received an impression of the appearance of that which is profitable or a duty? "No man." You have, then, in these thongs also something which is not hindered and is free. Wretched men, work out this, take care of this, seek for good here.

"And how is it possible that a man who has nothing, who is naked, houseless, without a hearth, squalid, without a slave, without a city, can pass a life that flows easily?" See, God has sent you a man to show you that it is possible. "Look at me, who am without a city, without a house, without possessions, without a slave; I sleep on the ground; I have no wife, no children; no praetorium, but only the earth and heavens, and one poor cloak. And what do I want? Am I not without sorrow? am I not without fear? Am I not free? When did any of you see me failing in the object of my desire? or ever falling into that which I would avoid? did I ever blame God or man? did I ever accuse any man? did any of you ever see me with sorrowful countenance? And how do I meet with those whom you are afraid of and admire? Do not I treat them like slaves? Who, when he sees me, does not think that he sees his king and master?"

This is the language of the Cynics, this their character, this is their purpose. You say "No": but their characteristic is the little wallet, and staff, and great jaws: the devouring of all that you give them, or storing it up, or the abusing unseasonably all whom they meet, or displaying their shoulder as a fine thing. Do you see how you are going, to undertake so great a business? First take a mirror: look at your shoulders; observe your loins, your thighs. You are going, my man, to be enrolled as a combatant in the Olympic games, no frigid and miserable contest. In the Olympic games a man is not permitted to be conquered only and to take his departure; but first he must be disgraced in the sight of all the world, not in the sight of Athenians only, or of Lacedaemonians or of Nicopolitans; next he must be whipped also if he has entered into the contests rashly: and before being whipped, he must suffer thirst and heat, and swallow much dust.

Reflect more carefully, know thyself, consult the divinity, without God attempt nothing; for if he shall advise you, be assured that he intends you to become great or to receive many blows. For this very amusing quality is conjoined to a Cynic: he must be flogged like an ass, and when he is flogged, he must love those who flog him, as if he were the father of all, and the brother of all. You say "No"; but if a man flogs you, stand in the public place and call out, "Caesar, what do I suffer in this state of peace under thy protection? Let us bring the offender before the proconsul." But what is Caesar to a Cynic, or what is a proconsul, or what is any other except him who sent the Cynic down hither, and whom he serves, namely Zeus? Does he call upon any other than Zeus? Is he not convinced that, whatever he suffers, it is Zeus who is exercising him? Hercules when he was exercised by Eurystheus did not think that he was wretched, but without hesitation he attempted to execute all that he had in hand. And is he who is trained to the contest and exercised by Zeus going to call out and to be vexed, he who is worthy to bear the sceptre of Diogenes? Hear what Diogenes says to the passers-by when he is in a fever, "Miserable wretches, will you not stay? but are you going so long a journey to Olympia to see the destruction or the fight of athletes; and will you not choose to see the combat between a fever and a man?" Would such a man accuse God who sent him down as if God were treating him unworthily, a man who gloried in his circumstances, and claimed to be an example to those who were passing by? For what shall he accuse him of? because he maintains a decency of behavior, because he displays his virtue more conspicuously? Well, and what does he say of poverty, about death, about pain? How did he compare his own happiness with that of the Great King? or rather he thought that there was no comparison between them. For where there are perturbations, and griefs, and fears, and desires not satisfied, and aversions of things which you cannot avoid, and envies and jealousies, how is there a road to happiness there? But where there are corrupt principles, there these things must of necessity be.

When the young man asked, if when a Cynic is sick, and a friend asks him to come to his house and be taken care of in his sickness, shall the Cynic accept the invitation, he replied: And where shall you find, I ask, a Cynic's friend? For the man who invites ought to be such another as that he may be worthy of being reckoned the Cynic's friend. He ought to be a partner in the Cynic's sceptre and his royalty, and a worthy minister, if he intends to be considered worthy of a Cynic's friendship, as Diogenes was a friend of Antisthenes, as Crates was a friend of Diogenes. Do you think that, if a man comes to a Cynic and salutes him, he is the Cynic's friend, and that the Cynic will think him worthy of receiving a Cynic into his house? So that, if you please, reflect on this also: rather look round for some convenient dunghill on which you shall bear your fever and which will shelter you from the north wind that you may not be chilled. But you seem to me to wish to go into some man's house and to be well fed there for a time. Why then do you think of attempting so great a thing?

"But," said the young man, "shall marriage and the procreation of children as a chief duty be undertaken by the Cynic?" If you grant me a community of wise men, Epictetus replies, perhaps no man will readily apply himself to the Cynic practice. For on whose account should he undertake this manner of life? However if we suppose that he does, nothing will prevent him from marrying and begetting children; for his wife will be another like himself, and his father-in-law another like himself, and his children will be brought up like himself. But in the present state of things which is like that of an army placed in battle order, is it not fit that the Cynic should without any distraction be employed only on the administration of God, able to go about among men, not tied down to the common duties of mankind, nor entangled in the ordinary relations of life, which if he neglects, he will not maintain the character of an honorable and good man? and if he observes them he will lose the character of the messenger, and spy and herald of God. For consider that it is his duty to do something toward his father-in-law, something to the other kinsfolk of his wife, something to his wife also. He is also excluded by being a Cynic from looking after the sickness of his own family, and from providing for their support. And, to say nothing of the rest, he must have a vessel for heating water for the child that he may wash it in the bath; wool for his wife when she is delivered of a child, oil, a bed, a cup: so the furniture of the house is increased. I say nothing of his other occupations and of his distraction. Where, then, now is that king, he who devotes himself to the public interests,

The people's guardian and so full of cares.

whose duty it is to look after others, the married and those who have children; to see who uses his wife well, who uses her badly; who quarrels; what family is well administered, what is not; going about as a physician does and feels pulses? He says to one, "You have a fever," to another, "You have a headache, or the gout": he says to one, "Abstain from food"; to another he says, "Eat"; or "Do not use the bath"; to another,

"You require the knife, or the cautery." How can he have time for this who is tied to the duties of common life? is it not his duty to supply clothing to his children, and to send them to the schoolmaster with writing tablets, and styles. Besides, must he not supply them with beds? for they cannot be genuine Cynics as soon as they are born. If he does not do this, it would be better to expose the children as soon as they are born than to kill them in this way. Consider what we are bringing the Cynic down to, how we are taking his royalty from him. "Yes, but Crates took a wife." You are speaking of a circumstance which arose from love and of a woman who was another Crates. But we are inquiring about ordinary marriages and those which are free from distractions, and making this inquiry we do not find the affair of marriage in this state of the world a thing which is especially suited to the Cynic.

"How, then, shall a man maintain the existence of society?" In the name of God, are those men greater benefactors to society who introduce into the world to occupy their own places two or three grunting children, or those who superintend as far as they can all mankind, and see what they do, how they live, what they attend to, what they neglect contrary to their duty? Did they who left little children to the Thebans do them more good than Epaminondas who died childless? And did Priamus, who begat fifty worthless sons, or Danaus or AEolus contribute more to the community than Homer? then shall the duty of a general or the business of a writer exclude a man from marriage or the begetting of children, and such a man shall not be judged to have accepted the condition of childlessness for nothing; and shall not the royalty of a Cynic be considered an equivalent for the want of children? Do we not perceive his grandeur and do we not justly contemplate the character of Diogenes; and do we, instead of this, turn our eyes to the present Cynics, who are dogs that wait at tables and in no respect imitate the Cynics of old except perchance in breaking wind, but in nothing else? For such matters would not have moved us at all nor should we have wondered if a Cynic should not marry or beget children. Man, the Cynic is the father of all men; the men are his sons, the women are his daughters: he so carefully visits all, so well does he care for all. Do you think that it is from idle impertinence that he rebukes those whom he meets? He does it as a father, as a brother, and as the minister of the father of all, the minister of Zeus.

If you please, ask me also if a Cynic shall engage in the administration of the state. Fool, do you seek a greater form of administration than that in which he is engaged? Do you ask if he shall appear among the Athenians and say something about the revenues and the supplies, he who must talk with all men, alike with Athenians, alike with Corinthians, alike with Romans, not about supplies, nor yet about revenues, nor about peace or war, but about happiness and unhappiness, about good fortune and bad fortune, about slavery and freedom? When a man has undertaken the administration of such a state, do you ask me if he shall engage in the administration of a state? ask me also if he shall govern: again I will say to you: Fool, what greater government shall he exercise than that which he exercises now?

It is necessary also for such a man to have a certain habit of body: for if he appears to be consumptive, thin and pale, his testimony has not then the same weight. For he must not only by showing the qualities of the soul prove to the vulgar that it is in his power independent of the things which they admire to be a good man, but he must also show by his body that his simple and frugal way of living in the open air does not injure even the body. "See," he says, "I am a proof of this, and my own body also is." So Diogenes used to do, for he used to go about fresh-looking, and he attracted the notice of the many by his personal appearance. But if a Cynic is an object of compassion, he seems to a beggar: all persons turn away from him, all are offended with him; for neither ought he to appear dirty so that he shall not also in this respect drive away men; but his very roughness ought to be clean and attractive.

There ought also to belong to the Cynic much natural grace and sharpness; and if this is not so, he is a stupid fellow, and nothing else; and he must have these qualities that he may be able readily and fitly to be a match for all circumstances that may happen. So Diogenes replied to one who said, "Are you the Diogenes who does not believe that there are gods?" "And, how," replied Diogenes, "can this be when I think that you are odious to the gods?" On another occasion in reply to Alexander, who stood by him when he was sleeping, and quoted Homer's line,

A man a councilor should not sleep all night,

he answered, when he was half-asleep,

The people's guardian and so full of cares.

But before all the Cynic's ruling faculty must be purer than the sun; and, if it is not, he must be a cunning knave and a fellow of no principle, since while he himself is entangled in some vice he will reprove others. For see how the matter stands: to these kings and tyrants their guards and arms give the power of reproving some persons, and of being able even to punish those who do wrong though they are themselves bad; but to a Cynic instead of arms and guards it is conscience which gives this power. When he knows that he has watched and labored for mankind, and has slept pure, and sleep has left him still purer, and that he thought whatever he has thought as a friend of the gods, as a minister, as a participator of the power of Zeus, and that on all occasions he is ready to say

Lead me, O Zeus, and thou O Destiny;

and also, "If so it pleases the gods, so let it be"; why should he not have confidence to speak freely to his own brothers, to his children, in a word to his kinsmen? For this reason he is neither overcurious nor a busybody when he is in this state of mind: for he is not a meddler with the affairs of others when he is superintending human affairs, but he is looking after his own affairs. If that is not so, you may also say that the general is a busybody, when he inspects his soldiers, and examines them, and watches them, and punishes the disorderly. But if, while you have a cake under your arm, you rebuke others, I will say to you: "Will you not rather go away into a corner and eat that which you have stolen"; what have you to do with the affairs of others? For who are you? are you the bull of the herd, or the queen of the bees? Show me the tokens of your supremacy, such as they have from nature. But if you are a drone claiming the sovereignty over the bees, do you not suppose that your fellow citizens will put you down as the bees do the drones?

The Cynic also ought to have such power of endurance as to seem insensible to the common sort and a stone: no man reviles him, no man strikes him, no man insults him, but he gives his body that any man who chooses may do with it what he likes. For he bears in mind that the inferior must be overpowered by the superior in that in which it is inferior; and the body is inferior to the many, the weaker to the stronger. He never then descends into such a contest in which he can be overpowered; but he immediately withdraws from things which belong to others, he claims not the things which are servile. where there is will and the use of appearances, there you will see how many eyes he has so that you may say, "Argus was blind compared with him." Is his assent ever hasty, his movement rash, does his desire ever fall in its object, does that which he would avoid befall him, is his purpose unaccomplished, does he ever find fault, is he ever humiliated, is he ever envious? To these he directs all his attention and energy; but as to everything else he snores supine. All is peace; there is no robber who takes away his will, no tyrant. But what say you as to his body? I say there is. And as to magistracies and honors? What does he care for them? When then any person would frighten him through them, he says to him, "Begone, look for children: masks are formidable to them; but I know that they are made of shell, and they have nothing inside."

About such a matter as this you are deliberating. Therefore, if you please, I urge you in God's name, defer the matter, and first consider your preparation for it. For see what Hector says to Andromache, "Retire rather," he says, "into the house and weave:

War is the work of men
Of all indeed, but specially 'tis mine.

So he was conscious of his own qualification, and knew her weakness.

CHAPTER 23

To those who read and discuss for the sake of ostentation

First say to yourself, who you wish to be: then do accordingly what you are doing; for in nearly all other things we see this to be so. Those who follow athletic exercises first determine what they wish to be, then do accordingly what follows. If a man is a runner in the long course, there is a certain kind of diet, of walking, rubbing and exercise: if a man is a runner in the stadium, all these things are different; if he is a Pentathlete, they are still more different. So you will find it also in the arts. If you are a carpenter, you will have such and such things: if a worker in metal, such things. For everything that we do, if we refer it to no end, we shall do it to no purpose; and if we refer it to the wrong end, we shall miss the mark. Further, there is a general end or purpose, and a particular purpose. First of all, we must act as a man. What is comprehended in this? We must not be like a sheep, though gentle, nor mischievous, like a wild beast. But the particular cud has reference to each person's mode of life and his will. The lute-player acts as a lute-player, the carpenter as a carpenter, the philosopher as a philosopher, the rhetorician as a rhetorician. When then you say, "Come and hear me read to you": take care first of all that you are not doing this without a purpose; then, if you have discovered that you are doing this with reference to a purpose, consider if it is the right purpose. Do you wish to do good or to be praised? Immediately you hear him saying, "To me what is the value of praise from the many?" and he says well, for it is of no value to a musician, so far as he is a musician, nor to a geometrician. Do you then wish to be useful? in what? tell us that we may run to your audience-room. Now can a man do anything useful to others, who has not received something useful himself? No, for neither can a man do anything useful in the carpenter's art, unless he is a carpenter; nor in the shoemaker's art, unless he is a shoemaker.

Do you wish to know then if you have received any advantage? Produce your opinions, philosopher. What is the thing which desire promises? Not to fall in the object. What does aversion promise? Not to fall into that which you would avoid. Well; do we fulfill their promise? Tell me the truth; but if you lie, I will tell you. Lately when your hearers came together rather coldly, and did not give you applause, you went away humbled. Lately again when you had been praised, you went about and said to all, "What did you think of me?" "Wonderful, master, I swear by all that is dear to me." "But how did I treat of that particular matter?" "Which?" "The passage in which I described Pan and the nymphs?" "Excellently." Then do you tell me that in desire and in aversion you are acting according to nature? Begone; try to persuade somebody else. Did you not praise a certain person contrary to your opinion? and did you not flatter a certain person who was the son of a senator? Would you wish your own children to be such persons? "I hope not." Why then did you praise and flatter him? "He is an ingenuous youth and listens well to discourses." How is this? "He admires me." You have stated your proof. Then what do you think? do not these very people secretly despise you? When, then, a man who is conscious that he has neither done any good nor ever thinks of it, finds a philosopher who says, "You have a great natural talent, and you have a candid and good disposition," what else do you think that he says except this, "This man has some need of me?" Or tell me what act that indicates a, great mind has he shown? Observe; he has been in your company a long time; he has listened to your discourses, he has heard you reading; has he become more modest? has he been turned to reflect on himself? has he perceived in what a bad state he is? has he cast away self-conceit? does he look for a person to teach him? "He does." A man who will teach him to live? No, fool, but how to talk; for it is for this that he admires you also. Listen and hear what he says: "This man writes with perfect art, much better than Dion." This is altogether another thing. Does he say, "This man is modest, faithful, free from perturbations?" and even if he did say it, I should say to him, "Since this man is faithful, tell me what this faithful man is." And if he could not tell me, I should add this, "First understand what you say, then speak."

You, then, who are in a wretched plight and gaping after applause and counting your auditors, do you intend to be useful to others? "To-day many more attended my discourse." "Yes, many; we suppose five hundred." "That is nothing; suppose that there were a thousand." "Dion never had so many hearers." "How could he?" "And they understand what is said beautifully." "What is fine, master, can move even a stone." See, these are the words of a philosopher. This is the disposition of a man who will do good to others; here is a man who has listened to discourses, who has read what is written about Socrates as Socratic, not as the compositions of Lysias and Isocrates. "I have often wondered by what arguments." Not so, but "by what argument": this is more exact than that. What, have you read the words at all in a different way from that in which you read little odes? For if you read them as you ought, you would not have been attending to such matters, but you would rather have been looking to these words: "Anytus and Meletus are able to kill me, but they cannot harm me": and "I am always of such a disposition as to pay regard to nothing of my own except to the reason which on inquiry seems to me the best." Hence who ever heard Socrates say, "I know something and I teach"; but he used to send different people to different teachers. Therefore they used to come to him and ask to be introduced to philosophy by him; and he would take them and recommend them. Not so; but as he accompanied them he would say, "Hear me to-day discoursing in the house of Quadratus." Why should I hear you? Do you wish to show me that you put words together cleverly? You put them together, man; and what good will it do you? "But only praise me." What do you mean by praising? "Say to me,

"Admirable, wonderful." Well, I say so. But if that is praise whatever it is which philosophers mean by the name of good, what have I to praise in you? If it is good to speak well, teach me, and will praise you. "What then? ought a man to listen to such things without pleasure?" I hope not. For my part I do not listen even to a lute-player without pleasure. Must I then for this reason stand and play the lute? Hear what Socrates says, "Nor would it be seemly for a man of my age, like a young man composing addresses, to appear before you." "Like a young man," he says. For in truth this small art is an elegant thing, to select words, and to put them together, and to come forward and gracefully to read them or to speak, and while he is reading to say, "There are not many who can do these things, I swear by all that you value."

Does a philosopher invite people to hear him? As the sun himself draws men to him, or as food does, does not the philosopher also draw to him those who will receive benefit? What physician invites a man to be treated by him? Indeed I now hear that even the physicians in Rome do invite patients, but when I lived there, the physicians were invited. "I invite you to come and hear that things are in a bad way for you, and that you are taking care of everything except that of which you ought to take care, and that you are ignorant of the good and the bad and are unfortunate and unhappy." A fine kind of invitation: and yet if the words of the philosopher do not produce this effect on you, he is dead, and so is the speaker. Rufus was used to say: "If you have leisure to praise me, I am speaking to no purpose." Accordingly he used to speak in such a way that every one of us who were sitting there supposed that some one had accused him before Rufus: he so touched on what was doing, he so placed before the eyes every man's faults.

The philosopher's school, ye men, is a surgery: you ought not to go out of it with pleasure, but with pain. For you are not in sound health when you enter: one has dislocated his shoulder, another has an abscess, a third a fistula, and a fourth a headache. Then do I sit and utter to you little thoughts and exclamations that you may praise me and go away, one with his shoulder in the same condition in which he entered, another with his head still aching, and a third with his fistula or his abscess just as they were? Is it for this then that young men shall quit home, and leave their parents and their friends and kinsmen and property, that they may say to you, "Wonderful!" when you are uttering your exclamations. Did Socrates do this, or Zeno, or Cleanthes?

What then? is there not the hortatory style? Who denies it? as there is the style of refutation, and the didactic style. Who, then, ever reckoned a fourth style with these, the style of display? What is the hortatory style? To be able to show both to one person and to many the struggle in which they are engaged, and that they think more about anything than about what they really wish. For they wish the things which lead to happiness, but they look for them in the wrong place. In order that this may be done, a thousand seats must be placed and men must be invited to listen, and you must ascend the pulpit in a fine robe or cloak and describe the death of Achilles. Cease, I entreat you by the gods, to spoil good words and good acts as much as you can. Nothing can have more power in exhortation than when the speaker shows to the hearers that he has need of them. But tell me who when he hears you reading or discoursing is anxious about himself or turns to reflect on himself? or when he has gone out says, "The philosopher hit me well: I must no longer do these things." But does he not, even if you have a great reputation, say to some person, "He spoke finely about Xerxes"; and another says, "No, but about the battle of Thermopylae"? Is this listening to a philosopher?

CHAPTER 24

That we ought not to be moved by a desire of those things which are not in our power

Let not that which in another is contrary to nature be an evil to you: for you are not formed by nature to be depressed with others nor to be unhappy with others, but to be happy with them. If a man is unhappy, remember that his unhappiness is his own fault: for God has made all men to be happy, to be free from perturbations. For this purpose he has given means to them, some things to each person as his own, and other things not as his own: some things subject to hindrance and compulsion and deprivation; and these things are not a man's own: but the things which are not subject to hindrances are his own; and the nature of good and evil, as it was fit to be done by him who takes care of us and protects us like a father, he has made our own. "But," you say, "I have parted from a certain person, and he is grieved." Why did he consider as his own that which belongs to another? why, when he looked on you and was rejoiced, did he not also reckon that you are mortal, that it is natural for you to part from him for a foreign country? Therefore he suffers the consequences of his own folly. But why do you or for what purpose bewail yourself? Is it that you also have not thought of these things? but like poor women who are good for nothing, you have enjoyed all things in which you took pleasure, as if you would always enjoy them, both places and men and conversation; and now you sit and weep because you do not see the same persons and do not live in the same places. Indeed you deserve this, to be more wretched than crows and ravens who have the power of flying where they please and changing their nests for others, and crossing the seas without lamenting or regretting their former condition. "Yes, but this happens to them because they are irrational creatures." Was reason, then, given to us by the gods for the purpose of unhappiness and misery, that we may pass our lives in wretchedness and lamentation? Must all persons be immortal and must no man go abroad, and must we ourselves not go abroad, but remain rooted like plants; and, if any of our familiar friends go abroad, must we sit and weep; and, on the contrary, when he returns, must we dance and clap our hands like children?

Shall we not now wean ourselves and remember what we have heard from the philosophers? if we did not listen to them as if they were jugglers: they tell us that this world is one city, and the substance out of which it has been formed is one, and that there must be a certain period, and that some things must give way to others, that some must be dissolved, and others come in their place; some to remain in the same place, and others to be moved; and that all things are full of friendship, first of the gods, and then of men who by nature are made to be of one family; and some must be with one another, and others must be separated, rejoicing in those who are with them, and not grieving for those who are removed from them; and man in addition to being by nature of a noble temper and having a contempt of all things which are not in the power of his will, also possesses this property, not to be rooted nor to be naturally fixed to the earth, but to go at different times to different places, sometimes from the urgency of certain occasions, and at others merely for the sake of seeing. So it was with Ulysses, who saw

Of many men the states, and learned their ways.

And still earlier it was the fortune of Hercules to visit all the inhabited world

Seeing men's lawless deeds and their good rules of law:

casting out and clearing away their lawlessness and introducing in their place good rules of law. And yet how many friends do you think that he had in Thebes, how many in Argos, how many in Athens? and how many do you think that he gained by going about? And he married also, when it seemed to him a proper occasion, and begot children, and left them without lamenting or regretting or leaving them as orphans; for he knew that no man is an orphan; but it is the father who takes care of all men always and continuously. For it was not as mere report that he had heard that Zeus is the father of for he thought that Zeus was his own father, and he called him so, and to him he looked when he was doing what he did. Therefore he was enabled to live happily in all places. And it is never possible for happiness and desire of what is not present to come together. that which is happy must have all that desires, must resemble a person who is filled with food, and must have neither thirst nor hunger. "But Ulysses felt a desire for his wife and wept as he sat on a rock." Do you attend to Homer and his stories in everything? Or if Ulysses really wept, what was he else than an unhappy man? and what good man is unhappy? In truth, the whole is badly administered, if Zeus does not take care of his own citizens that they may be happy like himself. But these things are not lawful nor right to think of: and if Ulysses did weep and lament, he was not a good man. For who is good if he knows not who he is? and who knows what he is, if he forgets that things which have been made are perishable, and that it is not possible for one human being to be with another always? To desire, then, things which are impossible is to have a slavish character and is foolish: it is the part of a stranger, of a man who fights against God in the only way that he can, by his opinions.

"But my mother laments when she does not see me." Why has she not learned these principles? and I do not say this, that we should not take care that she may not lament, but I say that we ought not to desire in every way what is not our own. And the sorrow of another is another's sorrow: but my sorrow is my own. I, then, will stop my own sorrow by every means, for it is in my power: and the sorrow of another I will endeavor to stop as far as I can; but I will not attempt to do it by every means; for if I do, I shall be fighting against God, I shall be opposing and shall be placing myself against him in the administration of the universe; and the reward of this fighting against God and of this disobedience not only will the children of my children pay, but I also shall myself, both by day and by night, startled by dreams, perturbed, trembling at every piece of news, and having my tranquility depending on the letters of others. Some person has arrived from Rome. "I only hope that there is no harm." But what harm can happen to you, where you are not? From Hellas some one is come: "I hope that there is no harm." In this way every place may be the cause of misfortune to you. Is it not enough for you to be unfortunate there where you are, and must you be so even beyond sea, and by the report of letters? Is this the way in which your affairs are in a state of security? "Well, then, suppose that my friends have died in the places which are far from me." What else have they suffered than that which is the condition of mortals? Or how are you desirous at the same time to live to old age, and at the same time not to see the death of any person whom you love? Know you not that in the course of a long time many and various kinds of things must happen; that a fever shall overpower one, a robber another, and a third a tyrant? Such is the condition of things around us, such are those who live with us in the world: cold and heat, and unsuitable ways of living, and journeys by land, and voyages by sea, and winds, and various circumstances which surround us, destroy one man, and banish another, and throw one upon an embassy and another into an army. Sit down, then, in a flutter at all these things, lamenting, unhappy, unfortunate, dependent on another, and dependent not on one or two, but on ten thousands upon ten thousands.

Did you hear this when you were with the philosophers? did you learn this? do you not know that human life is a warfare? that one man must keep watch, another must go out as a spy, and a third must fight? and it is not possible that all should be in one place, nor is it better that it be so. But you, neglecting to do the commands of the general, complain when anything more hard than usual is imposed on you, and you do not observe what you make the army become as far as it is in your power; that if all imitate you, no man will dig a trench, no man will put a rampart round, nor keep watch, nor expose himself to danger, but will appear to be useless for the purposes of an army. Again, in a vessel if you go as a sailor, keep to one place and stick to it. And if you are ordered to climb the mast, refuse; if to run to the head of the ship, refuse; and what master, of a ship will endure you? and will he not pitch you overboard as a useless thing, an impediment only and bad example to the other sailors? And so it is here also: every man's life is a kind of warfare, and it is long and diversified. You must observe the duty of a soldier and do everything at the nod of the general; if it is possible, divining what his wishes are: for there is no resemblance between that general and this, neither in strength nor in superiority of character. You are placed in a great office of command and not in any mean place; but you are always a senator. Do you not know that such a man must give little time to the affairs of his household, but be often away from home, either as a governor or one who is governed, or discharging some office, or serving in war or acting as a judge? Then do you tell me that you wish, as a plant, to be fixed to the same places and to be rooted? "Yes, for it is pleasant." Who says that it is not? but a soup is pleasant, and a handsome woman is pleasant. What else do those say who make pleasure their end? Do you not see of what men yon have uttered the language? that it is the language of Epicureans and catamites? Next while you are doing what they do and holding their opinions, do you speak to us the words of Zeno and of Socrates? Will you not throw away as far as you can the things belonging to others with which you decorate yourself, though they do not fit you at all? For what else do they desire than to sleep without hindrance and free from compulsion, and when they have risen to yawn at their leisure, and to wash the face, then write and read what they choose, and then talk about some trifling matter being praised by their friends whatever they may say, then to go forth for a walk, and having walked about a little to bathe, and then eat and sleep, such sleep as is the fashion of such men? why need we say how? for one can easily conjecture. Come, do you also tell your own way of passing the time which you desire, you who are an admirer of truth and of Socrates and Diogenes. What do you wish to do in Athens? the same, or something else? Why then do you call yourself a Stoic? Well, but they who falsely call themselves Roman citizens, are severely punished; and should those, who falsely claim so great and reverend a thing and name, get off unpunished? or is this not possible, but the law divine and strong and inevitable is this, which exacts the severest punishments from those who commit the greatest crimes? For what does this law say? "Let him who pretends to things which do not belong to him be a boaster, a vainglorious man: let him who disobeys the divine administration be base, and a slave; let him suffer grief, let him be envious, let him pity; and in a word let him be unhappy and lament."

"Well then; do you wish me to pay court to a certain person? to go to his doors?" If reason requires this to be done for the sake of country, for the sake of kinsmen, for the sake of mankind, why should you not go? You are not ashamed to go to the doors of a shoemaker, when you are in want of shoes, nor to the door of a gardener, when you want lettuces; and are you ashamed to go to the doors of the rich when you want anything? "Yes, for I have no awe of a shoemaker." Don't feel any awe of the rich. "Nor will I flatter the gardener." And do not flatter the rich. "How, then, shall I get what I want?" Do I say to you, "Go as if you were certain to get what you want"? And do not I only tell you that you may do what is becoming to yourself? "Why, then, should I still go?" That you may have gone, that you may have discharged the duty of a citizen, of a brother, of a friend.

And further remember that you have gone to the shoemaker, to the seller of vegetables, who have no power in anything great or noble, though he may sell dear. You go to buy lettuces: they cost an obolus, but not a talent. So it is here also. The matter is worth going for to the rich man's door. Well, I will go. It is worth talking about. Let it be so; I will talk with him. But you must also kiss his hand and flatter him with praise. Away with that, it is a talent's worth: it is not profitable to me, nor to the state nor to my friends, to have done that which spoils a good citizen and a friend. "But you seem not to have been eager about the matter, if you do not succeed." Have you again forgotten why you went? Know you not that a good man does nothing for the sake of appearance, but for the sake of doing right? "What advantage is it, then, to him to have done right?" And what advantage is it to a man who writes the name of Dion to write it as he ought? The advantage is to have written it. "Is there no reward then?" Do you seek a reward for a good man greater than doing what is good and just? At Olympia you wish for nothing more, but it seems to you enough to be crowned at the games. Does it seem to you so small and worthless a thing to be good and happy? For these purposes being introduced by the gods into this city, and it being now your duty to undertake the work of a man, do you still want nurses also and a mamma, and do foolish women by their weeping move you and make you effeminate? Will you thus never cease to be a foolish child? know you not that he who does the acts of a child, the older he is, the more ridiculous he is?

In Athens did you see no one by going to his house? "I visited any man that I pleased." Here also be ready to see, and you will see whom you please: only let it be without meanness, neither with desire nor with aversion, and your affairs will be well managed. But this result does not depend on going nor on standing at the doors, but it depends on what is within, on your opinions. When you have learned not to value things which are external, and not dependent on the will, and to consider that not one of them is your own, but that these things only are your own, to exercise the judgment well, to form opinions, to move toward an object, to desire, to turn from a thing, where is there any longer room for flattery, where for meanness? why do you still long for the quiet there, and for the places to which you are accustomed? Wait a little and you will again find these places familiar: then, if you are of so ignoble a nature, again if you leave these also, weep and lament.

"How then shall I become of an affectionate temper?" By being of a noble disposition, and happy. For it is not reasonable to be means-spirited nor to lament yourself, nor to depend on another, nor even to blame God or man. I entreat you, become an affectionate person in this way, by observing these rules. But if through this affection, as you name it, you are going to be a slave and wretched, there is no profit in being affectionate. And what prevents you from loving another as a person subject to mortality, as one who may go away from you. Did not Socrates love his own children? He did; but it was as a free man, as one who remembered that he must first be a friend to the gods. For this reason he violated nothing which was becoming to a good man, neither in making his defense nor by fixing a penalty on himself, nor even in the former part of his life when he was a senator or when be was a soldier. But we are fully supplied with every pretext for being of ignoble temper, some for the sake of a child, some for a mother, and others for brethren's sake. But it is not fit for us to be unhappy on account of any person, but to be happy on account of all, but chiefly on account of God who has made us for this end. Well, did Diogenes love nobody, who was so kind and so much a lover of all that for mankind in general he willingly undertook so much labor and bodily sufferings? He did love mankind, but how? As became a minister of God, at the same time caring for men, and being also subject to God. For this reason all the earth was his country, and no particular place; and when he was taken prisoner he did not regret Athens nor his associates and friends there, but even he became familiar with the pirates and tried to improve them; and being sold afterward he lived in Corinth as before at Athens; and he would have behaved the same, if he had gone to the country of the Perrhaebi. Thus is freedom acquired. For this reason he used to say, "Ever since Antisthenes made me free, I have not been a slave." How did Antisthenes make him free? Hear what he says: "Antisthenes taught me what is my own, and what is not my own; possessions are not my own, nor kinsmen, domestics, friends, nor reputation, nor places familiar, nor mode of life; all these belong to others." What then is your own? "The use of appearances. This be showed to me, that I possess it free from hindrance, and from compulsion, no person can put an obstacle in my way, no person can force me to use appearances otherwise than I wish." Who then has any power over me? Philip or Alexander, or Perdiccas or the Great King? How have they this power? For if a man is going to be overpowered by a man, he must long before be overpowered by things. If, then, pleasure is not able to subdue a man, nor pain, nor fame, nor wealth, but he is able, when he chooses, to spit out all his poor body in a man's face and depart from life, whose slave can he still be? But if he dwelt with pleasure in Athens, and was overpowered by this manner of life, his affairs would have been at every man's command; the stronger would have had the power of grieving him. How do you think that Diogenes would have flattered the pirates that they might sell him to some Athenian, that some time he might see that beautiful Piraeus, and the Long Walls and the Acropolis? In what condition would you see them? As a captive, a slave and mean: and what would be the use of it for you? "Not so: but I should see them as a free man." Show me, how you would be free. Observe, some person has caught you, who leads you away from your accustomed place of abode and says, "You are my slave, for it is in my power to hinder you from living as you please, it is in my power to treat you gently, and to humble you: when I choose, on the contrary you are cheerful and go elated to Athens." What do you say to him who treats you as a slave? What means have you of finding one who will rescue you from slavery? Or cannot you even look him in the face, but without saying more do you entreat to be set free? Man, you ought to go gladly to prison, hastening, going before those who lead you there. Then, I ask you, are you unwilling to live in Rome and desire to live in Hellas? And when you must die, will you then also fill us with your lamentations, because you will not see Athens nor walk about in the Lyceion? Have you gone abroad for this? was it for this reason you have sought to find some person from whom you might receive benefit? What benefit? That you may solve syllogisms more readily, or handle hypothetical arguments? and for this reason did you leave brother, country, friends, your family, that you might return when you had learned these things? So you did not go abroad to obtain constancy of mind, nor freedom from perturbation, nor in order that, being secure from harm, you may never complain of any person, accuse no person, and no man may wrong you, and thus you may maintain your relative position without impediment? This is a fine traffic that you have gone abroad for in syllogisms and sophistical arguments and hypothetical: if you like, take your place in the agora and proclaim them for sale like dealers in physic. Will you not deny even all that you have learned that you may not bring a bad name on your theorems as useless? What harm has philosophy done you? Wherein has Chrysippus injured you that you should prove by your acts that his labors are useless? Were the evils that you had there not enough, those which were the cause of your pain and lamentation, even if you had not gone abroad? Have you added more to the list? And if you again have other acquaintances and friends, you will have more causes for lamentation; and the same also if you take an affection for another country. Why, then, do you live to surround yourself with other sorrows upon sorrows through which you are unhappy? Then, I ask you, do you call this affection? What affection, man! If it is a good thing, it is the cause of no evil: if it is bad, I have nothing to do with it. I am formed by nature for my own good: I am not formed for my own evil.

What then is the discipline for this purpose? First of all the highest and the principal, and that which stands as it were at the entrance, is this; when you are delighted with anything, be delighted as with a thing which is not one of those which cannot be taken away, but as with something of such a kind, as an earthen pot is, or a glass cup, that, when it has been broken, you may remember what it was and may not be troubled. So in this matter also: if you kiss your own child, or your brother or friend, never give full license to the appearance, and allow not your pleasure to go as far as it chooses; but check it, and curb it as those who stand behind men in their triumphs and remind them that they are mortal. Do you also remind yourself in like manner, that he whom you love is mortal, and that what you love is nothing of your own: it has been given to you for the present, not that it should not be taken from you, nor has it been given to you for all time, but as a fig is given to you or a bunch of grapes at the appointed season of the year. But if you wish for these things in winter, you are a fool. So if you wish for your son or friend when it is not allowed to you, you must know that you are wishing for a fig in winter. For such as winter is to a fig, such is every event which happens from the universe to the things which are taken away according to its nature. And further, at the times when you are delighted with a thing, place before yourself the contrary appearances. What harm is it while you are kissing your child to say with a lisping voice, "To-morrow you will die"; and to a friend also, "To-morrow you will go away or I shall, and never shall we see one another again"? "But these are words of bad omen." And some incantations also are of bad omen; but because they are useful, I don't care for this; only let them be useful. "But do you call things to be of bad omen except those which are significant of some evil?" Cowardice is a word of bad omen, and meanness of spirit, and sorrow, and grief and shamelessness. These words are of bad omen: and yet we ought not to hesitate to utter them in order to protect ourselves against the things. Do you tell me that a name which is significant of any natural thing is of evil omen? say that even for the ears of corn to be reaped is of bad omen, for it signifies the destruction of the ears, but not of the world. Say that the falling of the leaves also is of bad omen, and for the dried fig to take the place of the green fig, and for raisins to be made from the grapes. For all these things are changes from a former state into other states; not a destruction, but a certain fixed economy and administration. Such is going away from home and a small change: such is death, a greater change, not from the state which now is to that which is not, but to that which is not now. "Shall I then no longer exist?" You will not exist, but you be something else, of which the world now has need: for you also came into existence not when you chose, but when the world had need of you.

Wherefore the wise and good man, remembering who he is and whence he came, and by whom he was produced, is attentive only to this, how he may fill his place with due regularity and obediently to God. "Dost Thou still wish me to exist? I will continue to exist as free, as noble in nature, as Thou hast wished me to exist: for Thou hast made me free from hindrance in that which is my own. But hast Thou no further need of me? I thank Thee; and so far I have remained for Thy sake, and for the sake of no other person, and now in obedience to Thee I depart." "How dost thou depart?" Again, I say, as Thou hast pleased, as free, as Thy servant, as one who has known Thy commands and Thy prohibitions. And so long as I shall stay in Thy service, whom dost Thou will me to be? A prince or a private man, a senator or a common person, a soldier or a general, a teacher or a master of a family? whatever place and position Thou mayest assign to me, as Socrates says, "I will die ten thousand times rather than desert them." And where dost Thou will me to be? in Rome or Athens, or Thebes or Gyara. Only remember me there where I am. If Thou sendest me to a place where there are no means for men living according to nature, I shall not depart in disobedience to Thee, but as if Thou wast giving me the signal to retreat: I do not leave Thee, let this be to from my intention, but perceive that Thou hast no need of me. If means of living according to nature be allowed me, I will seek no other place than that in which I am, or other men than those among whom I am.

Let these thoughts be ready to hand by night and by day: these you should write, these you should read: about these you should talk to yourself, and to others. Ask a man, "Can you help me at all for this purpose?" and further, go to another and to another. Then if anything that is said he contrary to your wish, this reflection first will immediately relieve you, that it is not unexpected. For it is a great thing in all cases to say, "I knew that I begot a son who is mortal." For so you also will say, "I knew that I am mortal, I knew that I may leave my home, I knew that I may be ejected from it, I knew that I may be led to prison." Then if you turn round, and look to yourself, and seek the place from which comes that which has happened, you will forthwith recollect that it comes from the place of things which are out of the power of the will, and of things which are not my own. "What then is it to me?" Then, you will ask, and this is the chief thing: "And who is it that sent it?" The leader, or the general, the state, the law of the state. Give it me then, for I must always obey the law in everything. Then, when the appearance pains you, for it is not in your power to prevent this, contend against it by the aid of reason, conquer it: do not allow it to gain strength nor to lead you to the consequences by raising images such as it pleases and as it pleases. If you be in Gyara, do not imagine the mode of living at Rome, and how many pleasures there were for him who lived there and how many there would be for him who returned to Rome: but fix your mind on this matter, how a man who lives in Gyara ought to live in Gyara like a man of courage. And if you be in Rome, do not imagine what the life in Athens is, but think only of the life in Rome.

Then in the place of all other delights substitute this, that of being conscious that you are obeying God, that, not in word but in deed, you are performing the acts of a wise and good man. For what a thing it is for a man to be able to say to himself, "Now, whatever the rest may say in solemn manner in the schools and may be judged to be saying in a way contrary to common opinion, this I am doing; and they are sitting and are discoursing of my virtues and inquiring about me and praising me; and of this Zeus has willed that I shall receive from myself a demonstration, and shall myself know if He has a soldier such as He ought to have, a citizen such as He ought to have, and if He has chosen to produce me to the rest of mankind as a witness of the things which are independent of the will: 'See that you fear without reason, that you foolishly desire what you do desire: seek not the good in things external; seek it in yourselves: if you do not, you will not find it.' For this purpose He leads me at one time hither, at another time sends me thither, shows me to men as poor, without authority, and sick; sends me to Gyara, leads me into prison, not because He hates me, far from him be such a meaning, for who hates the best of his servants? nor yet because He cares not for me, for He does not neglect any even of the smallest things;' but He does this for the purpose of exercising me and making use of me as a witness to others. Being appointed to such a service, do I still care about the place in which I am, or with whom I am, or what men say about me? and do I not entirely direct my thoughts to God and to His instructions and commands?"

Having these things always in hand, and exercising them by yourself, and keeping them in readiness, you will never be in want of one to comfort you and strengthen you. For it is not shameful to be without something to eat, but not to have reason sufficient for keeping away fear and sorrow. But if once you have gained exemption from sorrow and fear, will there any longer be a tyrant for you, or a tyrant's guard, or attendants on Caesar? Or shall any appointment to offices at court cause you pain, or shall those who sacrifice in the Capitol, on the occasion of being named to certain functions, cause pain to you who have received so great authority from Zeus? Only do not make a proud display of it, nor boast of it; but show it by your acts; and if no man perceives it, be satisfied that you are yourself in a healthy state and happy.

CHAPTER 25

To those who fall off from their purpose

Consider as to the things which you proposed to yourself at first, which you have secured and which you have not; and how you are pleased when you recall to memory the one and are pained about the other; and if it is possible, recover the things wherein you failed. For we must not shrink when we are engaged in the greatest combat, but we must even take blows. For the combat before us is not in wrestling and the Pancration, in which both the successful and the unsuccessful may have the greatest merit, or may have little, and in truth may be very fortunate or very unfortunate; but the combat is for good fortune and happiness themselves. Well then, even if we have renounced the contest in this matter, no man hinders us from renewing the combat again, and we are not compelled to wait for another four years that the games at Olympia may come again; but as soon as you have recovered and restored yourself, and employ the same zeal, you may renew the combat again; and if again you renounce it, you may again renew it; and if you once gain the victory, you are like him who has never renounced the combat. Only do not, through a habit of doing the same thing, begin to do it with pleasure, and then like a bad athlete go about after being conquered in all the circuit of the games like quails who have run away.

"The sight of a beautiful young girl overpowers me. Well, have I not been overpowered before? An inclination arises in me to find fault with a person; for have I not found fault with him before?" You speak to us as if you had come off free from harm, just as if a man should say to his physician who forbids him to bathe, "Have I not bathed before?" If, then, the physician can say to him, "Well, and what, then, happened to you after the bath? Had you not a fever, had you not a headache?" And when you found fault with a person lately, did you not do the act of a malignant person, of a trifling babbler; did you not cherish this habit in you by adding to it the corresponding acts? And when you were overpowered by the young girl, did you come off unharmed? Why, then, do you talk of what you did before? You ought, I think, remembering what you did, as slaves remember the blows which they have received, to abstain from the same faults. But the one case is not like the other; for in the case of slaves the pain causes the remembrance: but in the case of your faults, what is the pain, what is the punishment; for when have you been accustomed to fly from evil acts? Sufferings, then, of the trying character are useful to us, whether we choose or not.

CHAPTER 26

To those who fear want

Are you not ashamed at more cowardly and more mean than fugitive slaves? How do they when they run away leave their masters? on what estates do they depend, and what domestics do they rely on? Do they not, after stealing a little which is enough for the first days, then afterward move on through land or through sea, contriving one method after another for maintaining their lives? And what fugitive slave ever died of hunger? But you are afraid lest necessary things should fall you, and are sleepless by night. Wretch, are you so blind, and don't you see the road to which the want of necessaries leads? "Well, where does it lead?" To the same place to which a fever leads, or a stone that falls on you, to death. Have you not often said this yourself to your companions? have you not read much of this kind, and written much? and how often have you boasted that you were easy as to death?

"Yes: but my wife and children also suffer hunger." Well then, does their hunger lead to any other place? Is there not the same descent to some place for them also? Is not there the same state below for them? Do you not choose, then, to look to that place full of boldness against every want and deficiency, to that place to which both the richest and those who have held the highest offices, and kings themselves and tyrants must descend? or to which you will descend hungry, if it should so happen, but they burst by indigestion and drunkenness. What beggar did you hardly ever see who was not an old man, and even of extreme old age? But chilled with cold day and night, and lying on the ground, and eating only what is absolutely necessary they approach near to the impossibility of dying. Cannot you write? Cannot you teach children? Cannot you be a watchman at another person's door? "But it is shameful to come to such necessity." Learn, then, first what are the things which are shameful, and then tell us that you are a philosopher: but at present do not, even if any other man call you so, allow it.

Is that shameful to you which is not your own act, that of which you are not the cause, that which has come to you by accident, as a headache, as a fever? If your parents were poor, and left their property to others, and if while they live, they do not help you at all, is this shameful to you? Is this what you learned with the philosophers? Did you never hear that the thing which is shameful ought to be blamed, and that which is blamable is worthy of blame? Whom do you blame for an act which is not his own, which he did not do himself? Did you, then, make your father such as he is, or is it in your power to improve him? Is this power given to you? Well then, ought you to wish the things which are not given to you, or to be ashamed if you do not obtain them? And have you also been accustomed while you were studying philosophy to look to others and to hope for nothing from yourself? Lament then and groan and eat with fear that you may not have food to-morrow. Tremble about your poor slaves lest they steal, lest they run away, lest they die. So live, and continue to live, you who in name only have approached philosophy and have disgraced its theorems as far as you can by showing them to be useless and unprofitable to those who take them up; you who have never sought constancy, freedom from perturbation, and from passions: you who have not sought any person for the sake of this object, but many for the sake of syllogisms; you who have never thoroughly examined any of these appearances by yourself, "Am I able to bear, or am I not able to bear? What remains for me to do?" But as if all your affairs were well and secure, you have been resting on the third topic, that of things being unchanged, in order that you may possess unchanged—what? cowardice, mean spirit, the admiration of the rich, desire without attaining any end, and avoidance which fails in the attempt? About security in these things you have been anxious.

Ought you not to have gained something in addition from reason and, then, to have protected this with security? And whom did you ever see building a battlement all round and not encircling it with a wall? And what doorkeeper is placed with no door to watch? But you practice in order to be able to prove—what? You practice that you may not be tossed as on the sea through sophisms, and tossed about from what? Show me first what you hold, what you measure, or what you weigh; and show me the scales or the medimnus; or how long will you go on measuring the dust? Ought you not to demonstrate those things which make men happy, which make things go on for them in the way as they wish, and why we ought to blame no man, accuse no man, and acquiesce in the administration of the universe? Show me these. "See, I show them: I will resolve syllogisms for you." This is the measure, slave; but it is not the thing measured. Therefore you are now paying the penalty for what you neglected, philosophy: you tremble, you lie awake, you advise with all persons; and if your deliberations are not likely to please all, you think that you have deliberated ill. Then you fear hunger, as you suppose: but it is not hunger that you fear, but you are afraid that you will not have a cook, that you will not have another to purchase provisions for the table, a third to take off your shoes, a fourth to dress you, others to rub you, and to follow you, in order that in the bath, when you have taken off your clothes and stretched yourself out like those who are crucified you may be rubied on this side and on that, and then the aliptes may say, "Change his position, present the side, take hold of his head, show the shoulder"; and then when you have left the bath and gone home, you may call out, "Does no one bring something to eat?" And then, "Take away the tables, sponge them": you are afraid of this, that you may not be able to lead the life of a sick man. But learn the life of those who are in health, how slaves live, how laborers, how those live who are genuine philosophers; how Socrates lived, who had a wife and children; how Diogenes lived, and how Cleanthes, who attended to the school and drew water. If you choose to have these things, you will have them everywhere, and you will live in full confidence. Confiding in what? In that alone in which a man can confide, in that which is secure, in that which is not subject to hindrance, in that which cannot be taken away, that is, in your own will. And why have you made yourself so useless and good for nothing that no man will choose to receive you into his house, no man to take care of you? but if a utensil entire and useful were cast abroad, every man who found it would take it up and think it again; but no man will take you up, and every man will consider you a loss. So cannot you discharge the office of a dog, or of a cock? Why then do you choose to live any longer, when you are what you are?

Does any good man fear that he shall fall to have food? To the blind it does not fall, to the lame it does not: shall it fall to a good man? And to a good soldier there does not fail to one who gives him pay, nor to a laborer, nor to a shoemaker: and to the good man shall there be wanting such a person? Does God thus neglect the things that He has established, His ministers, His witnesses, whom alone He employs as examples to the uninstructed, both that He exists, and administers well the whole, and does not neglect human affairs, and that to a good man there is no evil either when he is living or when he is dead? What, then, when He does not supply him with food? What else does He do than like a good general He has given me the signal to retreat? I obey, I follow, assenting to the words of the Commander, praising, His acts: for I came when it pleased Him, and I will also go away when it pleases Him; and while I lived, it was my duty to praise God both by myself, and to each person severally and to many. He does not supply me with many things, nor with abundance, He does not will me to live luxuriously; for neither did He supply Hercules who was his own son; but another was king of Argos and Mycenae, and Hercules obeyed orders, and labored, and was exercised. And Eurystheus was what he was, neither kin, of Argos nor of Mycenae, for he was not even king of himself; but Hercules was ruler and leader of the whole earth and sea, who purged away lawlessness, and introduced justice and holiness; and he did these things both naked and alone. And when Ulysses was cast out shipwrecked, did want humiliate him, did it break his spirit? but how did he go off to the virgins to ask for necessaries, to beg which is considered most shameful?

As a lion bred in the mountains trusting in his strength.

Relying on what? Not on reputation nor on wealth nor on the power of a magistrate, but on his own strength, that is, on his opinions about the things which are in our power and those which, are not. For these are the only things which make men free, which make them escape from hindrance, which raise the head of those who are depressed, which make them look with steady eyes on the rich and on tyrants. And this was the gift given to the philosopher. But you will not come forth bold, but trembling about your trifling garments and silver vessels. Unhappy man, have you thus wasted your time till now?

"What, then, if I shall be sick?" You will be sick in such a way as you ought to be. "Who will take care of me?" God; your friends. "I shall lie down on a hard bed." But you will lie down like a man. "I shall not have a convenient chamber." You will be sick in an inconvenient chamber. "Who will provide for me the necessary food?" Those who provide for others also. You will be sick like Manes. "And what, also, will be the end of the sickness? Any other than death?" Do you then consider that this the chief of all evils to man and the chief mark of mean spirit and of cowardice is not death, but rather the fear of death? Against this fear then I advise you to exercise yourself: to this let all your reasoning tend, your exercises, and reading; and you will know that thus only are men made free.

The Discourses of Epictetus

BOOK FOUR

CHAPTER 1

About freedom

He is free who lives as he wishes to live; who is neither subject to compulsion nor to hindrance, nor to force; whose movements to action are not impeded, whose desires attain their purpose, and who does not fall into that which he would avoid. Who, then, chooses to live in error? No man. Who chooses to live deceived, liable to mistake, unjust, unrestrained, discontented, mean? No man. Not one then of the bad lives as he wishes; nor is he, then, free. And who chooses to live in sorrow, fear, envy, pity, desiring and failing in his desires, attempting to avoid something and falling into it? Not one. Do we then find any of the bad free from sorrow, free from fear, who does not fall into that which he would avoid, and does not obtain that which he wishes? Not one; nor then do we find any bad man free.

If, then, a man who has been twice consul should hear this, if you add, "But you are a wise man; this is nothing to you": he will pardon you. But if you tell him the truth, and say, "You differ not at all from those who have been thrice sold as to being yourself not a slave," what else ought you to expect than blows? For he says, "What, I a slave, I whose father was free, whose mother was free, I whom no man can purchase: I am also of senatorial rank, and a friend of Caesar, and I have been a consul, and I own many slaves." In the first place, most excellent senatorial man, perhaps your father also was a slave in the same kind of servitude, and your mother, and your grandfather and all your ancestors in an ascending series. But even if they were as free as it is possible, what is this to you? What if they were of a noble nature, and you of a mean nature; if they were fearless, and you a coward; if they had the power of self-restraint, and you are not able to exercise it.

"And what," you may say, "has this to do with being a slave?" Does it seem to you to be nothing to do a thing unwillingly, with compulsion, with groans, has this nothing to do with being a slave? "It is something," you say: "but who is able to compel me, except the lord of all, Caesar?" Then even you yourself have admitted that you have one master. But that he is the common master of all, as you say, let not this console you at all: but know that you are a slave in a great family. So also the people of Nicopolis are used to exclaim, "By the fortune of Caesar, are free."

However, if you please, let us not speak of Caesar at present. But tell me this: did you never love any person, a young girl, or slave, or free? What then is this with respect to being a slave or free? Were you never commanded by the person beloved to do something which you did not wish to do? have you never flattered your little slave? have you never kissed her feet? And yet if any man compelled you to kiss Caesar's feet, you would think it an insult and excessive tyranny. What else, then, is slavery? Did you never go out by night to some place whither you did not wish to go, did you not expend what you did not wish to expend, did you not utter words with sighs and groans, did you not submit to abuse and to be excluded? But if you are ashamed to confess your own acts, see what Thrasonides says and does, who having seen so much military service as perhaps not even you have, first of all went out by night, when Geta does not venture out, but if he were compelled by his master, would have cried out much and would have gone out lamenting his bitter slavery. Next, what does Thrasonides say? "A worthless girl has enslaved me, me whom no enemy, ever did." Unhappy man, who are the slave even of a girl, and a worthless girl. Why then do you still call yourself free? and why do you talk of your service in the army? Then he calls for a sword and is angry with him who out of kindness refuses it; and he sends presents to her who hates him, and entreats and weeps, and on the other hand, having had a little success, he is elated. But even then how? was he free enough neither to desire nor to fear?

Now consider in the case of animals, how we employ the notion of liberty. Men keep tame lions shut up, and feed them, and some take them about; and who will say that this lion is free? Is it not the fact that the more he lives at his ease, so much the more he is in a slavish condition? and who if he had perception and reason would wish to be one of these lions? Well, these birds when they are caught and are kept shut up, how much do they suffer in their attempts to escape? and some of them die of hunger rather than submit to such a kind of life. And as many of them as live, hardly live and with suffering pine away; and if they ever find any opening, they make their escape. So much do they desire their natural liberty, and to be independent and free from hindrance. And what harm is there to you in this? "What do you say? I am formed by nature to fly where I choose, to live in the open air, to sing when I choose: you deprive me of all this, and say, 'What harm is it to you?'" For this reason we shall say that those animals only are free which cannot endure capture, but, as soon as they are caught, escape from captivity by death. So Diogenes says that there is one way to freedom, and that is to die content: and he writes to the Persian king, "You cannot enslave the Athenian state any more than you can enslave fishes." "How is that? cannot I catch them?" "If you catch them," says Diogenes, "they will immediately leave you, as fishes do; for if you catch a fish, it dies; and if these men that are caught shall die, of what use to you is the preparation for war?" These are the words of a free man who had carefully examined the thing and, as was natural, had discovered it. But if you look for it in a different place from where it is, what wonder if you never find it?

The slave wishes to be set free immediately. Why? Do you think that he wishes to pay money to the collectors of twentieths? No; but because he imagines that hitherto through not having obtained this, he is hindered and unfortunate. "If I shall be set free, immediately it is all happiness, I care for no man, I speak to all as an equal and, like to them, I go where I choose, I come from any place I choose, and go where I choose." Then he is set free; and forthwith having no place where he can eat, he looks for some man to flatter, some one with whom he shall sup: then he either works with his body and endures the most dreadful things; and if he can obtain a manger, he falls into a slavery much worse than his former slavery; or even if he is become rich, being a man without any knowledge of what is good, he loves some little girl, and in his happiness laments and desires to be a slave again. He says, "what evil did I suffer in my state of slavery? Another clothed me, another supplied me with shoes, another fed me, another looked after me in sickness; and I did only a few services for him. But now a wretched man, what things I suffer, being a slave of many instead of to one. But however," he says, "if I shall acquire rings, then I shall live most prosperously and happily." First, in order to acquire these rings, he submits to that which he is worthy of; then, when he has acquired them, it is again all the same. Then he says, "if I shall be engaged in military service, I am free from all evils." He obtains military service. He suffers as much as a flogged slave, and nevertheless he asks for a second service and a third. After this, when he has put the finishing stroke to his career and is become a senator, then he becomes a slave by entering into the assembly, then he serves the finer and most splendid slavery—not to be a fool, but to learn what Socrates taught, what is the nature of each thing that exists, and that a man should not rashly adapt preconceptions to the several things which are. For this is the cause to men of all their evils, the not being able to adapt the general preconceptions to the several things. But we have different opinions. One man thinks that he is sick: not so however, but the fact is that he does not adapt his preconceptions right. Another thinks that he is poor; another that he has a severe father or mother; and another, again, that Caesar is not favorable to him. But all this is one and only one thing, the not knowing how to adapt the preconceptions. For who has not a preconception of that which is bad, that it is hurtful, that it ought to be avoided, that it ought in every way to be guarded against? One preconception is not repugnant to another, only where it comes to the matter of adaptation. What then is this evil, which is both hurtful, and a thing to be avoided? He answers, "Not to be Caesar's friend." He is gone far from the mark, he has missed the adaptation, he is embarrassed, he seeks the things which are not at all pertinent to the matter; for when he has succeeded in being Caesar's friend, nevertheless he has failed in finding what he sought. For what is that which every man seeks? To live secure, to be happy, to do everything as he wishes, not to be hindered, nor compelled. When then he is become the friend of Caesar, is he free from hindrance? free from compulsion, is he tranquil, is he happy? Of whom shall we inquire? What more trustworthy witness have we than this very man who is, become Caesar's friend? Come forward and tell us when did you sleep more quietly, now or before you became Caesar's friend? Immediately you hear the answer, "Stop, I entreat you, and do not mock me: you know not what miseries I suffer, and sleep does not come to me; but one comes and says, 'Caesar is already awake, he is now going forth': then come troubles and cares." Well, when did you sup with more pleasure, now or before? Hear what he says about this also. He says that if he is not invited, he is pained: and if he is invited, he sups like a slave with his master, all the while being anxious that he does not say or do anything foolish. And what do you suppose that he is afraid of; lest he should be lashed like a slave? How can he expect anything so good? No, but as befits so great a man, Caesar's friend, he is afraid that he may lose his head. And when did you bathe more free from trouble, and take your gymnastic exercise more quietly? In fine, which kind of life did you prefer? your present or your former life? I can swear that no man is so stupid or so ignorant of truth as not to bewail his own misfortunes the nearer he is in friendship to Caesar.

Since, then, neither those who are called kings live as they choose, nor the friends of kings, who finally are those who are free? Seek, and you will find; for you have aids from nature for the discovery of truth. But if you are not able yourself by going along these ways only to discover that which follows, listen to those who have made the inquiry. What do they say? Does freedom seem to you a good thing? "The greatest good." Is it possible, then, that he who obtains the greatest good can be unhappy or fare badly? "No." Whomsoever, then, you shall see unhappy, unfortunate, lamenting, confidently declare that they are not free. "I do declare it." We have now, then, got away from buying and selling and from such arrangements about matters of property; for if you have rightly assented to these matters, if the Great King is unhappy, he cannot be free, nor can a little king, nor a man of consular rank, nor one who has been twice consul. "Be it so."

Further, then, answer me this question also: Does freedom seem to you to be something great and noble and valuable? "How should it not seem so?" Is it possible, then, when a man obtains anything, so great and valuable and noble to be mean? "It is not possible." When, then, you see any man subject to another, or flattering him contrary to his own opinion, confidently affirm that this man also is not free; and not only if he do this for a bit of supper, but also if he does it for a government or a consulship: and call these men "little slaves" who for the sake of little matters do these things, and those who do so for the sake of great things call "great slaves," as they deserve to be. "This is admitted also."

Do you think that freedom is a thing independent and self-governing? "Certainly." Whomsoever, then, it is in the power of another to hinder and compel, declare that he is not free. And do not look, I entreat you, after his grandfathers and great-grandfathers, or inquire about his being bought or sold; but if you hear him saying from his heart and with feeling, "Master," even if the twelve fasces precede him, call him a slave. And if you hear him say, "Wretch that I am, how much I suffer," call him a slave. If, finally, you see him lamenting, complaining, unhappy, call him a slave though he wears a praetexta. If, then, he is doing nothing of this kind, do not yet say that he is free, but learn his opinions, whether they are subject to compulsion, or may produce hindrance, or to bad fortune; and if you find him such, call him a slave who has a holiday in the Saturnalia: say that his master is from home: he will return soon, and you will know what he suffers. "Who will return?" Whoever has in himself the power over anything which is desired by the man, either to give it to him or to take it away? "Thus, then, have we many masters?" We have: for we have circumstances as masters prior to our present masters; and these circumstances are many. Therefore it must of necessity be that those who have the power over any of these circumstances must be our masters. For no man fears Caesar himself, but he fears death, banishment, deprivation of his property, prison, and disgrace. Nor does any man love Caesar, unless Caesar is a person of great merit, but he loves wealth, the office of tribune, praetor or consul. When we love, and hate, and fear these things, it must be that those who have the power over them must be our masters. Therefore we adore them even as gods; for we think that what possesses the power of conferring the greatest advantage on us is divine. Then we wrongly assume that a certain person has the power of conferring the greatest advantages; therefore he is something divine. For if we wrongly assume that a certain person has the power of conferring the greatest advantages, it is a necessary consequence that the conclusion from these premises must be false.

What, then, is that which makes a man free from hindrance and makes him his own master? For wealth does not do it, nor consulship, nor provincial government, nor royal power; but something else must be discovered. What then is that which, when we write, makes us free from hindrance and unimpeded? "The knowledge of the art of writing." What, then, is it in playing the lute? "The science of playing the lute." Therefore in life also it is the science of life. You have, then, heard in a general way: but examine the thing also in the several parts. Is it possible that he who desires any of the things which depend on others can be free from hindrance? "No." Is it possible for him to be unimpeded? "No." Therefore he cannot be free. Consider then: whether we have nothing which is in our own power only, or whether we have all things, or whether some things are in our own power, and others in the power of others. "What do you mean?" When you wish the body to be entire, is it in your power or not? "It is not in my power." When you wish it to be healthy? "Neither is this in my power." When you wish it to be handsome? "Nor is this." Life or death? "Neither is this in my power." Your body, then, is another's, subject to every man who is stronger than yourself? "It is." But your estate, is it in your power to have it when you please, and as long as you please, and such as you please? "No." And your slaves? "No." And your clothes? "No." And your house? "No." And your horses? "Not one of these things." And if you wish by all means your children to live, or your wife, or your brother, or your friends, is it in your power? "This also is not in my power."

Whether, then, have you nothing which is in your own power, which depends on yourself only and cannot be taken from you, or have you anything of the kind? "I know not." Look at the thing, then, thus, examine it. Is any man able to make you assent to that which is false? "No man." In the matter of assent, then, you are free from hindrance and obstruction. "Granted." Well; and can a man force you to desire to move toward that to which you do not choose? "He can, for when he threatens me with death or bonds, he compels me to desire to move toward it." If, then, you despise death and bonds, do you still pay any regard to him? "No." Is, then, the despising of death an act of your own, or is it not yours? "It is my act." It is your own act, then, also to desire to move toward a thing: or is it not so? "It is my own act." But to desire to move away from a thing, whose act is that? This also is your act. "What, then, if I have attempted to walk, suppose another should hinder me." What part of you does he hinder? does he hinder the faculty of assent? "No: but my poor body." Yes, as he would do with a stone. "Granted; but I no longer walk." And who told you that walking is your act free from hindrance? for I said that this only was free from hindrance, to desire to move: but where there is need of body and its co-operation, you have heard long ago that nothing is your own. "Granted also." And who can compel you to desire what you do not wish? "No man." And to propose, or intend, or in short to make use of the appearances which present themselves, can any man compel you? "He cannot do this: but he will hinder me when I desire from obtaining what I desire." If you desire anything which is your own, and one of the things which cannot be hindered, how will he hinder you? "He cannot in any way." Who, then, tells you that he who desires the things that belong to another is free from hindrance?

"Must I, then, not desire health?" By no means, nor anything else that belongs to another: for what is not in your power to acquire or to keep when you please, this belongs to another. Keep, then, far from it not only your hands but, more than that, even your desires. If you do not, you have surrendered yourself as a slave; you have subjected your neck, if you admire anything not your own, to everything that is dependent on the power of others and perishable, to which you have conceived a liking. "Is not my hand my own?" It is a part of your own body; but it is by nature earth, subject to hindrance, compulsion, and the slave of everything which is stronger. And why do I say your hand?

You ought to possess your whole body as a poor ass loaded, as long as it is possible, as long as you are allowed. But if there be a press, and a soldier should lay hold of it, let it go, do not resist, nor murmur; if you do, you will receive blows, and nevertheless you will also lose the ass. But when you ought to feel thus with respect to the body, consider what remains to be done about all the rest, which is provided for the sake of the body. When the body is an ass, all the other things are bits belonging to the ass, pack-saddles, shoes, barley, fodder. Let these also go: get rid of them quicker and more readily than of the ass.

When you have made this preparation, and have practiced this discipline, to distinguish that which belongs to another from that which is your own, the things which are subject to hindrance from those which are not, to consider the things free from hindrance to concern yourself, and those which are not free not to concern yourself, to keep your desire steadily fixed to the things which do concern yourself, and turned from the things which do not concern yourself; do you still fear any man? "No one." For about what will you be afraid? about the things which are your own, in which consists the nature of good and evil? and who has power over these things? who can take them away? who can impede them? No man can, no more than he can impede God. But will you be afraid about your body and your possessions, about things which are not yours, about things which in no way concern you? and what else have you been studying from the beginning than to distinguish between your own and not your own, the things which are in your power and not in your power, the things subject to hindrance and not subject? and why have you come to the philosophers? was it that you may nevertheless be unfortunate and unhappy? You will then in this way, as I have supposed you to have done, be without fear and disturbance. And what is grief to you? for fear comes from what you expect, but grief from that which is present. But what further will you desire? For of the things which are within the power of the will, as being good and present, you have a proper and regulated desire: but of the things which are not in the power of the will you do not desire any one, and so you do not allow any place to that which is irrational, and impatient, and above measure hasty.

When, then, you are thus affected toward things, what man can any longer be formidable to you? For what has a man which is formidable to another, either when you see him or speak to him or, finally, are conversant with him? Not more than one horse has with respect to another, or one dog to another, or one bee to another bee. Things, indeed, are formidable to every man; and when any man is able to confer these things on another or to take them away, then he too becomes formidable. How then is an acropolis demolished? Not by the sword, not by fire, but by opinion. For if we abolish the acropolis which is in the city, can we abolish also that of fever, and that of beautiful women? Can we, in a word, abolish the acropolis which is in us and cast out the tyrants within us, whom we have dally over us, sometimes the same tyrants, at other times different tyrants? But with this we must begin, and with this we must demolish the acropolis and eject the tyrants, by giving up the body, the parts of it, the faculties of it, the possessions, the reputation, magisterial offices, honors, children, brothers, friends, by considering all these things as belonging to others. And if tyrants have been ejected from us, why do I still shut in the acropolis by a wall of circumvallation, at least on my account; for if it still stands, what does it do to me? why do I still eject guards? For where do I perceive them? against others they have their faces, and their spears, and their swords. But I have never been hindered in my will, nor compelled when I did not will. And how is this possible? I have placed my movements toward action in obedience to God. Is it His will that I shall have fever? It is my will also. Is it His will that I should move toward anything? It is my will also. Is it His will that I should obtain anything? It is my wish also. Does He not will? I do not wish. Is it His will that I be put to the rack? It is my will then to die; it is my will then to be put to the rack. Who, then, is still able to hinder me contrary to my own judgment, or to compel me? No more than he can hinder or compel Zeus.

Thus the more cautious of travelers also act. A traveler has heard that the road is infested by robbers; he does not venture to enter on it alone, but he waits for the companionship on the road either of an ambassador, or of a quaestor, or of a proconsul, and when he has attached himself to such persons he goes along the road safely. So in the world the wise man acts. There are many companies of robbers, tyrants, storms, difficulties, losses of that which is dearest. "Where is there any place of refuge? how shall he pass along without being attacked by robbers? what company shall he wait for that he may pass along in safety? to whom shall he attach himself? To what person generally? to the rich man, to the man of consular rank? and what is the use of that to me? Such a man is stripped himself, groans and laments. But what if the fellow-companion himself turns against me and becomes my robber, what shall I do? I will be 'a friend of Caesar': when I am Caesar's companion no man will wrong me. In the first place, that I may become illustrious, what things must I endure and suffer? how often and by how many must I he robbed? Then, if I become Caesar's friend, he also is mortal. And if Caesar from any circumstance becomes my enemy, where is it best for me to retire? Into a desert? Well, does fever not come there? What shall be done then? Is it not possible to find a safe fellow traveler, a faithful one, strong, secure against all surprises?" Thus he considers and perceives that if he attaches himself to God, he will make his journey in safety.

"How do you understand 'attaching yourself to God'?" In this sense, that whatever God wills, a man also shall will; and what God does not will, a man shall not will. How, then, shall this he done? In what other way than by examining the movements of God and his administration What has He given to me as my own and in my own power? what has He reserved to Himself? He has given to me the things which are in the power of the will: He has put them in my power free from impediment and hindrance. How was He able to make the earthly body free from hindrance? And accordingly He has subjected to the revolution of the whole, possessions, household things, house, children, wife. Why, then, do I fight against God? why do I will what does not depend on the will? why do I will to have absolutely what is not granted to ma? But how ought I to will to have things? In the way in which they are given and as long as they are given. But He who has given takes away. Why then do I resist? I do not say that I shall be fool if I use force to one who is stronger, but I shall first be unjust. For whence had I things when I came into the world? My father gave them to me. And who gave them to him? and who made the sun? and who made the fruits of the earth? and who the seasons? and who made the connection of men with one another and their fellowship?

Then after receiving everything from another and even yourself, are you angry and do you blame the Giver if he takes anything from you? Who are you, and for what purpose did you come into the world? Did not He introduce you here, did He not show you the light, did he not give you fellow-workers, and perception, and reason? and as whom did He introduce you here? did He not introduce you as a subject to death, and as one to live on the earth with a little flesh, and to observe His administration, and to join with Him in the spectacle and the festival for a short time? Will you not, then, as long as you have been permitted, after seeing the spectacle and the solemnity, when he leads you out, go with adoration of Him and thanks for what you have seen, and heard? "No; but I would, still enjoy the feast." The initiated, too, would wish to be longer in the initiation: and perhaps also those, at Olympia to see other athletes; but the solemnity is ended: go away like a grateful and modest man; make room for others: others also must be born, as you were, and being born they must have a place, and houses and necessary things. And if the first do not retire, what remains? Why ire you insatiable? Why are you not content? why do you contract the world? "Yes, but I would have my little children with me and my wife." What, are they yours? do they not belong to the Giver, and to Him who made you? then will you not give up what belongs to others? will you not give way to Him who is superior? "Why, then, did He introduce me into the world on these conditions," And if the conditions do not suit you depart. He has no need of a spectator who is not satisfied. He wants those who join in the festival, those who take part in the chorus, that they may rather applaud, admire, and celebrate with hymns the solemnity. But those who can bear no trouble, and the cowardly He will not willingly see absent from the great assembly; for they did not when they were present behave as they ought to do at a festival nor fill up their place properly, but they lamented, found fault with the deity, fortune, their companions; not seeing both what they had. and their own powers, which they received for contrary purposes, the powers of magnanimity, of a generous mind, manly spirit, and what we are now inquiring about, freedom. "For what purpose, then, have I received these things? To use them. "How long;" So long as He who his lent them chooses. "What if they are necessary to me?" Do not attach yourself to them and they will not be necessary: do not say to yourself that they are necessary, and then they are not necessary.

This study you ought to practice from morning to evening, beginning, with the smallest things and those most liable to damage, with an earthen pot, with a cup. Then proceed in this way to a tunic to a little dog, to a horse, to a small estate in land: then to yourself, to your body, to the parts of your body, to your brothers. Look all round and throw these things from you. Purge your opinions so that nothing cleave to you of the things which are not your own, that nothing grow to you, that nothing give you pain when it is torn from you; and say, while you are daily exercising yourself as you do there, not that you are philosophizing, for this is an arrogant expression, but that you are presenting an asserter of freedom: for this is really freedom. To this freedom Diogenes was called by Antisthenes, and he said that he could no longer be enslaved by any man. For this reason when he was taken prisoner, how did he behave to the pirates? Did he call any of them master? and I do not speak of the name, for I am not afraid of the word, but of the state of mind by which the word is produced. How did he reprove them for feeding badly their captives? How was he sold? Did he seek a master? no; but a slave, And, when he was sold, how did he behave to his master? Immediately he disputed with him and said to his master that he ought not to be dressed as he was, nor shaved in such a manner; and about the children he told them how he ought to bring them up. And what was strange in this? for if his master had bought an exercise master, would he have employed him in the exercises of the palaestra as a servant or as a master? and so if he had bought a physician or an architect. And so, in every matter, it is absolutely necessary that he who has skill must be the superior of him who has not. Whoever, then, generally possesses the science of life, what else must he be than master? For who is master of a ship? "The man who governs the helm." Why? Because he who will not obey him suffers for it. "But a master can give me stripes." Can he do it, then, without suffering for it?' "So I also used to think." But because he can not do it without suffering for it, for this reason it is not in his power: and no man can do what is unjust without suffering for it. "And what is the penalty for him who puts his own slave in chains, what do you think that is?" The fact of putting the slave in chains: and you also will admit this, if you choose to maintain the truth, that man is not a wild beast, but a tame animal. For when is a a vine doing badly? When it is in a condition contrary to its nature. When is a cock? Just the same. Therefore a man also is so. What then is a man's nature? To bite, to kick, and to throw into prison and to behead? No; but to do good, to co-operate with others, to wish them well. At that time, then, he is in a bad condition, whether you choose to admit it or not, when he is acting foolishly.

"Socrates, then, did not fare badly?" No; but his judges aid his accusers did. "Nor did Helvidius at Rome fare badly?" No; but his murderer did. "How do you mean?" The same as you do when you say that a cock has not fared badly when he has gained the victory and been severely wounded; but that the cock has fared badly when he has been defeated and is unhurt: nor do you call a dog fortunate who neither pursues game nor labors, but when you see him sweating, when you see him in pain and panting violently after running. What paradox do we utter if we say that the evil in everything's that which is contrary to the nature of the thing? Is that a paradox? for do you not say this in the case of all other things? Why then in the case of man only do you think differently, But because we say that the nature of man is tame and social and faithful, you will not say that this is a paradox? "It is not." What then is it a paradox to say that a man is not hurt when he is whipped, or put in chains, or beheaded? does he not, if he suffers nobly, come off even with increased advantage and profit? But is he not hurt, who suffers in a most pitiful and disgraceful way, who in place of a man becomes a wolf, or viper or wasp?

Well then let us recapitulate the things which have been agreed on. The man who is not under restraint is free, to whom things are exactly in that state in which he wishes them to be; but he who can be restrained or compelled or hindered, or thrown into any circumstances against his will, is a slave. But who is free from restraint? He who desires nothing that belongs to others. And what are the things which belong to others? Those which are not in our power either to have or not to have, or to have of a certain kind or in a certain manner. Therefore the body belongs to another, the parts of the body belong to another, possession belongs to another. If, then, you are attached to any of these things as your own, you will pay the penalty which it is proper for him to pay who desires what belongs to another. This road leads to freedom, that is the only way of escaping from slavery, to be able to say at last with all your soul

Lead me, O Zeus, and thou O destiny,
The way that I am bid by you to go.

But what do you say, philosopher? The tyrant summons you to say something which does not become you. Do you say it or do you not? Answer me. "Let me consider." Will you consider now? But when you were in the school, what was it which you used to consider? Did you not study what are the things that are good and what are bad, and what things are neither one nor the other? "I did." What then was our opinion? "That just and honorable acts were good; and that unjust and disgraceful acts were bad." Is life a good thing? "No." Is death a bad thing? "No." Is prison? "No." But what did we think about mean and faithless words and betrayal of a friend and flattery of a tyrant? "That they are bad." Well then, you are not considering, nor have you considered nor deliberated. For what is the matter for consideration: is it whether it is becoming for me, when I have it in my power, to secure for myself the greatest of good things, and not to secure for myself the greatest evils? A fine inquiry indeed, and necessary, and one that demands much deliberation. Man, why do you mock us? Such an inquiry is never made. If you really imagined that base things were bad and honorable things were good, and that all other things were neither good nor bad, you would not even have approached this inquiry, nor have come near it; but immediately you would have been able to distinguish them by the understanding as you would do by the vision. For when do you inquire if black things are white, if heavy things are light, and do not comprehend the manifest evidence of the senses? How, then, do you now say that you are considering whether things which are neither good nor bad ought to be avoided more than things which are bad? But you do not possess these opinions; and neither do these things seem to you to he neither good nor bad, but you think that they are the greatest evils; nor do you think those other things to be evils, but matters which do not concern us at all. For thus from the beginning you have accustomed yourself. "Where am I? In the schools: and are any listening to me? I am discoursing among philosophers. But I have gone out of the school. Away with this talk of scholars and fools." Thus a friend is overpowered by the testimony of a philosopher: thus a philosopher becomes a parasite; thus he lets himself for hire for money: thus in the senate a man does not say what he thinks; in private he proclaims his opinions. You are a cold and miserable little opinion, suspended from idle words as from a hair. But keep yourself strong and fit for the uses of life and initiated by being exercised in action. How do you hear? I do not say that your child is dead — for how could you bear that? — but that your oil is spilled, your wine drunk up. Do you act in such a way that one standing by you while you are making a great noise, may say this only, "Philosopher, you say something different in the school. Why do you deceive us? Why, when you are only a worm, do you say that you are a man?" I should like to be present when one of the philosophers is lying with a woman, that I might see how he is exerting himself, and what words he is uttering, and whether he remembers his title of philosopher, and the words which he hears or says or reads.

"And what is this to liberty?" Nothing else than this, whether you who are rich choose or not. "And who is your evidence for this?" who else than yourselves? who have a powerful master, and who live in obedience to his nod and motion, and who faint if he only looks at you with a scowling countenance; you who court old women and old men, and say, "I cannot do this: it is not in my power." Why is it not in your power? Did you not lately contend with me and say that you are free "But Aprulla has hindered me." Tell the truth, then, slave, and do not run away from your masters, nor deny, nor venture to produce any one to assert your freedom, when you have so many evidences of your slavery. And indeed when a man is compelled by love to do something contrary to his opinion, and at the same time sees the better but has not the strength to follow it, one might consider him still more worthy of excuse as being held by a certain violent and, in a manner, a divine power. But who could endure you who are in love with old women and old men, and wipe the old women's noses, and wash them and give them presents, and also wait on them like a slave when they are sick, and at the same time wish them dead, and question the physicians whether they are sick unto death? And again, when in order to obtain these great and much admired magistracies and honors, you kiss the hands of these slaves of others, and so you are not the slave even of free men. Then you walk about before me in stately fashion, praetor or a consul. Do I not know how you became a praetor, by what means you got your consulship, who gave it to you? I would not even choose to live, if I must live by help of Felicion and endure his arrogance and servile insolence: for I know what a slave is, who is fortunate, as he thinks, and puffed up by pride.

"You then," a man may say, "are you free?" I wish, by the Gods, and pray to be free; but I am not yet able to face my masters, I still value my poor body, I value greatly the preservation of it entire, though I do not possess it entire. But I can point out to you a free man, that you may no longer seek an example. Diogenes was free. How was he free?—not because he was born of free parents, but because he was himself free, because he had cast off all the handles of slavery, and it was not possible for any man to approach him, nor had any man the means of laying hold of him to enslave him. He had everything easily loosed, everything only hanging to him. If you laid hold of his property, he would rather have let it go and be yours than he would have followed you for it: if you had laid hold of his leg, he would have let go his leg; if of all his body, all his poor body; his intimates, friends, country, just the same. For he knew from whence he had them, and from whom, and on what conditions. His true parents indeed, the Gods, and his real country he would never have deserted, nor would he have yielded to any man in obedience to them or to their orders, nor would any man have died for his country more readily. For he was not used to inquire when he should be considered to have done anything on behalf of the whole of things, but he remembered that everything which is done comes from thence and is done on behalf of that country and is commanded by him who administers it. Therefore see what Diogenes himself says and writes: "For this reason," he says, "Diogenes, it is in your power to speak both with the King of the Persians and with Archidamus the king of the Lacedaemonians, as you please." Was it because he was born of free parents? I suppose all the Athenians and all the Lacedaemonians, because they were born of slaves, could not talk with them as they wished, but feared and paid court to them. Why then does he say that it is in his power? "Because I do not consider the poor body to be my own, because I want nothing, because law is everything to me, and nothing else is." These were the things which permitted him to be free.

And that you may not think that I show you the example of a man who is a solitary person, who has neither wife nor children, nor country, nor friends nor kinsmen, by whom he could be bent and drawn in various directions, take Socrates and observe that he had a wife and children, but he did not consider them as his own; that he had a country, so long as it was fit to have one, and in such a manner as was fit; friends and kinsmen also, but he held all in subjection to law and to the obedience due to it. For this reason he was the first to go out as a soldier, when it was necessary; and in war he exposed himself to danger most unsparingly, and when he was sent by the tyrants to seize Leon, he did not even deliberate about the matter, because he thought that it was a base action, and he knew that he must die, if it so happened. And what difference did that make to him? for he intended to preserve something else, not his poor flesh, but his fidelity, his honorable character. These are things which could not be assailed nor brought into subjection. Then, when he was obliged to speak in defense of his life, did he behave like a man who had children, who had a wife? No, but he behaved like a man who has neither. And what did he do when he was to drink the poison, and when he had the power of escaping from prison, and when Crito said to him, "Escape for the sake of your children," what did Socrates say? Did he consider the power of escape as an unexpected gain? By no means: he considered what was fit and proper; but the rest he did not even look at or take into the reckoning. For he did not choose, he said, to save his poor body, but to save that which is increased and saved by doing what is just, and is impaired and destroyed by doing what is unjust. Socrates will not save his life by a base act; he who would not put the Athenians to the vote when they clamored that he should do so, he who refused to obey the tyrants, he who discoursed in such a manner about virtue and right behavior. It is not possible to save such a man's life by base acts, but he is saved by dying, not by running away. For the good actor also preserves his character by stopping when he ought to stop, better than when he goes on acting beyond the proper time. What then shall the children of Socrates do? "If," said Socrates, "I had gone off to Thessaly, would you have taken care of them; and if I depart to the world below, will there be no man to take care of them?" See how he gives to death a gentle name and mocks it. But if you and I had been in his place, we should have immediately answered as philosophers that those who act unjustly must be repaid in the same way, and we should have added, "I shall be useful to many, if my life is saved, and if I die, I shall be useful to no man." For, if it had been necessary, we should have made our escape by slipping through a small hole. And how in that case should we have been useful to any man? for where would they have been then staying? or if we were useful to men while we were alive, should we not have been much more useful to them by dying when we ought to die, and as we ought? And now, Socrates being dead, no less useful to men, and even more useful, is the remembrance of that which he did or said when he was alive.

Think of these things, these opinions, these words: look to these examples, if you would be free, if you desire the thing according to its worth. And what is the wonder if you buy so great a thing at the price of things so many and so great? For the sake of this which is called "liberty," some hang themselves, others throw themselves down precipices, and sometimes even whole cities have perished: and will you not for the sake of the true and unassailable and secure liberty give back to God when He demands them the things which He has given? Will you not, as Plato says, study not to die only, but also to endure torture, and exile, and scourging, and, in a word, to give up all which is not your own? If you will not, you will be a slave among slaves, even you be ten thousand times a consul; and if you make your way up to the Palace, you will no less be a slave; and you will feel, that perhaps philosophers utter words which are contrary to common opinion, as Cleanthes also said, but not words contrary to reason. For you will know by experience that the words are true, and that there is no profit from the things which are valued and eagerly sought to those who have obtained them; and to those who have not yet obtained them there is an imagination that when these things are come, all that is good will come with them; then, when they are come, the feverish feeling is the same, the tossing to and fro is the same, the satiety, the desire of things which are not present; for freedom is acquired not by the full possession of the things which are desired, but by removing the desire. And that you may know that this is true, as you have labored for those things, so transfer your labor to these; be vigilant for the purpose of acquiring an opinion which will make you free; pay court to a philosopher instead of to a rich old man: be seen about a philosopher's doors: you will not disgrace yourself by being seen; you will not go away empty nor without profit, if you go to the philosopher as you ought, and if not, try at least: the trial is not disgraceful.

CHAPTER 2

On familiar intimacy

To This matter before all you must attend: that you be never so closely connected with any of your former intimates or friends as to come down to the same acts as he does. If you do not observe this rule, you will ruin yourself. But if the thought arises in your mind. "I shall seem disobliging to him, and he will not have the same feeling toward me," remember that nothing is done without cost, nor is it possible for a man if he does not do the same to be the same man that he was. Choose, then, which of the two you will have, to be equally loved by those by whom you were formerly loved, being the same with your former self; or, being superior, not to obtain from your friends the same that you did before. For if this is better, turn away to it, and let not other considerations draw you in a different direction. For no man is able to make progress, when he is wavering between opposite things, but if you have preferred this to all things, if you choose to attend to this only, to work out this only, give up everything else. But if you will not do this, your wavering will produce both these results: you will neither improve as you ought, nor will you obtain what you formerly obtained. For before, by plainly desiring the things which were worth nothing, you pleased your associates. But you cannot excel in both kinds, and it is necessary that so far as you share in the one, you must fall short in the other. You cannot, when you do not drink with those with whom you used to drink, he agreeable to them as you were before. Choose, then, whether you will be a hard drinker and pleasant to your former associates or a sober man and disagreeable to them. You cannot, when you do not sing with those with whom you used to sing, be equally loved by them. Choose, then, in this matter also which of the two you will have. For if it is better to be modest and orderly than for a man to say, "He is a jolly fellow," give up the rest, renounce it, turn away from it, have nothing to do with such men. But if this behavior shall not please you, turn altogether to the opposite: become a catamite, an adulterer, and act accordingly, and you will get what you wish. And jump up in the theatre and bawl out in praise of the dancer. But characters so different cannot be mingled: you cannot act both Thersites and Agamemnon. If you intend to be Thersites, you must be humpbacked and bald: if Agamemnon, you must be tall and handsome, and love those who are placed in obedience to you.

CHAPTER 3

What things we should exchange for other things

Keep this thought in readiness, when you lose anything external, what you acquire in place of it; and if it be worth more, never say, "I have had a loss"; neither if you have got a horse in place of an ass, or an ox in place of a sheep, nor a good action in place of a bit of money, nor in place of idle talk such tranquility as befits a man, nor in place of lewd talk if you have acquired modesty. If you remember this, you will always maintain your character such as it ought to be. But if you do not, consider that the times of opportunity are perishing, and that whatever pains you take about yourself, you are going to waste them all and overturn them. And it needs only a few things for the loss and overturning of all, namely a small deviation from reason. For the steerer of a ship to upset it, he has no need of the same means as he has need of for saving it: but if he turns it a little to the wind, it is lost; and if he does not do this purposely, but has been neglecting his duty a little, the ship is lost. Something of the kind happens in this case also: if you only fall to nodding a little, all that you have up to this time collected is gone. Attend therefore to the appearances of things, and watch over them; for that which you have to preserve is no small matter, but it is modesty and fidelity and constancy, freedom from the affects, a state of mind undisturbed, freedom from fear, tranquility, in a word, "liberty." For what will you sell these things? See what is the value of the things which you will obtain in exchange for these. "But shall I not obtain any such thing for it?" See, and if you do in return get that, see what you receive in place of it. "I possess decency, he possesses a tribuneship: be possesses a praetorship, I possess modesty. But I do not make acclamations where it is not becoming: I will not stand up where I ought not; for I am free, and a friend of God, and so I obey Him willingly. But I must not claim anything else, neither body nor possession, nor magistracy, nor good report, nor in fact anything. For He does not allow me to claim them: for if He had chosen, He would have made them good for me; but He has not done so, and for this reason I cannot transgress his commands." Preserve that which is your own good in everything; and as to every other thing, as it is permitted, and so far as to behave consistently with reason in respect to them, content with this only. If you do not, you will be unfortunate, you will fall in all things, you will be hindered, you will be impeded. These are the laws which have been sent from thence; these are the orders. Of these laws a man ought to be an expositor, to these he ought to submit, not to those of Masurius and Cassius.

CHAPTER 4

To those who are desirous of passing life in tranquility

Remember that not only the desire of power and of riches makes us mean and subject to others, but even the desire of tranquility, and of leisure. and of traveling abroad, and of learning. For, to speak plainly, whatever the external thing may be, the value which we set upon it places us in subjection to others. What, then, is the difference between desiring, to be a senator or not desiring to be one; what is the difference between desiring power or being content with a private station; what is the difference between saying, "I am unhappy, I have nothing, to do, but I am bound to my books as a corpse"; or saying, "I am unhappy, I have no leisure for reading"? For as salutations and power are things external and independent of the will, so is a book. For what purpose do you choose to read? Tell me. For if you only direct your purpose to being amused or learning something, you are a silly fellow and incapable of enduring labor. But if you refer reading to the proper end, what else is this than a tranquil and happy life? But if reading does not secure for you a happy and tranquil life, what is the use of it? But it does secure this," the man replies, "and for this reason I am vexed that I am deprived of it." And what is this tranquil and happy life, which any man can impede; I do not say Caesar or Caesar's friend, but a crow, a piper, a fever, and thirty thousand other things? But a tranquil and happy life contains nothing so sure is continuity and freedom from obstacle. Now I am called to do something: I will go, then, with the purpose of observing the measures which I must keep, of acting with modesty, steadiness, without desire and aversion to things external; and then that I may attend to men, what they say, how they are moved; and this not with any bad disposition, or that I may have something to blame or to ridicule; but I turn to myself, and ask if I also commit the same faults. "How then shall I cease to commit them?" Formerly I also acted wrong, but now I do not: thanks to God.

Come, when you have done these things and have attended to them, have you done a worse act than when you have read a thousand verses or written as many? For when you eat, are you grieved because you are not reading? are you not satisfied with eating according to what you have learned by reading, and so with bathing and with exercise? Why, then, do you not act consistently in all things, both when you approach Caesar and when you approach any person? If you maintain yourself free from perturbation, free from alarm, and steady; if you look rather at the things which are done and happen than are looked at yourself; if you do not envy those who are preferred before you; if surrounding circumstances do not strike you with fear or admiration, what do you want? Books? How or for what purpose? for is not this a preparation for life? and is not life itself made up of certain other things than this? This is just as if an athlete should weep when he enters the stadium, because he is not being exercised outside of it. It was for this purpose that you used to practice exercise; for this purpose were used the halters, the dust, the young men as antagonists; and do you seek for those things now when it is the time of action? This is just as if in the topic of assent when appearances present themselves, some of which can he comprehended, and some cannot be comprehended, we should not choose to distinguish them but should choose to read what has been written about comprehension.

What then is the reason of this? The reason is that we have never read for this purpose, we have never written for this purpose, so that we may in our actions use in a way conformable to nature the appearances presented to us; but we terminate in this, in learning what is said, and in being able to expound it to another, in resolving a syllogism, and in handling the hypothetical syllogism. For this reason where our study is, there alone is the impediment. Would you have by all means the things which are not in your power? Be prevented then, be hindered, fail in your purpose. But if we read what is written about action, not that we may see what is said about action, but that we may act well: if we read what is said about desire and aversion, in order that we may neither fall in our desires, nor fall into that which we try to avoid: if we read what is said about duty, in order that, remembering the relations, we may do nothing irrationally nor contrary to these relations; we should not be vexed in being hindered as to our readings, but we should be satisfied with doing, the acts which are conformable, and we should be reckoning not what so far we have been accustomed to reckon; "To-day I have read so many verses, I have written so many"; but, "To-day I have employed my action as it is taught by the philosophers; I have not employed any desire; I have used avoidance only with respect to things which are within the power of my will; I have not been afraid of such a person, I have not been prevailed upon by the entreaties of another; I have exercised my patience, my abstinence my co-operation with others"; and so we should thank God for what we ought to thank Him.

But now we do not know that we also in another way are like the many. Another man is afraid that he shall not have power: you are afraid that you will. Do not do so, my man; but as you ridicule him who is afraid that he, shall not have power, so ridicule yourself also. For it makes no difference whether you are thirsty like a man who has a fever, or have a dread of water like a man who is mad. Or how will you still be able to say as Socrates did, "If so it pleases God, so let it be"? Do you think that Socrates, if he had been eager to pass his leisure in the Lyceum or in the Academy and to discourse dally with the young men, would have readily served in military expeditions so often as he did; and would he not have lamented and groaned, "Wretch that I am; I must now be miserable here, when I might be sunning myself in the Lyceum"? Why, was this your business, to sun yourself? And is it not your business to be happy, to be free from hindrance, free from impediment? And could he still have been Socrates, if he had lamented in this way: how would he still have been able to write Paeans in his prison?

In short, remember this, that what you shall prize which is beyond your will, so far you have destroyed your will. But these things are out of the power of the will, not only power, but also a private condition: not only occupation, but also leisure. "Now, then, must I live in this tumult?" Why do you say "tumult"? "I mean among many men." Well what is the hardship? Suppose that you are at Olympia: imagine it to be a panegyris, where one is calling out one thing, another is doing another thing, and a third is pushing another person: in the baths there is a crowd: and who of us is not pleased with this assembly and leaves it unwillingly, Be not difficult to please nor fastidious about what happens. "Vinegar is disagreeable, for it is sharp; honey is disagreeable, for it disturbs my habit of body. I do not like vegetables." So also, "I do not like leisure; it is a desert: I do not like a crowd; it is confusion." But if circumstances make it necessary for you to live alone or with a few, call it quiet and use the thing as you ought: talk with yourself, exercise the appearances, work up your preconceptions. If you fall into a crowd, call it a celebration of games, a panegyris, a festival: try to enjoy the festival with other men. For what is a more pleasant sight to him who loves mankind than a number of men? We see with pleasure herds of horses or oxen: we are delighted when we see many ships: who is pained when he sees many men? "But they deafen me with their cries." Then your hearing is impeded. What, then, is this to you? Is, then, the power of making use of appearances hindered? And who prevents you from using, according to nature, inclination to a thing and aversion from it; and movement toward a thing and movement from it? What tumult is able to do this?

Do you only bear in mind the general rules: "What is mine, what is not mine; what is given to me; what does God will that I should do now? what does He not will?" A little before he willed you to be at leisure, to talk with yourself, to write about these things, to read, to hear, to prepare yourself. You had sufficient time for this. Now He says to you: "Come now to the contest; show us what you have learned, how you have practiced the athletic art. How long will you be exercised alone? Now is the opportunity for you to learn whether you are an athlete worthy of victory, or one of those who go about the world and are defeated." Why, then, are; you vexed? No contest is without confusion. There be many who exercise themselves for the contests, many who call out to those who exercise themselves, many masters, many spectators. "But my wish is to live quietly." Lament, then, and groan as you deserve to do. For what other is a greater punishment than this to the untaught man and to him who disobeys the divine commands: to be grieved, to lament, to envy, in a word, to be disappointed and to he unhappy? Would you not release yourself from these things? "And how shall I release myself?" Have you not often heard that you ought to remove entirely desire, apply aversion to those things only which are within your power, that you ought to give up everything, body, property, fame, books, tumult, power, private station? for whatever way you turn, you are a slave, you are subjected, you are hindered, you are compelled, you are entirely in the power of others. But keep the words of Cleanthes in readiness,

Lead me, O Zeus, and thou necessity.

Is it your will that I should go to Rome? I will go to Rome. To Gyara? I will go to Gyara. I will go to Athens? I will go to Athens. To prison? I will go to prison. If you should once say, "When shall a man go to Athens?" you are undone. It is a necessary consequence that this desire, if it is not accomplished, must make you unhappy; and if it is accomplished, it must make you vain, since you are elated at things at which you ought not to be elated; and on the other hand, if you are impeded, it must make you wretched because you fall into that which you would not fall into. Give up then all these things. "Athens is a good place." But happiness is much better; and to be free from passions, free from disturbance, for your affairs not to depend on any man. "There is tumult at Rome and visits of salutation." But happiness is an equivalent for all troublesome things. If, then, the time comes for these things, why do you not take away the wish to avoid them? what necessity is there to carry to avoid a burden like an ass, and to be beaten with a stick? But if you do not so, consider that you must always be a slave to him who has it in his power to effect your release, and also to impede you, and you must serve him as an evil genius.

There is only one way to happiness, and let this rule be ready both in the morning and during the day and by night; the rule is not to look toward things which are out of the power of our will, to think that nothing is our own, to give up all things to the Divinity, to Fortune; to make them the superintendents of these things, whom Zeus also has made so; for a man to observe that only which is his own, that which cannot be hindered; and when we read, to refer our reading to this only, and our writing and our listening. For this reason, I cannot call the man industrious, if I hear this only, that he reads and writes; and even if a man adds that he reads all night, I cannot say so, if he knows not to what he should refer his reading. For neither do you say that a man is industrious if he keeps awake for a girl; nor do I. But if he does it for reputation, I say that he is a lover of reputation. And if he does it for money, I say that he is a lover of money, not a lover of labor; and if he does it through love of learning, I say that he is a lover of learning. But if he refers his labor to his own ruling power, that he may keep it in a state conformable to nature and pass his life in that state, then only do I say that he is industrious. For never commend a man on account of these things which are common to all, but on account of his opinions; for these are the things which belong to each man, which make his actions bad or good. Remembering these rules, rejoice in that which is present, and be content with the things which come in season. If you see anything which you have learned and inquired about occurring, to you in your course of life, be delighted at it. If you have laid aside or have lessened bad disposition and a habit of reviling; if you have done so with rash temper, obscene words, hastiness, sluggishness; if you are not moved by what you formerly were, and not in the same way as you once were, you can celebrate a festival daily, to-day because you have behaved well in one act, and to-morrow because you have behaved well in another. How much greater is this a reason for making sacrifices than a consulship or the government of a province? These things come to you from yourself and from the gods. Remember this, Who gives these things and to whom, and for what purpose. If you cherish yourself in these thoughts, do you still think that it makes any difference where yon shall be happy, where you shall please God? Are not the gods equally distant from all places? Do they not see from all places alike that which is going on?

CHAPTER 5

Against the quarrelsome and ferocious

The wise and good man neither himself fights with any person, nor does he allow another, so far as he can prevent it. And an example of this as well as of all other things is proposed to us in the life of Socrates, who not only himself on all occasions avoided fights, but would not allow even others to quarrel. See in Xenophon's Symposium how many quarrels he settled; how further he endured Thrasymachus and Polus and Callicles; how he tolerated his wife, and how he tolerated his son who attempted to confute him aid to cavil with him. For he remembered well that no man has in his power another man's ruling principle. He wished, therefore nothing else than that which was his own. And what is this? Not that this or that man may act according to nature; for that is a thing which belongs to another; but that while others are doing their own acts, as they choose, he may never the less be in a condition conformable to nature and live in it, only doing what is his own to the end that others also may be in a state conformable to nature. For this is the object always set before him by the wise and good man. Is it to be commander of an army? No: but if it is permitted him, his object is in this matter to maintain his own ruling principle. Is it to marry? No; but if marriage is allowed to him, in this matter his object is to maintain himself in a condition conformable to nature. But if he would have his son not to do wrong, or his wife, he would have what belongs to another not to belong to another; and to he instructed is this: to learn what things are a man's own and what belongs to another.

How, then, is there left any place for fighting, to a man who has this opinion? Is he surprised at anything which happens, and does it appear new to him? Does he not expect that which comes from the bad to be worse and more grievous than what actually befalls him? And does he not reckon as pure gain whatever they may do which falls short of extreme wickedness? "Such a person has reviled you." Great thanks to him for not having, struck you. "But he has struck me also." Great thanks that he did not wound you "But he wounded me also." Great thanks that he did not kill you. For when did he learn or in what school that man is a tame animal, that men love one another, that an act of injustice is a great harm to him who does it. Since then he has not to him who does it. Since then he has not learned this and is not convinced of it, why shall he not follow that which seems to be for his own "Your neighbor has thrown stones." Have you then done anything wrong? "But the things in the house have been broken." Are you then a utensil? No; but a free power of will. What, then, is given to you in answer to this? If you are like a wolf, you must bite in return, and throw more stones. But if you consider what is proper for a man, examine your store-house, see with at faculties you came into the world. Have you the disposition of a wild beast, Have you the disposition of revenge for an injury? When is a horse wretched? When he is deprived of his natural faculties; not when he cannot crow like a cock, but when he cannot run. When is a dog wretched? Not when he cannot fly, but when he cannot track his game. Is, then, a man also unhappy in this way, not because he cannot strangle lions or embrace statues, for he did not come into the world in the possession of certain powers from nature for this purpose, but because he has lost his probity and his fidelity? People ought to meet and lament such a man for the misfortunes into which he has fallen; not indeed to lament because a man his been born or has died, but because it has happened to him in his lifetime to have lost the things which are his own, not that which he received from his father, not his land and house, and his inn, and his slaves; for not one of these things is a man's own, but all belong to others, are servile and subject to account, at different times given to different persons by those who have them in their power: but I mean the things which belong to him as a man, the marks in his mind with which he came into the world, such as we seek also on coins, and if we find them, we approve of the coins, and if we do not find the marks, we reject them. What is the stamp on this Sestertius? "The stamp of Trajan." Present it. "It is the stamp of Nero." Throw it away: it cannot be accepted, it is counterfeit. So also in this case. What is the stamp of his opinions? "It is gentleness, a sociable disposition, a tolerant temper, a disposition to mutual affection." Produce these qualities. I accept them: I consider this man a citizen, I accept him as a neighbor, a companion in my voyages. Only see that he has not Nero's stamp. Is he passionate, is he full of resentment, is he faultfinding? If the whim seizes him, does he break the heads of those who come in his way? Why, then did you say that he is a man? Is everything judged by the bare form? If that is so, say that the form in wax is all apple and has the smell and the taste of an apple. But the external figure is not enough: neither then is the nose enough and the eyes to make the man, but he must have the opinions of a man. Here is a man who does not listen to reason, who does not know when he is refuted: he is an ass: in another man the sense of shame is become dead: he is good for nothing, he is anything rather than a man. This man seeks whom he may meet and kick or bite, so that he is not even a sheep or an ass, but a kind of wild beast.

"What then would you have me to be despised?" By whom? by those who know you? and how and how shall those who know you despise a man who is gentle and modest? Perhaps you mean by those who do not know you? What is that to you? For no other artisan cares for the opinion of those who know not his art. "But they will be more hostile to me for this reason." Why do you say "me"? Can any man injure your will, or prevent you from using in a natural way the appearances which are presented to you, "In no way can he." Why, then, are still disturbed and why do you choose to show yourself afraid? And why do you not come forth and proclaim that you are at peace with all men whatever they may do, and laugh at those chiefly who think that they can harm you? "These slaves," you can say, "know not either who I am nor where lies my good or my evil, because they have no access to the things which are mine."

In this way, also, those who occupy a strong city mock the besiegers; "What trouble these men are now taking for nothing: our wall is secure, we have food for a very long time, and all other resources." These are the things which make a city strong and impregnable: but nothing else than his opinions makes a man's soul impregnable. For what wall is so strong, or what body is so hard, or what possession is so safe, or what honor so free from assault? All things everywhere are perishable, easily taken by assault, and, if any man in any way is attached to them, he must be disturbed, expect what is bad, he must fear, lament, find his desires disappointed, and fall into things which he would avoid. Then do we not choose to make secure the only means of safety which are offered to us, and do we not choose to withdraw ourselves from that which is perishable and servile and to labor at the things, which are imperishable and by nature free; and do we not remember that no man either hurts another or does good to another, but that a man's opinion about each thing is that which hurts him, is that which overturns him; this is fighting, this is civil discord, this is war? That which made Eteocles and Polynices enemies was nothing else than this opinion which they had about royal power, their opinion about exile, that the one is the extreme of evils, the other the greatest good. Now this is the nature of every man to seek the good, to avoid the bad; to consider him who deprives us of the one and involves us in the other an enemy and treacherous, even if he be a brother, or a son or a father. For nothing is more akin to us than the good: therefore if these things are good and evil, neither is a father a friend to sons, nor a brother to a brother, but all the world is everywhere full of enemies, treacherous men, and sycophants. But if the will, being what it ought to be, is the only good; and if the will, being such as it ought not to be, is the only evil, where is there any strife, where is there reviling? about what? about the things which do not concern us? and strife with whom? with the ignorant, the unhappy, with those who are deceived about the chief things?

Remembering this Socrates managed his own house and endured a very ill-tempered wife and a foolish son. For in what did she show her bad temper? In pouring water on his head as much as she liked, and in trampling on the cake. And what is this to me, if I think that these things are nothing to me? But this is my business; and neither tyrant shall check my will nor a master; nor shall the many check me who am only one, nor shall the stronger check me who am the weaker; for this power of being free from check is given by God to every man. For these opinions make love in a house, concord in a state, among nations peace, and gratitude to God; they make a man in all things cheerful in externals as about things which belong to others, as about things which are of no value. We indeed are able to write and to read these things, and to praise them when they are read, but we do not even come near to being convinced of them. Therefore what is said of the Lacedaemonians, "Lions at home, but in Ephesus foxes," will fit in our case also, "Lions in the school, but out of it foxes."

CHAPTER 6

Against those who lament over being pitied

"I am grieved," a man says, "at being pitied." Whether, then, is the fact of your being pitied a thing which concerns you or those who pity you? Well, is it in your power to stop this pity? "It is in my power, if I show them that I do not require pity." And whether, then, are you in the condition of not deserving pity, or are you not in that condition? "I think I am not: but these persons do not pity me for the things for which, if they ought to pity me, it would be proper, I mean, for my faults; but they pity me for my poverty, for not possessing honorable offices, for diseases and deaths and other such things." Whether, then, are you prepared to convince the many that not one of these things is an evil, but that it is possible for a man who is poor and has no office and enjoys no honor to be happy; or to show yourself to them as rich and in power? For the second of these things belong, to a man who is boastful, silly and good for nothing. And consider by what means the pretense must be supported. It will be necessary for you to hire slaves and to possess a few silver vessels, and to exhibit them in public, if it is possible, though they are often the same, and to attempt to conceal the fact that they are the same, and to have splendid garments, and all other things for display, and to show that you are a man honored by the great, and to try to sup at their houses, or to be supposed to sup there, and as to your person to employ some mean arts, that you may appear to be more handsome and nobler than you are. These things you must contrive, if you choose to go by the second path in order not to be pitied. But the first way is both impracticable and long, to attempt the very thing which Zeus has not been able to do, to convince all men what things are good and bad. Is this power given to you? This only is given to you, to convince yourself; and you have not convinced yourself. Then I ask you, do you attempt to persuade other men? and who has lived so long with you as you with yourself? and who has so much power of convincing you as you have of convincing yourself; and who is better disposed and nearer to you than you are to yourself? How, then, have you not convinced yourself in order to learn? At present are not things upside down? Is this what you have been earnest about doing, to learn to be free from grief and free from disturbance, and not to be humbled, and to be free? Have you not heard, then, that there is only one way which leads to this end, to give up the things which do not depend on the will, to withdraw from them, and to admit that they belong to others? For another man, then, to have an opinion about you, of what kind is it? "It is a thing independent of the will." Then is it nothing to you? "It is nothing." When, then, you are still vexed at this and disturbed, do you think that you are convinced about good and evil?

Will you not, then, letting others alone, be to yourself both scholar and teacher? "The rest of mankind will look after this, whether it is to their interest to be and to pass their lives in a state contrary to nature: but to me no man is nearer than myself. What, then, is the meaning of this, that I have listened to the words of the philosophers and I assent to them, but in fact I am no way made easier? Am I so stupid? And yet, in all other things such as I have chosen, I have not been found very stupid; but I learned letters quickly, and to wrestle, and geometry, and to resolve syllogisms. Has not, then, reason convinced me? and indeed no other things have I from the beginning so approved and chosen: and now I read about these things, hear about them, write about them; I have so far discovered no reason stronger than this. In what, then, am I deficient? Have the contrary opinions not been eradicated from me? Have the notions themselves not been exercised nor used to be applied to action, but as armor are laid aside and rusted and cannot fit me? And yet neither in the exercises of the palaestra, nor in writing or reading am I satisfied with learning, but I turn up and down the syllogisms which are proposed, and I make others, and sophistical syllogisms also. But the necessary theorems, by proceeding from which a man can become free from grief, fear, passions, hindrance, and a free man, these I do not exercise myself in nor do I practice in these the proper practice. Then I care about what others will say of me, whether I shall appear to them worth notice, whether I shall appear happy."

Wretched man, will you not see what you. are saying about yourself? What do you appear to yourself to be? in your opinions, in your desires, in your aversions from things, in your movements, in your preparation, in your designs, and in other acts suitable to a man? But do you trouble yourself about this, whether others pity you? "Yes, but I am pitied not as I ought to be." Are you then pained at this? and is he who is pained, an object of pity? "Yes." How, then, are you pitied not as you ought to be? For by the very act that you feel about being pitied, you make yourself deserving of pity. What then says Antisthenes? Have you not heard? "It is a royal thing, O Cyrus, to do right and to be ill-spoken of." My head is sound, and all think that I have the headache. What do I care for that? I am free from fever, and people sympathize with me as if I had a fever: "Poor man, for so long a time you have not ceased to have fever." I also say with a sorrowful countenance: "In truth it is now a long time that I have been ill." "What will happen then?" "As God may please": and at the same time I secretly laugh at those who are pitying me. What, then, hinders the same being done in this case also? I am poor, but I have a right opinion about poverty. Why, then, do I care if they pity me for my poverty? I am not in power; but others are: and I have the opinion which I ought to have about having and not having power. Let them look to it who pity me; but I am neither hungry nor thirsty nor do I suffer cold; but because they are hungry or thirsty they think that I too am. What, then, shall I do for them? Shall I go about and proclaim and say: "Be not mistaken, men, I am very well, I do not trouble myself about poverty, nor want of power, nor in a word about anything else than right opinions. These I have free from restraint, I care for nothing at all." What foolish talk is this? How do I possess right opinions when I am not content with being what I am, but am uneasy about what I am supposed to be?

"But," you say, "others will get more and be preferred to me." What, then, is more reasonable than for those who have labored about anything to have more in that thing in which they have labored? They have labored for power, you have labored about opinions; and they have labored for wealth, you for the proper use of appearances. See if they have more than you in this about which you have labored, and which they neglect; if they assent better than you with respect to the natural rules of things; if they are less disappointed than you in their desires; if they fall less into things which they would avoid than you do; if in their intentions, if in the things which they propose to themselves, if in their purposes, if in their motions toward an object they take a better aim; if they better observe a proper behavior, as men, as sons, as parents, and so on as to the other names by which we express the relations of life. But if they exercise power, and you do not, will you not choose to tell yourself the truth, that you do nothing for the sake of this, and they do all? But it is most unreasonable that he who looks after anything should obtain less than he who does not look after it.

"Not so: but since I care about right opinions, it more reasonable for me to have power." Yes in the matter about which you do care, in opinions. But in a matter in which they have cared more than you, give way to them. The case is just the same as if, because you have right opinions, you thought that in using the bow you should hit the mark better than an archer, and in working in metal you should succeed better than a smith. Give up, then, your earnestness about opinions and employ yourself about the things which you wish to acquire; and then lament, if you do not succeed; for you deserve to lament. But now you say that you are occupied with other things, that you are looking after other things; but the many say this truly, that one act has no community with another. He who has risen in the morning seeks whom he shall salute, to whom he shall say something agreeable, to whom he shall send a present, how he shall please the dancing man, how by bad behavior to one he may please another. When he prays, he prays about these things; when he sacrifices, he sacrifices for these things: the saying of Pythagoras

Let sleep not come upon thy languid eyes

he transfers to these things. "Where have I failed in the matters pertaining to flattery?" "What have I done?" Anything like a free man, anything like a noble-minded man? And if he finds anything of the kind, he blames and accuses himself: "Why did you say this?

Was it not in your power to lie? Even the philosophers say that nothing hinders us from telling a lie." But do you, if indeed you have cared about nothing else except the proper use of appearances, as soon as you have risen in the morning reflect, "What do I want in order to be free from passion, and free from perturbation? What am I? Am I a poor body, a piece of property, a thing of which something is said? I am none of these. But what am I? I am a rational animal. What then is required of me?" Reflect on your acts. "Where have I omitted the things which conduce to happiness? What have I done which is either unfriendly or unsocial? what have I not done as to these things which I ought to have done?"

So great, then, being, the difference in desires, actions, wishes, would you still have the same share with others in those things about which you have not labored, and they have labored? Then are you surprised if they pity you, and are you vexed? But they are not vexed if you pity them. Why? Because they are convinced that they have that which is good, and you are not convinced. For this reason you are not satisfied with your own, but you desire that which they have: but they are satisfied with their own, and do not desire what you have: since, if you were really convinced that with respect to what is good, it is you who are the possessor of it and that they have missed it, you would not even have thought of what they say about you.

CHAPTER 7

On freedom from fear

What makes the tyrant formidable? "The guards," you say, "and their swords, and the men of the bedchamber and those who exclude them who would enter." Why, then, if you bring a boy to the tyrant when he is with his guards, is he not afraid; or is it because the child does not understand these things? If, then, any man does understand what guards are and that they have swords, and comes to the tyrant for this very purpose because he wishes to die on account of some circumstance and seeks to die easily by the hand of another, is he afraid of the guards? "No, for he wishes for the thing which makes the guards formidable." If, then, neither any man wishing to die nor to live by all means, but only as it may be permitted, approaches the tyrant, what hinders him from approaching the tyrant without fear? "Nothing." If, then, a man has the same opinion about his property as the man whom I have instanced has about his body; and also about his children and his wife, and in a word is so affected by some madness or despair that he cares not whether he possesses them or not, but like children who are playing, with shells care about the play, but do not trouble themselves about the shells, so he too has set no value on the materials, but values the pleasure that he has with them and the occupation, what tyrant is then formidable to him or what guards or what swords?

Then through madness is it possible for a man to be so disposed toward these things, and the Galilaens through habit, and is it possible that no man can learn from reason and from demonstration that God has made all the things in the universe and the universe itself completely free from hindrance and perfect, and the parts of it for the use of the whole? All other animals indeed are incapable of comprehending the administration of it; but the rational animal, man, has faculties for the consideration of all these and for understanding that it is a part, and what kind of a part it is, and that it is right for the parts to be subordinate to the whole. And besides this being naturally noble, magnanimous and free, man sees that of the things which surround him some are free from hindrance and in his power, and the other things are subject to hindrance and in the power of others; that the things which are free from hindrance are in the power of the will; and those which are subject to hindrance are the things which are not in the power of the will. And, for this reason, if he thinks that his good and his interest be in these things only which are free from hindrance and in his own power, he will be free, prosperous, happy, free from harm, magnanimous pious, thankful to God for all things; in no matter finding fault with any of the things which have not been put in his power, nor blaming any of them. But if he thinks that his good and his interest are in externals and in things which are not in the power of his will, he must of necessity be hindered, be impeded, be a slave to those who have the power over things which he admires and fears; and he must of necessity be impious because he thinks that he is harmed by God, and he must be unjust because he always claims more than belongs to him; and he must of necessity be abject and mean.

What hinders a man, who has clearly separated these things, from living with a light heart and bearing easily the reins, quietly expecting everything which can happen, and enduring that which has already happened? "Would you have me to bear poverty?" Come and you will know what poverty is when it has found one who can act well the part of a poor man. "Would you have me to possess power?" Let me have power, and also the trouble of it. "Well, banishment?" Wherever I shall go, there it will be well with me; for here also where I am, it was not because of the place that it was well with me, but because of my opinions which I shall carry off with me: for neither can any man deprive me of them; but my opinions alone are mine and they cannot he taken from me, and I am satisfied while I have them, wherever I may be and whatever I am doing. "But now it is time to die." Why do you say "to die"? Make no tragedy show of the thing, but speak of it as it is: it is now time for the matter to be resolved into the things out of which it was composed. And what is the formidable thing here? what is going to perish of the things which are in the universe? what new thing or wondrous is going to happen? Is it for this reason that a tyrant is formidable? Is it for this reason that the guards appear to have swords which are large and sharp? Say this to others; but I have considered about all these things; no man has power over me. I have been made free; I know His commands, no man can now lead me as a slave. I have a proper person to assert my freedom; I have proper judges. Are you not the master of my body? What, then, is that to me? Are you not the master of my property? What, then, is that to me? Are you not the master of my exile or of my chains? Well, from all these things and all the poor body itself I depart at your bidding, when you please. Make trial of your power, and you will know how far it reaches.

Whom then can I still fear? Those who are over the bedchamber? Lest they should do, what? Shut me out? If they find that I wish to enter, let them shut me out. "Why, then, do you go to the doors?" Because I think it befits me, while the play lasts, to join in it. "How, then, are you not shut out?" Because, unless some one allows me to go in, I do not choose to ,o in, but am always content with that I which happens; for I think that what God chooses is better than what I choose. I will attach myself as a minister and follower to Him; I have the same movements as He has, I have the same desires; in a word, I have the same will. There is no shutting out for me, but for those who would force their in. Why, then, do not I force my way in? Because I know that nothing good is distributed within to those who enter. But when I hear any man called fortunate because he is honored by Caesar, I say, "What does he happen to get?" A province. Does he also obtain an opinion such as he ought? The office of a Prefect. Does he also obtain the power of using his office well? Why do I still strive to enter? A man scatters dried figs and nuts: the children seize them and fight with one another; men do not, for they think them to be a small matter. But if a man should throw about shells, even the children do not seize them. Provinces are distributed: let children look to that. Money is distributed: let children look to that. Praetorships, consulships are distributed: let children scramble for them, let them be shut out, beaten, kiss the hands of the giver, of the slaves: but to me these are only dried figs and nuts. What then? If you fail to get them, while Caesar is scattering them about, do not be troubled: if a dried fig come into your lap, take it and eat it; for so far you may value even a fig. But if I shall stoop down and turn another over, or be turned over by another, and shall flatter those who have got into chamber, neither is a dried fig worth the trouble, nor anything else of the things which are not good, which the philosophers have persuaded me not to think good.

Show me the swords of the guards. "See how big they are, and how sharp." What, then, do these big and sharp swords do? "They kill." And what does a fever do? "Nothing else." And what else a tile? "Nothing else." Would you then have me to wonder at these things and worship them, and go about as the slave of all of them? I hope that this will not happen: but when I have once learned that everything which has come into existence must also go out of it, that the universe may not stand still nor be impeded, I no longer consider it any difference whether a fever shall do it, or a tile, or a soldier. But if a man must make a comparison between these things, I know that the soldier will do it with less trouble, and quicker. When, then, I neither fear anything which a tyrant can do to me, nor desire anything which he can give, why do I still look on with wonder? Why am I still confounded? Why do I fear the guards? Why am I pleased if he speaks to me in a friendly way, and receives me, and why do I tell others how he spoke to me? Is he a Socrates, is he a Diogenes that his praise should be a proof of what I am? Have I been eager to imitate his morals? But I keep up the play and go to him, and serve him so long as he does not bid me to do anything foolish or unreasonable. But if he says to me, "Go and bring Leon of Salamis," I say to him, "Seek another, for I am no longer playing." "Lead him away." I follow; that is part of the play. "But your head will be taken off." Does the tyrant's head always remain where it is, and the heads of you who obey him? "But you will be cast out unburied." If the corpse is I, I shall be cast out; but if I am different from the corpse, speak more properly according as the fact is, and do not think of frightening me. These things are formidable to children and fools. But if any man has once entered a philosopher's school and knows not what he is, he deserves to be full of fear and to flatter those whom afterward he used to flatter; if he has not yet learned that he is not flesh nor bones nor sinews, but he is that which makes use of these parts of the body and governs them and follows the appearances of things.

"Yes, but this talk makes us despise the laws." And what kind of talk makes men more obedient to the laws who employ such talk? And the things which are in the power of a fool are not law. And yet see how this talk makes us disposed as we ought to be even to these men; since it teaches us to claim in opposition to them none of the things in which they are able to surpass us. This talk teaches us, as to the body, to give it up, as to property, to give that up also, as to children, parents, brothers, to retire from these, to give up all; It only makes an exception of the opinions, which even Zeus has willed to be the select property of every man. What transgression of the laws is there here, what folly? Where you are superior and stronger, there I give way to you: on the other hand, where I am superior, do you yield to me; for I have studied this, and you have not. It is your study to live in houses with floors formed of various stones, how your slaves and dependents shall serve you, how you shall wear fine clothing, have many hunting men, lute players, and tragic actors. Do I claim any of these? have you made any study of opinions and of your own rational faculty? Do you know of what parts it is composed, how they are brought together, how they are connected, what powers it has, and of what kind? Why then are you vexed, if another, who has made it his study, has the advantage over you in these things? "But these things are the greatest." And who hinders you from being employed about these things and looking after them? And who has a better stock of books, of leisure, of persons to aid you? Only turn your mind at last to these things, attend, if it be only a short time, to your own ruling faculty: consider what this is that you possess, and whence it came, this which uses all others, and tries them, and selects and rejects. But so long as you employ yourself about externals you will possess them as no man else does; but you will have this such as you choose to have it, sordid and neglected.

CHAPTER 8

Against those who hastily rush into the use of the philosophic dress

Never praise nor blame a man because of the things which are common, and do not ascribe to him any skill or want of skill; and thus you will be free from rashness and from malevolence. "This man bathes very quickly." Does he then do wrong? Certainly not. But what does he do? He bathes very quickly. Are all things then done well? By no means: but the acts which proceed from right opinions are done well; and those which proceed from bad opinions are done ill. But do you, until you know the opinion from which a man does each thing, neither praise nor blame the act. But the opinion is not easily discovered from the external things. "This man is a carpenter." Why? "Because he uses an ax." What, then, is this to the matter? "This man is a musician because he sings." And what does that signify? "This man is a philosopher. Because he wears a cloak and long hair." And what does a juggler wear? For this reason if a man sees any philosopher acting indecently, immediately he says, "See what the philosopher is doing"; but he ought because of the man's indecent behavior rather to say that he is not a philosopher. For if this is the preconceived notion of a philosopher and what he professes, to wear a cloak and long hair, men would say well; but if what he professes is this rather, to keep himself free from faults, why do we not rather, because he does not make good his professions, take from him the name of philosopher? For so we do in the case of all other arts. When a man sees another handling an ax badly, he does not say, "What is the use of the carpenter's art? See how badly carpenters do their work"; but he says just the contrary, "This man is not a carpenter, for he uses an ax badly." In the same way if a man hears another singing badly, he does not say, "See how musicians sing"; but rather, "This man is not a musician." But it is in the matter of philosophy only that people do this. When they see a man acting contrary to the profession of a philosopher, they do not take away his title, but they assume him to be a philosopher, and from his acts deriving the fact that he is behaving indecently they conclude that there is no use in philosophy.

What, then, is the reason of this? Because we attach value to the notion of a carpenter, and to that of a musician, and to the notion of other artisans in like manner, but not to that of a philosopher, and we judge from externals only that it is a thing confused and ill defined. And what other kind of art has a name from the dress and the hair; and has not theorems and a material and an end? What, then, is the material of the philosopher? Is it a cloak? No, but reason. What is his end? is it to wear a cloak? No, but to possess the reason in a right state. Of what kind are his theorems? Are they those about the way in which the beard becomes great or the hair long? No, but rather what Zeno says, to know the elements of reason, what kind of a thing each of them is, and how they are fitted to one another, and what things are consequent upon them. Will you not, then, see first if he does what he professes when he acts in an unbecoming manner, and then blame his study? But now when you yourself are acting in a sober way, you say in consequence of what he seems to you to be doing wrong, "Look at the philosopher," as if it were proper to call by the name of philosopher one who does these things; and further, "This is the conduct of a philosopher." But you do not say, "Look at the carpenter," when you know that a carpenter is an adulterer or you see him to be a glutton; nor do you say, "See the musician." Thus to a certain degree even you perceive the profession of a philosopher, but you fall away from the notion, and you are confused through want of care.

But even the philosophers themselves as they are called pursue the thing by beginning with things which are common to them and others: as soon as they have assumed a cloak and grown a beard, they say, "I am a philosopher." But no man will say, "I am a musician," if he has bought a plectrum and a lute: nor will he say, "I am a smith," if he has put on a cap and apron. But the dress is fitted to the art; and they take their name from the art, and not from the dress. For this reason Euphrates used to say well, "A long time I strove to be a philosopher without people knowing it; and this," he said, "was useful to me: for first I knew that when I did anything well, I did not do it for the sake of the spectators, but for the sake of myself: I ate well for the sake of myself; I had my countenance well composed and my walk: all for myself and for God. Then, as I struggled alone, so I alone also was in danger: in no respect through me, if I did anything base or unbecoming, was philosophy endangered; nor did I injure the many by doing anything wrong as a philosopher. For this reason those who did not know my purpose used to wonder how it was that, while I conversed and lived altogether with all philosophers, I was not a philosopher myself. And what was the harm for me to be known to be a philosopher by my acts and not by outward marks?" See how I eat, how I drink, how I sleep, how I bear and forbear, how I co-operate, how I employ desire, how I employ aversion, how I maintain the relations, those which are natural or those which are acquired, how free from confusion, how free from hindrance. Judge of me from this, if you can. But if you are so deaf and blind that you cannot conceive even Hephaestus to be a good smith, unless you see the cap on his head, what is the harm in not being recognized by so foolish a judge?

So Socrates was not known to be a philosopher by most persons; and they used to come to him and ask to be introduced to philosophers. Was he vexed then as we are, and did he say, "And do you not think that I am a philosopher?" No, but he would take them and introduce them, being satisfied with one thing, with being a philosopher; and being pleased also with not being thought to be a philosopher, he was not annoyed: for he thought of his own occupation. What is the work of an honorable and good man? To have many pupils? By no means. They will look to this matter who are earnest about it. But was it his business to examine carefully difficult theorems? Others will look after these matters also. In what, then, was he, and who was he and whom did he wish to be? He was in that wherein there was hurt and advantage. "If any man can damage me," he says, "I am doing nothing: if I am waiting for another man to do me good, I am nothing. If I anguish for anything, and it does not happen, I am unfortunate." To such a contest he invited every man, and I do not think that he would have declined the contest with any one. What do you suppose? was it by proclaiming and saying, "I am such a man?" Far from it, but by being such a man. For further, this is the character of a fool and a boaster to say, "I am free from passions and disturbance: do not be ignorant, my friends, that while you are uneasy and disturbed about things of no value, I alone am free from all perturbation." So is it not enough for you to feel no pain, unless you make this proclamation: "Come together all who are suffering gout, pains in the head, fever, ye who are lame, blind, and observe that I am sound from every ailment." This is empty and disagreeable to hear, unless like Aesculapius you are able to show immediately by what kind of treatment they also shall be immediately free from disease, and unless you show your own health as an example.

For such is the Cynic who is honored with the sceptre and the diadem of Zeus, and says, "That you may see, O men, that you seek happiness and tranquility not where it is, but where it is not, behold I am sent to you by God as an example. I who have neither property nor house, nor wife nor children, nor even a bed, nor coat nor household utensil; and see how healthy I am: try me, and if you see that I am free from perturbations, hear the remedies and how I have been cured." This is both philanthropic and noble. But see whose work it is, the work of Zeus, or of him whom He may judge worthy of this service, that he may never exhibit anything to the many, by which he shall make of no effect his own testimony, whereby he gives testimony to virtue, and bears evidence against external things:

His beauteous face pales his cheeks
He wipes a tear.

And not this only, but he neither desires nor seeks anything, nor man nor place nor amusement, as children seek the vintage or holidays; always fortified by modesty as others are fortified by walls and doors and doorkeepers.

But now, being only moved to philosophy, as those who have a bad stomach are moved to some kinds of food which they soon loathe, straightway toward the sceptre and to the royal power. They let the hair grow, they assume the cloak, they show the shoulder bare, they quarrel with those whom they meet; and if they see a man in a thick winter coat, they quarrel with him. Man, first exercise yourself in winter weather: see your movements that they are not those of a man with a bad stomach or those of a longing woman. First strive that it be not known what you are: be a philosopher to yourself a short time. Fruit grows thus: the seed must be buried for some time, hid, grow slowly in order that it may come to perfection. But if it produces the ear before the jointed stem, it is imperfect, a produce of the garden of Adonis. Such a poor plant are you also: you have blossomed too soon; the cold weather will scorch you up. See what the husbandmen say about seeds when there is warm weather too early. They are afraid lest the seeds should be too luxuriant, and then a single frost should lay hold of them and show that they are too forward. Do you also consider, my man: you have shot out too soon, you have hurried toward a little fame before the proper season: you think that you are something, a fool among fools: you will be caught by the frost, and rather you have been frost-bitten in the root below, but your upper parts still blossom a little, and for this reason you think that you are still alive and flourishing. Allow us to ripen in the natural way: why do you bare us? why do you force us? we are not yet able to bear the air. Let the root grow, then acquire the first joint, then the second, and then the third: in this way, then, the fruit will naturally force itself out, even if I do not choose. For who that is pregnant and I filled with such great principles does not also perceive his own powers and move toward the corresponding acts? A bull is not ignorant of his own nature and his powers, when a wild beast shows itself, nor does he wait for one to urge him on; nor a dog when he sees a wild animal. But if I have the powers of a good man, shall I wait for you to prepare me for my own acts? At present I have them not, believe me. Why then do you wish me to be withered up before the time, as you have been withered up?

CHAPTER 9

To a person who had been changed to a character of shamelessness

When you see another man in the possession of power, set against this the fact that you have not the want of power; when you see another rich, see what you possess in place of riches: for if you possess nothing in place of them, you are miserable; but if you have not the want of riches, know that you possess more than this man possesses and what is worth much more. Another man possesses a handsome woman: you have the satisfaction of not desiring a handsome wife. Do these things appear to you to he small? And how much would these persons give, these very men who are rich and in possession of power, and live with handsome women, to be able to despise riches and power and these very women whom they love and enjoy? Do you not know, then, what is the thirst of a man who has a fever? He possesses that which is in no degree like the thirst of a man who is in health: for the man who is in health ceases to be thirsty after he has drunk; but the sick man, being pleased for a short time, has a nausea; he converts the drink into bile, vomits, is griped, and more thirsty. It is such a thing to have desire of riches and to possess riches, desire of power and to possess power, desire of a beautiful woman and to sleep with her: to this is added jealousy, fear of being deprived of the thing which you love, indecent words, indecent thoughts, unseemly acts.

"And what do I lose?" you will say. My man, you were modest, and you are so no longer. Have you lost nothing? In place of Chrysippus and Zeno you read Aristides and Evenus; have you lost nothing? In place of Socrates and Diogenes, you admire him who is able to corrupt and seduce most women. You wish to appear handsome and try to make yourself so, though you are not. You like to display splendid clothes that you may attract women; and if you find any fine oil, yon imagine that you are happy. But formerly you did not think of any such thing, but only where there should be decent talk, a worthy man, and a generous conception. Therefore you slept like a man, walked forth like a man, wore a manly dress, and used to talk in a way becoming a good man; then do you say to me, "I have lost nothing?" So do men lose nothing more than coin? Is not modesty lost? Is not decent behavior lost? is it that he who has lost these things has sustained no loss? Perhaps you think that not one of these things is a loss. But there was a time when you reckoned this the only loss and damage, and you were anxious that no man should disturb you from these words and actions.

Observe, you are disturbed from these good words and actions by nobody but by yourself. Fight with yourself, restore yourself to decency, to modesty, to liberty. If any man ever told you this about me, that a person forces me to be an adulterer, to wear such a dress as yours, to perfume myself with oils, would you not have gone and with your own hand have killed the man who thus calumniated me? Now will you not help yourself? and how much easier is this help? There is no need to kill any man, nor to put him in chains, nor to treat him with contumely, nor to enter the Forum, but it is only necessary for you to speak to yourself who will be the most easily persuaded, with whom no man has more power of persuasion than yourself. First of all, condemn what you are doing, and then, when you have condemned it, do not despair of yourself, and be not in the condition of those men of mean spirit, who, when they have once given in, surrender themselves completely and are carried away as if by a torrent. But see what the trainers of boys do. Has the boy fallen? "Rise," they say, "wrestle again till you are made strong." Do you also do something of the same kind: for be well assured that nothing is more tractable than the human soul. You must exercise the will, and the thing is done, it is set right: as on the other hand, only fall a-nodding, and the thing is lost: for from within comes ruin and from within comes help. "Then what good do I gain?" And what greater good do you seek than this? From a shameless man you will become a modest man, from a disorderly you will become an orderly man, from a faithless you will become a faithful man, from a man of unbridled habits a sober man. If you seek anything more than this, go on doing what you are doing: not even a God can now help you.

CHAPTER 10

What things we ought to despise, and what things we ought to value

The difficulties of all men are about external things, their helplessness is about externals. "What shall I do, how will it be, how will it turn out, will this happen, will that?" All these are the words of those who are turning themselves to things which are not within the power of the will. For who says, "How shall I not assent to that which is false? how shall I not turn away from the truth?" If a man be of such a good disposition as to be anxious about these things, I will remind him of this: "Why are you anxious? The thing is in your own power: be assured: do not be precipitate in assenting before you apply the natural rule." On the other side, if a man is anxious about desire, lest it fail in its purpose and miss its end, and with respect to the avoidance of things, lest he should fall into that which he would avoid, I will first kiss him, because he throws away the things about which others are in a flutter, and their fears, and employs his thoughts about his own affairs and his own condition. Then I shall say to him: "If you do not choose to desire that which you will fall to obtain nor to attempt to avoid that into which you will fall, desire nothing which belongs to others, nor try to avoid any of the things which are not in your power. If you do not observe this rule, you must of necessity fall in your desires and fall into that which you would avoid. What is the difficulty here? where is there room for the words, 'How will it be?' and 'How will it turn out?' and, 'Will this happen or that?'

Now is not that which will happen independent of the will? "Yes." And the nature of good and of evil, is it not in the things which are within the power of the will? "Yes." Is it in your power, then, to treat according to nature everything which happens? Can any person hinder you? "No man." No longer then say to me, "How will it be?" For however it may be, you will dispose of it well, and the result to you will be a fortunate one. What would Hercules have been if he had said, "How shall a great lion not appear to me, or a great boar, or savage men?" And what do you care for that? If a great boar appear, you will fight a greater fight: if bad men appear, you relieve the earth of the bad. "Suppose, then, that I may lose my life in this way." You will die a good man, doing a noble act. For since we must certainly die, of necessity a man must be found doing something, either following the employment of a husbandman, or digging, or trading, or serving in a consulship or suffering from indigestion or from diarrhea. What then do you wish to be doing, when you are found by death? I for my part would wish to be found doing something which belongs to a man, beneficent, suitable to the general interest, noble. But if I cannot be found doing things so great, I would be found doing at least that which I cannot be hindered from doing, that which is permitted me to do, correcting, myself, cultivating the faculty which makes use of appearances, laboring at freedom from the affects, rendering to the relations of life their due; if I succeed so far, also touching on the third topic, safety in the forming judgments about things. If death surprises me when I am busy about these things, it is enough for me if I can stretch out my hands to God and say:

"The means which I have received from Thee for seeing Thy administration and following it, I have not neglected: I have not dishonored Thee by my acts: see how I have used my perceptions, see how I have used my preconceptions: have I ever blamed Thee? have I been discontented with anything that happens, or wished it to be otherwise? have I wished to transgress the relations? That Thou hast given me life, I thank Thee for what Thou has given me: so long as I have used the things which are Thine, I am content; take them back and place them wherever Thou mayest choose; for Thine were all things, Thou gavest them to me." Is it not enough to depart in this state of mind, and what life is better and more becoming than that of a man who is in this state of mind? and what end is more happy?

But that this may be done, a man must receive no small things, nor are the things small which he must lose. You cannot both wish to be a consul and to have these things, and to be eager to have lands and these things also; and to be solicitous about slaves and about yourself. But if you wish for anything which belongs to another, that which is your own is lost. This is the nature of the thing: nothing is given or had for nothing. And where is the wonder? If you wish to be a consul, you must keep awake, run about, kiss hands, waste yourself with exhaustion at other men's doors, say and do many things unworthy of a free man, send gifts to many, daily presents to some. And what is the thing that is got? Twelve bundles of rods, to sit three or four times on the tribunal, to exhibit the games in the Circus and to give suppers in small baskets. Or, if you do not agree about this, let some one show me what there is besides these things. In order, then, to secure freedom from passions, tranquility, to sleep well when you do sleep, to be really awake when you are awake, to fear nothing, to be anxious about nothing, will you spend nothing and give no labor? But if anything belonging to you be lost while you are thus busied, or be wasted badly, or another obtains what you ought to have obtained, will you immediately be vexed at what has happened? Will you not take into the account on the other side what you receive and for what, how much for how much? Do you expect to have for nothing things so great? And how can you? One work has no community with another. You cannot have both external things after bestowing care on them and your own ruling faculty: but if you would have those, give up this. If you do not, you will have neither this nor that, while you are drawn in different ways to both. The oil will be spilled, the household vessels will perish: but I shall be free from passions. There will be a fire when I am not present, and the books will be destroyed: but I shall treat appearances according to nature. "Well; but I shall have nothing to eat." If I am so unlucky, death is a harbor; and death is the harbour for all; this is the place of refuge; and for this reason not one of the things in life is difficult: as soon as you choose, you are out of the house, and are smoked no more. Why, then, are you anxious, why do you lose your sleep, why do you not straightway, after considering wherein your good is and your evil, say, "Both of them are in my power? Neither can any man deprive me of the good, nor involve me in the bad against my will. Why do I not throw myself down and snore? for all that I have is safe. As to the things which belong to others, he will look to them who gets them, as they may be given by Him who has the power. Who am I who wish to have them in this way or in that? is a power of selecting them given to me? has any person made me the dispenser of them? Those things are enough for me over which I have power: I ought to manage them as well as I can: and all the rest, as the Master of them may choose."

When a man has these things before his eyes, does he keep awake and turn hither and thither? What would he have, or what does he regret, Patroclus or Antilochus or Menelaus? For when did he suppose that any of his friends was immortal, and when had he not before his eyes that on the morrow or the day after he or his friend must die? "Yes," he says, "but I thought that he would survive me and bring up my son." You were a fool for that reason, and you were thinking of what was uncertain. Why, then, do you not blame yourself, and sit crying like girls? "But he used to set my food before me." Because he was alive, you fool, but now he cannot: but Automedon will set it before you, and if Automedon also dies, you will find another. But if the pot, in which your meat was cooked, should be broken, must you die of hunger, because you have not the pot which you are accustomed to? Do you not send and buy a new pot? He says:

"No greater ill could fall on me."

Why is this your ill? Do you, then, instead of removing it, blame your mother for not foretelling it to you that you might continue grieving from that time? What do you think? do you not suppose that Homer wrote this that we may learn that those of noblest birth, the strongest and the richest, the most handsome, when they have not the opinions which they ought to have, are not prevented from being most wretched and unfortunate?

CHAPTER 11

About Purity

Some persons raise a question whether the social feeling is contained in the nature of man; and yet I think that these same persons would have no doubt that love of purity is certainly contained in it, and that, if man is distinguished from other animals by anything, he is distinguished by this. When, then, we see any other animal cleaning itself, we are accustomed to speak of the act with surprise, and to add that the animal is acting like a man: and, on the other hand, if a man blames an animal for being dirty, straightway as if we were making an excuse for it, we say that of course the animal is not a human creature. So we suppose that there is something superior in man, and that we first receive it from the Gods. For since the Gods by their nature are pure and free from corruption, so far as men approach them by reason, so far do they cling to purity and to a love of purity. But since it is impossible that man's nature can be altogether pure being mixed of such materials, reason is applied, as far as it is possible, and reason endeavors to make human nature love

The first, then, and highest purity is that which is in the soul; and we say the same of impurity. Now you could not discover the impurity of the soul as you could discover that of the body: but as to the soul, what else could you find in it than that which makes it filthy in respect to the acts which are her own? Now the acts of the soul are movement toward an object or movement from it, desire, aversion, preparation, design, assent. What, then, is it which in these acts makes the soul filthy and impure? Nothing else than her own bad judgments. Consequently, the impurity of the soul is the soul's bad opinions; and the purification of the soul is the planting in it of proper opinions; and the soul is pure which has proper opinions, for the soul alone in her own acts is free from perturbation and pollution.

Now we ought to work at something like this in the body also, as far as we can. It was impossible for the defluxions of the nose not to run when man has such a mixture in his body. For this reason, nature has made hands and the nostrils themselves as channels for carrying off the humors. If, then, a man sucks up the defluxions, I say that he is not doing the act of a man. It was impossible for a man's feet not to be made muddy and not be soiled at all when he passes through dirty places. For this reason, nature has made water and hands. It was impossible that some impurity should not remain in the teeth from eating: for this reason, she says, wash the teeth. Why? In order that you may be a man and not a wild beast or a hog. It was impossible that from the sweat and the pressing of the clothes there should not remain some impurity about the body which requires to be cleaned away. For this reason water, oil, hands, towels, scrapers, nitre, sometimes all other kinds of means are necessary for cleaning the body. You do not act so: but the smith will take off the rust from the iron, and be will have tools prepared for this purpose, and you yourself wash the platter when you are going to eat, if you are not completely impure and dirty: but will you not wash the body nor make it clean? "Why?" he replies. I will tell you again; in the first place, that you may do the acts of a man; then, that you may not be disagreeable to those with whom you associate. You do something of this kind even in this matter, and you do not perceive it: you think that you deserve to stink. Let it be so: deserve to stink. Do you think that also those who sit by you, those who recline at table with you, that those who kiss you deserve the same? Either go into a desert, where you deserve to go, or live by yourself, and smell yourself. For it is just that you alone should enjoy your own impurity. But when you are in a city, to behave so inconsiderately and foolishly, to what character do you think that it belongs? If nature had entrusted to you a horse, would you have overlooked and neglected him? And now think that you have been entrusted with your own body as with a horse; wash it, wipe it, take care that no man turns away from it, that no one gets out of the way for it. But who does not get out of the way of a dirty man, of a stinking man, of a man whose skin is foul, more than he does out of the way of a man who is daubed with muck? That smell is from without, it is put upon him; but the other smell is from want of care, from within, and in a manner from a body in putrefaction.

"But Socrates washed himself seldom." Yes, but his body was clean and fair: and it was so agreeable and sweet that tile most beautiful and the most noble loved him, and desired to sit by him rather than by the side of those who had the handsomest forms. It was in his power neither to use the bath nor to wash himself, if he chose; and yet the rare use of water had an effect. If you do not choose to wash with warm water, wash with cold. But Aristophanes says:

Those who are pale, unshod, 'tis those I mean.

For Aristophanes says of Socrates that he also walked the air and stole clothes from the palaestra. But all who have written about Socrates bear exactly the contrary evidence in his favor; they say that he was pleasant not only to hear, but also to see. On the other hand they write the same about Diogenes. For we ought not even by the appearance of the body to deter the multitude from philosophy; but as in other things, a philosopher should show himself cheerful and tranquil, so also he should in the things that relate to the body: "See, ye men, that I have nothing, that I want nothing: see how I am without a house, and without a city, and an exile, if it happens to be so, and without a hearth I live more free from trouble and more happily than all of noble birth and than the rich. But look at my poor body also and observe that it is not injured by my hard way of living." But if a man says this to me, who has the appearance and face of a condemned man, what God shall persuade me to approach philosophy, if it makes men such persons? Far from it; I would not choose to do so, even if I were going to become a wise man. I indeed would rather that a young man, who is making his first movements toward philosophy, should come to me with his hair carefully trimmed than with it dirty and rough, for there is seen in him a certain notion of beauty and a desire of that which is becoming; and where he supposes it to be, there also he strives that it shall be. It is only necessary to show him, and to say: "Young man, you seek beauty, and you do well: you must know then that it grows in that part of you where you have the rational faculty: seek it there where you have the movements toward and the movements from things, where you have the desire toward, and the aversion from things: for this is what you have in yourself of a superior kind; but the poor body is naturally only earth: why do you labor about it to no purpose? if you shall learn nothing else, you will learn from time that the body is nothing." But if a man comes to me daubed with filth, dirty, with a mustache down to his knees, what can I say to him, by what kind of resemblance can I lead him on? For about what has he busied himself which resembles beauty, that I may be able to change him and "Beauty is not in this, but in that?" Would you have me to tell him, that beauty consists not in being daubed with muck, but that it lies in the rational part? Has he any desire of beauty? has he any form of it in his mind? Go and talk to a hog, and tell him not to roll in the mud.

For this reason the words of Xenocrates touched Polemon also; since he was a lover of beauty, for he entered, having in him certain incitements to love of beauty, but he looked for it in the wrong place. For nature has not made even the animals dirty which live with man. Does a horse ever wallow in the mud or a well-bred dog? But the hog, and the dirty geese, and worms and spiders do, which are banished furthest from human intercourse. Do you, then, being a man, choose to be not as one of the animals which live with man, but rather a worm, or a spider? Will you not wash yourself somewhere some time in such manner as you choose? Will you not wash off the dirt from your body? Will you not come clean that those with whom you keep company may have pleasure in being with you? But do you go with us even into the temples in such a state, where it is not permitted to spit or blow the nose, being a heap of spittle and of snot?

When then? does any man require you to ornament yourself? Far from it; except to ornament that which we really are by nature, the rational faculty, the opinions, the actions; but as to the body only so far as purity, only so far as not to give offense. But if you are told that you ought not to wear garments dyed with purple, go and daub your cloak with muck or tear it. "But how shall I have a neat cloak?" Man, you have water;

wash it. Here is a youth worthy of being loved, here is an old man worthy of loving and being loved in return, a fit person for a man to entrust to him a son's instruction, to whom daughters and young men shall come, if opportunity shall so happen, that the teacher shall deliver his lessons to them on a dunghill. Let this not be so: every deviation comes from something which is in man's nature; but this is near being something not in man's nature.

CHAPTER 12

On attention

When you have remitted your attention for a short time, do not imagine this, that you will recover it when you choose; but let but let this thought be present to you, that in consequence of the fault committed to-day your affairs must be in a worse condition for all that follows. For first, and what causes most trouble, a habit of not attending is formed in you; then a habit of deferring your attention. And continually from time to time you drive away, by deferring it, the happiness of life, proper behavior, the being and living conformably to nature. If, then, the procrastination of attention is profitable, the complete omission of attention is more profitable; but if it is not profitable, why do you not maintain your attention constant? "To-day I choose to play." Well then, ought you not to play with attention? "I choose to sing." What, then, hinders you from doing so with attention? Is there any part of life excepted, to which attention does not extend? For will you do it worse by using attention, and better by not attending at all? And what else of things in life is done better by those who do not use attention? Does he who works in wood work better by not attending to it? Does the captain of a ship manage it better by not attending? and is any of the smaller acts done better by inattention? Do you not see that, when you have let your mind loose, it is no longer in your power to recall it, either to propriety, or to modesty, or to moderation: but you do everything that comes into your mind in obedience to your inclinations?

To what things then ought I to attend? First to those general (principles) and to have them in readiness, and without them not to sleep, not to rise, not to drink, not to eat, not to converse with men; that no man is master of another man's will, but that in the will alone is the good and the bad. No man, then, has the power either to procure for me any good or to involve me in any evil, but I alone myself over myself have power in these things. When, then, these things are secured to me, why need I be disturbed about external things? What tyrant is formidable, what disease, what poverty, what offense? "Well, I have not pleased a certain person." Is he then my work, my judgment? "No." Why then should I trouble myself about him? "But he is supposed to be some one." He will look to that himself; and those who think so will also. But I have One Whom I ought to please, to Whom I ought to subject myself, Whom I ought to obey, God and those who are next to Him. He has placed me with myself, and has put my will in obedience to myself alone, and has given me rules for the right use of it; and when I follow these rules in syllogisms, I do not care for any man who says anything else: in sophistical argument, I care for no man. Why then in greater matters do those annoy me who blame me? What is the cause of this perturbation? Nothing else than because in this matter I am not disciplined. For all knowledge despises ignorance and the ignorant; and not only the sciences, but even the arts. Produce any shoemaker that you please, and he ridicules the many in respect to his own work. Produce any carpenter.

First, then, we ought to have these in readiness, and to do nothing without them, and we ought to keep the soul directed to this mark, to pursue nothing external, and nothing which belongs to others, but to do as He has appointed Who has the power; we ought to pursue altogether the things which are in the power of the will, and all other things as it is permitted. Next to this we ought to remember who we are, and what is our name, and to endeavor to direct our duties toward the character of our several relations in this manner: what is the season for singing, what is the season for play, and in whose presence; what will be the consequence of the act; whether our associates will despise us, whether we shall despise them; when to jeer, and whom to ridicule; and on what occasion to comply and with whom; and finally, in complying how to maintain our own character. But wherever you have deviated from any of these rules, there is damage immediately, not from anything external, but from the action itself.

What then? is it possible to be free from faults? It is not possible; but tills is possible, to direct your efforts incessantly to being faultless. For we must be content if by never remitting this attention we shall escape at least a few errors. But now when you have said, "To-morrow I will begin to attend," you must be told that you are saying this, "To-day I will be shameless, disregardful of time and place, mean; it will be in the power of others to give me pain; to-day I will be passionate and envious." See how many evil things you are permitting yourself to do. If it is good to use attention to-morrow, how much better is it to do so to-day? if to-morrow it is in your interest to attend, much more is it to-day, that you may be able to do so to-morrow also, and may not defer it again to the third day.

CHAPTER 13

Against or to those who readily tell their own affairs

When a man has seemed to us to have talked with simplicity about his own affairs, how is it that at last we are ourselves also induced to discover to him our own secrets and we think this to be candid behavior? In the first place, because it seems unfair for a man to have listened to the affairs of his neighbor, and not to communicate to him also in turn our own affairs: next, because we think that we shall not present to them the appearance of candid men when we are silent about our own affairs. Indeed men are often accustomed to say, "I have told you all my affairs, will you tell me nothing of your own? where is this done?" Besides, we have also this opinion that we can safely trust him who has already told us his own affairs; for the notion rises in our mind that this man could never divulge our affairs because he would be cautious that we also should not divulge his. In this way also the incautious are caught by the soldiers at Rome. A soldier sits by you in a common dress and begins to speak ill of Caesar; then you, as if you had received a pledge of his fidelity by his having begun the abuse, utter yourself also what you think, and then you are carried off in chains.

Something of this kind happens to us generally. Now as this man has confidently entrusted his affairs to me, shall I also do so to any man whom I meet? For when I have heard, I keep silence, if I am of such a disposition; but he goes forth and tells all men what he has heard. Then if I hear what has been done, if I be a man like him, I resolve to be revenged, I divulge what he has told me; I both disturb others and am disturbed myself. But if I remember that one man does not injure another, and that every man's acts injure and profit him, I secure this, that I do not anything like him, but still I suffer what I do suffer through my own silly talk.

"True: but it is unfair when you have heard the secrets of your neighbor for you in turn to communicate nothing to him." Did I ask you for your secrets, my man? did you communicate your affairs on certain terms, that you should in return hear mine also? If you are a babbler and think that all who meet you are friends, do you wish me also to be like you? But why, if you did well in entrusting your affairs to me, and it is not well for me to entrust mine to you, do you wish me to be so rash? It is just the same as if I had a cask which is water-tight, and you one with a hole in it, and you should come and deposit with me your wine that I might put it into my cask, and then should complain that I also did not entrust my wine to you, for you have a cask with a hole in it. How then is there any equality here? You entrusted your affairs to a man who is faithful and modest, to a man who thinks that his own actions alone are injurious and useful, and that nothing external is. Would you have me entrust mine to you, a man who has dishonored his own faculty of will, and who wishes to gain some small bit of money or some office or promotion in the court, even if you should be going to murder your own children, like Medea? Where is this equality? But show yourself to me to be faithful, modest, and steady: show me that you have friendly opinions; show that your cask has no hole in it; and you will see how I shall not wait for you to trust me with your affairs, but I myself shall come to you and ask you to hear mine. For who does not choose to make use of a good vessel? Who does not value a benevolent and faithful adviser? who will not willingly receive a man who is ready to bear a share, as we may say, of the difficulty of his circumstances, and by this very act to ease the burden, by taking a part of it.

"True: but I trust you; you do not trust me." In the first place, not even do you trust me, but you are a babbler, and for this reason you cannot hold anything; for indeed, if it is true that you trust me, trust your affairs to me only; but now, whenever you see a man at leisure, you seat yourself by him and say: "Brother, I have no friend more benevolent than you nor dearer; I request you to listen to my affairs." And you do this even to those who are not known to you at all. But if you really trust me, it is plain that you trust me because I am faithful and modest, not because I have told my affairs to you. Allow me, then, to have the same opinion about you. Show me that, if one man tells his affairs to another, he who tells them is faithful and modest. For if this were so, I would go about and tell my affairs to every man, if that would make me faithful and modest. But the thing is not so, and it requires no common opinions. If, then, you see a man who is busy about things not dependent on his will and subjecting his will to them, you must know that this man has ten thousand persons to compel and hinder him. He has no need of pitch or the wheel to compel him to declare what he knows: but a little girl's nod, if it should so happen, will move him, the blandishment of one who belongs to Caesar's court, desire of a magistracy or of an inheritance, and things without end of that sort. You must remember, then, among general principles that secret discourses require fidelity and corresponding opinions. But where can we now find these easily? Or if you cannot answer that question, let some one point out to me a man who can say: "I care only about the things which are my own, the things which are not subject to hindrance, the things which are by nature free." This I hold to be the nature of the good: but let all other things be as they are allowed; I do not concern myself.

THE ENCHIRIDIDON, OR MANUAL

I. Of things some are in our power, and others are not. In our power are opinion, movement towards a thing, desire, aversion, turning from a thing; and in a word, whatever are our acts. Not in our power are the body, property, reputation, offices (magisterial power), and in a word, whatever are not our own acts. And the things in our power are by nature free, not subject to restraint or hindrance; but the things not in our power are weak, slavish, subject to restraint, in the power of others. Remember then, that if you think the things which are by nature slavish to be free, and the things which are in the power of others to be your own, you will be hindered, you will lament, you will be disturbed, you will blame both gods and men; but if you think that only which is your own to be your own, and if you think that what is another's, as it really is, belongs to another, no man will ever compel you, no man will hinder you, you will never blame any man, you will accuse no man, you will do nothing involuntarily (against your will), no man will harm you, you will have no enemy, for you will not suffer any harm.

If then you desire (aim at) such great things remember that you must not (attempt to) lay hold of them with a small effort; but you must leave alone some things entirely, and postpone others for the present. But if you wish for these things also (such great things), and power (office) and wealth, perhaps you will not gain even these very things (power and wealth) because you aim also at those former things (such great things); certainly you will fail in those things through which alone happiness and freedom are secured. Straightway then practise saying to every harsh appearance: You are an appearance, and in no manner what you appear to be. Then examine it by the rules which you possess, and by this first and chiefly, whether it relates to the things which are in our power or to things which are not in our power; and if it relates to anything which is not in our power, be ready to say that it does not concern you.

II. Remember that desire contains in it the profession (hope) of obtaining that which you desire; and the profession (hope) in aversion (turning from a thing) is that you will not fall into that which you attempt to avoid; and he who fails in his desire is unfortunate; and he who falls into that which he would avoid is unhappy. If then you attempt to avoid only the things contrary to nature which are within your power you will not be involved in any of the things which you would avoid. But if you attempt to avoid disease, or death, or poverty, you will be unhappy. Take away then aversion from all things which are not in our power, and transfer it to the things contrary to nature which are in our power. But destroy desire completely for the present. For if you desire anything which is not in our power, you must be unfortunate; but of the things in our power, and which it would be good to desire, nothing yet is before you. But employ only the power of moving towards an object and retiring from it; and these powers indeed only slightly and with exceptions and with remission.

III. In everything which pleases the soul, or supplies a want, or is loved, remember to add this to the (description, notion): What is the nature of each thing, beginning from the smallest? If you love an earthen vessel, say it is an earthen vessel which you love; for when it has been broken you will not be disturbed. If you are kissing your child or wife, say that it is a human being whom you are kissing, for when the wife or child dies you will not be disturbed.

IV. When you are going to take in hand any act remind yourself what kind of an act it is. If you are going to bathe, place before yourself what happens in the bath; some splashing the water, others pushing against one another, others abusing one another, and some stealing; and thus with more safety you will undertake the matter, if you say to yourself, I now intend to bathe, and to maintain my will in a manner conformable to nature. And so you will do in every act; for thus if any hindrance to bathing shall happen let this thought be ready. It was not this only that I intended, but I intended also to maintain my will in a way conformable to nature; but I shall not maintain it so if I am vexed at what happens.

V. Men are disturbed not by the things which happen, but by the opinions about the things; for example, death is nothing terrible, for if it were it would have seemed so to Socrates; for the opinion about death that it is terrible, is the terrible thing. When then we are impeded, or disturbed, or grieved, let us never blame others, but ourselves—that is, our opinions. It is the act of an ill-instructed man to blame others for his own bad condition; it is the act of one who has begun to be instructed, to lay the blame on himself; and of one whose instruction is completed, neither to blame another, nor himself.

VI. Be not elated at any advantage (excellence) which belongs to another. If a horse when he is elated should say, I am beautiful, one might endure it. But when you are elated, and say, I have a beautiful horse, you must know that you are elated at having a good horse. What then is your own? The use of appearances. Consequently when in the use of appearances you are conformable to nature, then be elated, for then you will be elated at something good which is your own.

VII. As on a voyage when the vessel has reached a port, if you go out to get water it is an amusement by the way to pick up a shellfish or some bulb, but your thoughts ought to be directed to the ship, and you ought to be constantly watching if the captain should call, and then you must throw away all those things, that you may not be bound and pitched into the ship like sheep. So in life also, if there be given to you instead of a little bulb and a shell a wife and child, there will be nothing to prevent (you from taking them). But if the captain should call, run to the ship and leave all those things without regard to them. But if you are old, do not even go far from the ship, lest when you are called you make default.

VIII. Seek not that the things which happen should happen as you wish; but wish the things which happen to be as they are, and you will have a tranquil flow of life.

IX. Disease is an impediment to the body, but not to the will, unless the will itself chooses. Lameness is an impediment to the leg, but not to the will. And add this reflection on the occasion of everything that happens; for you will find it an impediment to something else, but not to yourself.

X. On the occasion of every accident (event) that befalls you, remember to turn to yourself and inquire what power you have for turning it to use. If you see a fair man or a fair woman, you will find that the power to resist is temperance (continence). If labor (pain) be presented to you, you will find that it is endurance. If it be abusive words, you will find it to be patience. And if you have been thus formed to the (proper) habit, the appearances will not carry you along with them.

XI. Never say about anything, I have lost it, but say I have restored it. Is your child dead? It has been restored. Is your wife dead? She has been restored. Has your estate been taken from you? Has not then this also been restored? But he who has taken it from me is a bad man. But what is it to you, by whose hands the giver demanded it back? So long as he may allow you, take care of it as a thing which belongs to another, as travellers do with their inn.

XII. If you intend to improve, throw away such thoughts as these: if I neglect my affairs, I shall not have the means of living: unless I chastise my slave, he will be bad. For it is better to die of hunger and so to be released from grief and fear than to live in abundance with perturbation; and it is better for your slave to be bad than for you to be unhappy. Begin then from little things. Is the oil spilled? Is a little wine stolen? Say on the occasion, at such price is sold freedom from perturbation; at such price is sold tranquillity, but nothing is got for nothing. And when you call your slave, consider that it is possible that he does not hear; and if he does hear, that he will do nothing which you wish. But matters are not so well with him, but altogether well with you, that it should be in his power for you to be not disturbed.

XIII. If you would improve, submit to be considered without sense and foolish with respect to externals. Wish to be considered to know nothing; and if you shall seem to some to be a person of importance, distrust yourself. For you should know that it is not easy both to keep your will in a condition conformable to nature and (to secure) external things: but if a man is careful about the one, it is an absolute necessity that he will neglect the other.

XIV. If you would have your children and your wife and your friends to live for ever, you are silly; for you would have the things which are not in your power to be in your power, and the things which belong to others to be yours. So if you would have your slave to be free from faults, you are a fool; for you would have badness not to be badness, but something else. But if you wish not to fail in your desires, you are able to do that. Practise then this which you are able to do. He is the master of every man who has the power over the things which another person wishes or does not wish, the power to confer them on him or to take them away. Whoever then wishes to be free let him neither wish for anything nor avoid anything which depends on others: if he does not observe this rule, he must be a slave.

XV. Remember that in life you ought to behave as at a banquet. Suppose that something is carried round and is opposite to you. Stretch out your hand and take a portion with decency. Suppose that it passes by you. Do not detain it. Suppose that it is not yet come to you. Do not send your desire forward to it, but wait till it is opposite to you. Do so with respect to children, so with respect to a wife, so with respect to magisterial offices, so with respect to wealth, and you will be some time a worthy partner of the banquets of the gods. But if you take none of the things which are set before you, and even despise them, then you will be not only a fellow banqueter with the gods, but also a partner with them in power. For by acting thus Diogenes and Heracleitus and those like them were deservedly divine, and were so called.

XVI. When you see a person weeping in sorrow either when a child goes abroad or when he is dead, or when the man has lost his property, take care that the appearance do not hurry you away with it, as if he were suffering in external things. But straightway make a distinction in your own mind, and be in readiness to say, it is not that which has happened that afflicts this man, for it does not afflict another, but it is the opinion about this thing which afflicts the man. So far as words then do not be unwilling to show him sympathy, and even if it happens so, to lament with him. But take care that you do not lament internally also.

XVII. Remember that thou art an actor in a play, of such a kind as the teacher (author) may choose; if short, of a short one; if long, of a long one: if he wishes you to act the part of a poor man, see that you act the part naturally; if the part of a lame man, of a magistrate, of a private person, (do the same). For this is your duty, to act well the part that is given to you; but to select the part, belongs to another.

XVIII. When a raven has croaked inauspiciously, let not the appearance hurry you away with it; but straightway make a distinction in your mind and say, None of these things is signified to me, but either to my poor body, or to my small property, or to my reputation, or to my children, or to my wife: but to me all significations are auspicious if I choose. For whatever of these things results, it is in my power to derive benefit from it.

XIX. You can be invincible, if you enter into no contest in which it is not in your power to conquer. Take care then when you observe a man honored before others or possessed of great power or highly esteemed for any reason, not to suppose him happy, and be not carried away by the appearance. For if the nature of the good is in our power, neither envy nor jealousy will have a place in us. But you yourself will not wish to be a general or senator or consul, but a free man: and there is only one way to this, to despise (care not for) the things which are not in our power.

XX. Remember that it is not he who reviles you or strikes you, who insults you, but it is your opinion about these things as being insulting. When then a man irritates you, you must know that it is your own opinion which has irritated you. Therefore especially try not to be carried away by the appearance. For if you once gain time and delay, you will more easily master yourself.

XXI. Let death and exile and every other thing which appears dreadful be daily before your eyes; but most of all death: and you will never think of anything mean nor will you desire anything extravagantly.

XXII. If you desire philosophy, prepare yourself from the beginning to be ridiculed, to expect that many will sneer at you, and say, He has all at once returned to us as a philosopher; and whence does he get this supercilious look for us? Do you not show a supercilious look; but hold on to the things which seem to you best as one appointed by God to this station. And remember that if you abide in the same principles, these men who first ridiculed will afterwards admire you; but if you shall have been overpowered by them, you will bring on yourself double ridicule.

XXIII. If it should ever happen to you to be turned to externals in order to please some person, you must know that you have lost your purpose in life. Be satisfied then in everything with being a philosopher; and if you wish to seem also to any person to be a philosopher, appear so to yourself, and you will be able to do this.

XXIV. Let not these thoughts afflict you, I shall live unhonored and be nobody nowhere. For if want of honor is an evil, you cannot be in evil through the means (fault) of another any more than you can be involved in anything base. Is it then your business to obtain the rank of a magistrate, or to be received at a banquet? By no means. How then can this be want of honor (dishonor)? And how will you be nobody nowhere, when you ought to be somebody in those things only which are in your power, in which indeed it is permitted to you to be a man of the greatest worth? But your friends will be without assistance! What do you mean by being without assistance? They will not receive money from you, nor will you make them Roman citizens. Who then told you that these are among the things which are in our power, and not in the power of others? And who can give to another what he has not himself? Acquire money then, your friends say, that we also may have something. If I can acquire money and also keep myself modest and faithful and magnanimous, point out the way, and I will acquire it. But if you ask me to lose the things which are good and my own, in order that you may gain the things which are not good, see how unfair and silly you are. Besides, which would you rather have, money or a faithful and modest friend? For this end then rather help me to be such a man, and do not ask me to do this by which I shall lose that character. But my country, you say, as far as it depends on me, will be without my help. I ask again, what help do you mean? It will not have porticos or baths through you. And what does this mean? For it is not furnished with shoes by means of a smith, nor with arms by means of a shoemaker. But it is enough if every man fully discharges the work that is his own: and if you provided it with another citizen faithful and modest, would you not be useful to it? Yes. Then you also cannot be useless to it. What place then, you say, shall I hold in the city? Whatever you can, if you maintain at the same time your fidelity and modesty. But if when you wish to be useful to the state, you shall lose these qualities, what profit could you be to it, if you were made shameless and faithless?

XXV. Has any man been preferred before you at a banquet, or in being saluted, or in being invited to a consultation? If these things are good, you ought to rejoice that he has obtained them; but if bad, be not grieved because you have not obtained them. And remember that you cannot, if you do not the same things in order to obtain what is not in our own power, be considered worthy of the same (equal) things. For how can a man obtain an equal share with another when he does not visit a man's doors as that other man does; when he does not attend him when he goes abroad, as the other man does;

when he does not praise (flatter) him as another does? You will be unjust then and insatiable, if you do not part with the price, in return for which those things are sold, and if you wish to obtain them for nothing. Well, what is the price of lettuces? An obolus perhaps. If then a man gives up the obolus, and receives the lettuces, and if you do not give up the obolus and do not obtain the lettuces, do not suppose that you receive less than he who has got the lettuces; for as he has the lettuces, so you have the obolus which you did not give. In the same way then in the other matter also you have not been invited to a man's feast, for you did not give to the host the price at which the supper is sold; but he sells it for praise (flattery), he sells it for personal attention. Give then the price, if it is for your interest, for which it is sold. But if you wish both not to give the price and to obtain the things, you are insatiable and silly. Have you nothing then in place of the supper? You have indeed, you have the not flattering of him, whom you did not choose to flatter; you have the not enduring of the man when he enters the room.

XXVI. We may learn the wish (will) of nature from the things in which we do not differ from one another: for instance, when your neighbor's slave has broken his cup, or anything else, we are ready to say forthwith, that it is one of the things which happen. You must know then that when your cup also is broken, you ought to think as you did when your neighbor's cup was broken. Transfer this reflection to greater things also. Is another man's child or wife dead? There is no one who would not say, This is an event incident to man. But when a man's own child or wife is dead, forthwith he calls out, Woe to me, how wretched I am! But we ought to remember how we feel when we hear that it has happened to others.

XXVII. As a mark is not set up for the purpose of missing the aim, so neither does the nature of evil exist in the world.

XXVIII. If any person was intending to put your body in the power of any man whom you fell in with on the way, you would be vexed; but that you put your understanding in the power of any man whom you meet, so that if he should revile you, it is disturbed and troubled, are you not ashamed at this?

XXIX. In every act observe the things which come first, and those which follow it; and so proceed to the act. If you do not, at first you will approach it with alacrity, without having thought of the things which will follow; but afterwards, when certain base (ugly) things have shown themselves, you will be ashamed. A man wishes to conquer at the Olympic games. I also wish indeed, for it is a fine thing. But observe both the things which come first, and the things which follow; and then begin the act. You must do everything according to rule, eat according to strict orders, abstain from delicacies, exercise yourself as you are bid at appointed times, in heat, in cold, you must not drink cold water, nor wine as you choose; in a word, you must deliver yourself up to the exercise master as you do to the physician, and then proceed to the contest. And sometimes you will strain the hand, put the ankle out of joint, swallow much dust, sometimes be flogged, and after all this be defeated. When you have considered all this, if you still choose, go to the contest: if you do not you will behave like children, who at one time play at wrestlers, another time as flute players, again as gladiators, then as trumpeters, then as tragic actors. So you also will be at one time an athlete, at another a gladiator, then a rhetorician, then a philosopher, but with your whole soul you will be nothing at all; but like an ape you imitate everything that you see, and one thing after another pleases you. For you have not undertaken anything with consideration, nor have you surveyed it well; but carelessly and with cold desire. Thus some who have seen a philosopher and having heard one speak, as Euphrates speaks—and who can speak as he does?—they wish to be philosophers themselves also. My man, first of all consider what kind of thing it is; and then examine your own nature, if you are able to sustain the character. Do you wish to be a pentathlete or a wrestler? Look at your arms, your thighs, examine your loins. For different men are formed by nature for different things. Do you think that if you do these things, you can eat in the same manner, drink in the same manner, and in the same manner loathe certain things? You must pass sleepless nights, endure toil, go away from your kinsmen, be despised by a slave, in everything have the inferior part, in honor, in office, in the courts of justice, in every little matter. Consider these things, if you would exchange for them, freedom from passions, liberty, tranquillity. If not, take care that, like little children, you be not now a philosopher, then a servant of the publicani, then a rhetorician, then a procurator (manager) for Cæsar. These things are not consistent. You must be one man, either good or bad. You must either cultivate your own ruling faculty, or external things. You must either exercise your skill on internal things or on external things; that is you must either maintain the position of a philosopher or that of a common person.

XXX. Duties are universally measured by relations. Is a man a father? The precept is to take care of him, to yield to him in all things, to submit when he is reproachful, when he inflicts blows. But suppose that he is a bad father. Were you then by nature made akin to a good father? No; but to a father. Does a brother wrong you? Maintain then your own position towards him, and do not examine what he is doing, but what you must do that your will shall be conformable to nature. For another will not damage you, unless you choose: but you will be damaged then when you shall think that you are damaged. In this way then you will discover your duty from the relation of a neighbor, from that of a citizen, from that of a general, if you are accustomed to contemplate the relations.

XXXI. As to piety towards the gods you must know that this is the chief thing, to have right opinions about them, to think that they exist, and that they administer the All well and justly; and you must fix yourself in this principle (duty), to obey them, and to yield to them in everything which happens, and voluntarily to follow it as being accomplished by the wisest intelligence. For if you do so, you will never either blame the gods, nor will you accuse them of neglecting you. And it is not possible for this to be done in any other way than by withdrawing from the things which are not in our power, and by placing the good and the evil only in those things which are in our power. For if you think that any of the things which are not in our power is good or bad, it is absolutely necessary that, when you do not obtain what you wish, and when you fall into those things which you do not wish, you will find fault and hate those who are the cause of them; for every animal is formed by nature to this, to fly from and to turn from the things which appear harmful and the things which are the cause of the harm, but to follow and admire the things which are useful and the causes of the useful. It is impossible then for a person who thinks that he is harmed to be delighted with that which he thinks to be the cause of the harm, as it is also impossible to be pleased with the harm itself. For this reason also a father is reviled by his son, when he gives no part to his son of the things which are considered to be good; and it was this which made Polynices and Eteocles enemies, the opinion that royal power was a good. It is for this reason that the cultivator of the earth reviles the gods, for this reason the sailor does, and the merchant, and for this reason those who lose their wives and their children. For where the useful (your interest) is, there also piety is. Consequently he who takes care to desire as he ought and to avoid as he ought, at the same time also cares after piety. But to make libations and to sacrifice and to offer first-fruits according to the custom of our fathers, purely and not meanly nor carelessly nor scantily nor above our ability, is a thing which belongs to all to do.

XXXII. When you have recourse to divination, remember that you do not know how it will turn out, but that you are come to inquire from the diviner. But of what kind it is, you know when you come, if indeed you are a philosopher. For if it is any of the things which are not in our power, it is absolutely necessary that it must be neither good nor bad. Do not then bring to the diviner desire or aversion: if you do, you will approach him with fear. But having determined in your mind that everything which shall turn out (result) is indifferent, and does not concern you, and whatever it may be, for it will be in your power to use it well, and no man will hinder this, come then with confidence to the gods as your advisers. And then when any advice shall have been given, remember whom you have taken as advisers, and whom you will have neglected, if you do not obey them. And go to divination, as Socrates said that you ought, about those matters in which all the inquiry has reference to the result, and in which means are not given either by reason nor by any other art for knowing the thing which is the subject of the inquiry.

Wherefore when we ought to share a friend's danger, or that of our country, you must not consult the diviner whether you ought to share it. For even if the diviner shall tell you that the signs of the victims are unlucky, it is plain that this is a token of death, or mutilation of part of the body, or of exile. But reason prevails, that even with these risks, we should share the dangers of our friend, and of our country. Therefore attend to the greater diviner, the Pythian god, who ejected from the temple him who did not assist his friend, when he was being murdered.

XXXIII. Immediately prescribe some character and some form to yourself, which you shall observe both when you are alone and when you meet with men.

And let silence be the general rule, or let only what is necessary be said, and in few words. And rarely, and when the occasion calls, we shall say something; but about none of the common subjects, not about gladiators, nor horse-races, nor about athletes, nor about eating or drinking, which are the usual subjects; and especially not about men, as blaming them or praising them, or comparing them. If then you are able, bring over by your conversation, the conversation of your associates, to that which is proper; but if you should happen to be confined to the company of strangers, be silent.

Let not your laughter be much, nor on many occasions, nor excessive.

Refuse altogether to take an oath, if it is possible; if it is not, refuse as far as you are able.

Avoid banquets which are given by strangers and by ignorant persons. But if ever there is occasion to join in them, let your attention be carefully fixed, that you slip not into the manners of the vulgar (the uninstructed). For you must know, that if your companion be impure, he also who keeps company with him must become impure, though he should happen to be pure.

Take (apply) the things which relate to the body as far as the bare use, as food, drink, clothing, house, and slaves; but exclude everything which is for show or luxury.

As to pleasure with women, abstain as far as you can before marriage; but if you do indulge in it, do it in the way which is conformable to custom. Do not however be disagreeable to those who indulge in these pleasures, or reprove them; and do not often boast that you do not indulge in them yourself.

If a man has reported to you, that a certain person speaks ill of you, do not make any defence (answer) to what has been told you; but reply, The man did not know the rest of my faults, for he would not have mentioned these only.

It is not necessary to go to the theatres often: but if there is ever a proper occasion for going, do not show yourself as being a partisan of any man except yourself, that is, desire only that to be done which is done, and for him only to gain the prize who gains the prize; for in this way you will meet with no hindrance. But abstain entirely from shouts and laughter at any (thing or person), or violent emotions. And when you are come away, do not talk much about what has passed on the stage, except about that which may lead to your own improvement. For it is plain, if you do talk much, that you admired the spectacle (more than you ought).

Do not go to the hearing of certain persons' recitations, nor visit them readily. But if you do attend, observe gravity and sedateness, and also avoid making yourself disagreeable.

When you are going to meet with any person, and particularly one of those who are considered to be in a superior condition, place before yourself what Socrates or Zeno would have done in such circumstances, and you will have no difficulty in making a proper use of the occasion.

When you are going to any of those who are in great power, place before yourself that you will not find the man at home, that you will be excluded, that the door will not be opened to you, that the man will not care about you. And if with all this it is your duty to visit him, bear what happens, and never say to yourself that it was not worth the trouble. For this is silly, and marks the character of a man who is offended by externals.

In company take care not to speak much and excessively about your own acts or dangers; for as it is pleasant to you to make mention of your own dangers, it is not so pleasant to others to hear what has happened to you. Take care also not to provoke laughter; for this is a slippery way towards vulgar habits, and is also adapted to diminish the respect of your neighbors. It is a dangerous habit also to approach obscene talk. When then, anything of this kind happens, if there is a good opportunity, rebuke the man who has proceeded to this talk; but if there is not an opportunity, by your silence at least, and blushing and expression of dissatisfaction by your countenance, show plainly that you are displeased at such talk.

XXXIV. If you have received the impression of any pleasure, guard yourself against being carried away by it; but let the thing wait for you, and allow yourself a certain delay on your own part. Then think of both times, of the time when you will enjoy the pleasure, and of the time after the enjoyment of the pleasure, when you will repent and will reproach yourself. And set against these things how you will rejoice, if you have abstained from the pleasure, and how you will commend yourself. But if it seem to you seasonable to undertake (do) the thing, take care that the charm of it, and the pleasure, and the attraction of it shall not conquer you; but set on the other side the consideration, how much better it is to be conscious that you have gained this victory.

XXXV. When you have decided that a thing ought to be done, and are doing it, never avoid being seen doing it, though the many shall form an unfavorable opinion about it. For if it is not right to do it, avoid doing the thing; but if it is right, why are you afraid of those who shall find fault wrongly?

XXXVI. As the proposition, it is either day, or it is night, is of great importance for the disjunctive argument, but for the conjunctive, is of no value, so in a symposium (entertainment) to select the larger share is of great value for the body, but for the maintenance of the social feeling is worth nothing. When, then, you are eating with another, remember, to look not only to the value for the body of the things set before you, but also to the value of the behavior towards the host which ought to be observed.

XXXVII. If you have assumed a character above your strength, you have both acted in this manner in an unbecoming way, and you have neglected that which you might have fulfilled.

XXXVIII. In walking about, as you take care not to step on a nail, or to sprain your foot, so take care not to damage your own ruling faculty; and if we observe this rule in every act, we shall undertake this act with more security.

XXXIX. The measure of possession (property) is to every man the body, as the foot is of the shoe. If then you stand on this rule (the demands of the body), you will maintain the measure; but if you pass beyond it, you must then of necessity be hurried as it were down a precipice. As also in the matter of the shoe, if you go beyond the (necessities of the) foot, the shoe is gilded, then of a purple color, then embroidered; for there is no limit to that which has once passed the true measure.

XL. Women forthwith from the age of fourteen are called by the men mistresses. Therefore, since they see that there is nothing else that they can obtain, but only the power of lying with men, they begin to decorate themselves, and to place all their hopes in this. It is worth our while then to take care that they may know that they are valued (by men) for nothing else than appearing (being) decent and modest and discreet.

XLI. It is a mark of a mean capacity to spend much time on the things which concern the body, such as much exercise, much eating, much drinking, much easing of the body, much copulation. But these things should be done as subordinate things; and let all your care be directed to the mind.

XLII. When any person treats you ill or speaks ill of you, remember that he does this or says this because he thinks that it is his duty. It is not possible then for him to follow that which seems right to you, but that which seems right to himself. Accordingly if he is wrong in his opinion, he is the person who is hurt, for he is the person who has been deceived; for if a man shall suppose the true conjunction to be false, it is not the conjunction which is hindered, but the man who has been deceived about it. If you proceed then from these opinions, you will be mild in temper to him who reviles you; for say on each occasion, It seemed so to him.

XLIII. Everything has two handles, the one by which it may be borne, the other by which it may not. If your brother acts unjustly, do not lay hold of the act by that handle wherein he acts unjustly, for this is the handle which cannot be borne; but lay hold of the other, that he is your brother, that he was nurtured with you, and you will lay hold of the thing by that handle by which it can be borne.

XLIV. These reasonings do not cohere: I am richer than you, therefore I am better than you; I am more eloquent than you, therefore I am better than you. On the contrary, these rather cohere: I am richer than you, therefore my possessions are greater than yours; I am more eloquent than you, therefore my speech is superior to yours. But you are neither possession nor speech.

XLV. Does a man bathe quickly (early)? do not say that he bathes badly, but that he bathes quickly. Does a man drink much wine? do not say that he does this badly, but say that he drinks much. For before you shall have determined the opinion how do you know whether he is acting wrong? Thus it will not happen to you to comprehend some appearances which are capable of being comprehended, but to assent to others.

XLVI. On no occasion call yourself a philosopher, and do not speak much among the uninstructed about theorems (philosophical rules, precepts); but do that which follows from them. For example, at a banquet do not say how a man ought to eat, but eat as you ought to eat. For remember that in this way Socrates also altogether avoided ostentation.

Persons used to come to him and ask to be recommended by him to philosophers, and he used to take them to philosophers, so easily did he submit to being overlooked. Accordingly, if any conversation should arise among uninstructed persons about any theorem, generally be silent; for there is great danger that you will immediately vomit up what you have not digested. And when a man shall say to you that you know nothing, and you are not vexed, then be sure that you have begun the work (of philosophy). For even sheep do not vomit up their grass and show to the shepherds how much they have eaten; but when they have internally digested the pasture, they produce externally wool and milk. Do you also show not your theorems to the uninstructed, but show the acts which come from their digestion.

XLVII. When at a small cost you are supplied with everything for the body, do not be proud of this; nor, if you drink water, say on every occasion, I drink water. But consider first how much more frugal the poor are than we, and how much more enduring of labor. And if you ever wish to exercise yourself in labor and endurance, do it for yourself, and not for others. Do not embrace statues; but if you are ever very thirsty, take a draught of cold water and spit it out, and tell no man.

XLVIII. The condition and characteristic of an uninstructed person is this: he never expects from himself profit (advantage) nor harm, but from externals. The condition and characteristic of a philosopher is this: he expects all advantage and all harm from himself. The signs (marks) of one who is making progress are these: he censures no man, he praises no man, he blames no man, he accuses no man, he says nothing about himself as if he were somebody or knew something; when he is impeded at all or hindered, he blames himself; if a man praises him he ridicules the praiser to himself; if a man censures him he makes no defence; he goes about like weak persons, being careful not to move any of the things which are placed, before they are firmly fixed; he removes all desire from himself, and he transfers aversion to those things only of the things within our power which are contrary to nature; he employs a moderate movement towards everything; whether he is considered foolish or ignorant he cares not; and in a word he watches himself as if he were an enemy and lying in ambush.

XLIX. When a man is proud because he can understand and explain the writings of Chrysippus, say to yourself, If Chrysippus had not written obscurely, this man would have had nothing to be proud of. But what is it that I wish? To understand nature and to follow it. I inquire therefore who is the interpreter? and when I have heard that it is Chrysippus, I come to him (the interpreter). But I do not understand what is written, and therefore I seek the interpreter. And so far there is yet nothing to be proud of. But when I shall have found the interpreter, the thing that remains is to use the precepts (the lessons). This itself is the only thing to be proud of. But if I shall admire the exposition, what else have I been made unless a grammarian instead of a philosopher? except in one thing, that I am explaining Chrysippus instead of Homer. When, then, any man says to me, Read Chrysippus to me, I rather blush, when I cannot show my acts like to and consistent with his words.

L. Whatever things (rules) are proposed to you (for the conduct of life) abide by them, as if they were laws, as if you would be guilty of impiety if you transgressed any of them. And whatever any man shall say about you, do not attend to it; for this is no affair of yours. How long will you then still defer thinking yourself worthy of the best things, and in no matter transgressing the distinctive reason? Have you accepted the theorems (rules), which it was your duty to agree to, and have you agreed to them? what teacher then do you still expect that you defer to him the correction of yourself? You are no longer a youth, but already a full-grown man. If, then, you are negligent and slothful, and are continually making procrastination after procrastination, and proposal (intention) after proposal, and fixing day after day, after which you will attend to yourself, you will not know that you are not making improvement, but you will continue ignorant (uninstructed) both while you live and till you die. Immediately then think it right to live as a full-grown man, and one who is making proficiency, and let everything which appears to you to be the best be to you a law which must not be transgressed. And if anything laborious or pleasant or glorious or inglorious be presented to you, remember that now is the contest, now are the Olympic games, and they cannot be deferred; and that it depends on one defeat and one giving way that progress is either lost or maintained. Socrates in this way became perfect, in all things improving himself, attending to nothing except to reason. But you, though you are not yet a Socrates, ought to live as one who wishes to be a Socrates.

LI. The first and most necessary place in philosophy is the use of theorems, for instance, that we must not lie; the second part is that of demonstrations, for instance, How is it proved that we ought not to lie? The third is that which is confirmatory of these two, and explanatory, for example, How is this a demonstration? For what is demonstration, what is consequence, what is contradiction, what is truth, what is falsehood? The third part (topic) is necessary on account of the second, and the second on account of the first; but the most necessary and that on which we ought to rest is the first. But we do the contrary. For we spend our time on the third topic, and all our earnestness is about it; but we entirely neglect the first. Therefore we lie; but the demonstration that we ought not to lie we have ready to hand.

LII. In every thing (circumstance) we should hold these maxims ready to hand:

The Enchiridion of Epictetus

Lead me, O Zeus, and thou O Destiny,
The way that I am bid by you to go:
To follow I am ready. If I choose not,
I make myself a wretch, and still must follow.

But whoso nobly yields unto necessity,
We hold him wise, and skill'd in things divine.

And the third also: O Crito, if so it pleases the gods, so let it be;
Anytus and Melitus are able indeed to kill me, but they cannot harm me.

FRAGMENTS OF THE LOST BOOKS OF EPICTETUS

I. The life which is implicated with fortune (depends on fortune) is like a winter torrent: for it is turbulent, and full of mud, and difficult to cross, and tyrannical, and noisy, and of short duration.

II. A soul which is conversant with virtue is like an ever flowing source, for it is pure and tranquil and potable and sweet and communicative (social), and rich and harmless and free from mischief.

III. If you wish to be good, first believe that you are bad.

IV. It is better to do wrong seldom and to own it, and to act right for the most part, than seldom to admit that you have done wrong and to do wrong often.

V. Check (punish) your passions, that you may not be punished by them.

VI. Do not so much be ashamed of that (disgrace) which proceeds from men's opinion as fly from that which comes from the truth.

VII. If you wish to be well spoken of, learn to speak well (of others): and when you have learned to speak well of them, try to act well, and so you will reap the fruit of being well spoken of.

VIII. Freedom and slavery, the one is the name of virtue, and the other of vice: and both are acts of the will. But where there is no will, neither of them touches (affects) these things. But the soul is accustomed to be master of the body, and the things which belong to the body have no share in the will. For no man is a slave who is free in his will.

IX. It is an evil chain, fortune (a chain) of the body, and vice of the soul. For he who is loose (free) in the body, but bound in the soul is a slave: but on the contrary he who is bound in the body, but free (unbound) in the soul, is free.

X. The bond of the body is loosened by nature through death, and by vice through money: but the bond of the soul is loosened by learning, and by experience and by discipline.

XI. If you wish to live without perturbation and with pleasure, try to have all who dwell with you good. And you will have them good, if you instruct the willing, and dismiss those who are unwilling (to be taught): for there will fly away together with those who have fled away both wickedness and slavery; and there will be left with those who remain with you goodness and liberty.

XII. It is a shame for those who sweeten drink with the gifts of the bees, by badness to embitter reason which is the gift of the gods.

XIII. No man who loves money, and loves pleasure, and loves fame, also loves mankind, but only he who loves virtue.

XIV. As you would not choose to sail in a large and decorate and gold-laden ship (or ship ornamented with gold), and to be drowned; so do not choose to dwell in a large and costly house and to be disturbed (by cares).

XV. When we have been invited to a banquet, we take what is set before us : but if a guest should ask the host to set before him fish or sweet cakes, he would be considered to be an unreasonable fellow. But in the world we ask the Gods for what they do not give; and we do this though the things are many which they have given.

XVI. They are amusing fellows, said he (Epictetus), who are proud of the things which are not in our power. A man says, I am better than you, for I possess much land, and you are wasting with hunger. Another says, I am of consular rank. Another says, I am a Procurator. Another, I have curly hair. But a horse does not say to a horse, I am superior to you, for I possess much fodder, and much barley, and my bits are of gold and my harness is embroidered: but he says, I am swifter than you. And every animal is better or worse from his own merit (virtue) or his own badness. Is there then no virtue in man only? and must we look to the hair, and our clothes and to our ancestors ?

XVII. The sick are vexed with the physician who gives them no advice, and think that he has despaired of them. But why should they not have the same feeling towards the philosopher, and think that he has despaired of their coming to a sound state of mind, if he says nothing at all that is useful to a man?

El Paso Norte Press
Special Edition Books

The Art of War – Special Edition

- The Art of War by Sun Tzu – Special Edition
- The Art of War & The Prince – Special Edition
- The Art of War by Baron de Jomini – Special Edition
- The Art of War by Mao Tse-tung – Special Edition

Asian Philosophy Collection

- Tao – The Way – Special Edition
- The Teachings of Confucius – Special Edition
- Zen: Religion of the Samurai
- The Samurai Series

Greco-Roman Studies

- Ethics and Politics – Aristotle
- The History of the Peloponnesian War – Thucydides
- Hellenica – A History of My Times: Books I-VII Complete
- Anabasis: The March Up Country – Xenophon
- Caesar's Commentaries – Julius Caesar

Classic Literature

- Beowulf – In Old English & New English
- Siddhartha – In German & English – Herman Hesse
- The Aeneid of Virgil
- The Iliad & The Odyssey – Homer

Available at online and local bookstores.
For full catalog, please visit

www.elpasonortepress.com

www.ingramcontent.com/pod-product-compliance
Lightning Source LLC
Chambersburg PA
CBHW080918170426
43201CB00016B/2182